purchasing power

purchasing power

Black Kids and American Consumer Culture

ELIZABETH CHIN

University of Minnesota Press
Minneapolis • London

The photograph in chapter 2 is reprinted by permission of The New York Times Company. All other photographs in the book were taken by the author.

Copyright 2001 by the Regents of the University of Minnesota

An earlier version of chapter 4 appeared in *Servicescapes: The Concept and Place in Contemporary Markets,* edited by John Sherry, copyright 1998 NTC Business Books. Used by permission.

An earlier version of chapter 6 originally appeared as "Ethnically Correct Dolls: Toying with the Race Industry," *American Anthropologist* 101, no. 2; reprinted by permission of the American Anthropological Association. Not for further reproduction.

Published by the University of Minnesota Press
111 Third Avenue South, Suite 290
Minneapolis, MN 55401–2520
http://www.upress.umn.edu

Library of Congress Cataloging-in-Publication Data

Chin, Elizabeth, 1963–
    Purchasing power : black kids and American consumer culture /
Elizabeth Chin.
        p.   cm.
    Includes bibliographical references and index.
    ISBN 0-8166-3510-2 (HC : acid-free paper) — ISBN 0-8166-3511-0
(PB : acid-free paper)
        1. Consumption (Economics)—Connecticut—New Haven.   2. Purchasing
power—Connecticut—New Haven.   3. Afro-American children—Connecticut—
New Haven.   4. Afro-American consumers—Connecticut—New Haven.   I. Title.
        HC107.C8 C47 2001
        306.3'089'96073—dc21

                                                                00-012081

Printed in the United States of America on acid-free paper

The University of Minnesota is an equal-opportunity educator and employer.

12 11 10 09 08 07 06 05 04 03 02 01   10 9 8 7 6 5 4 3 2 1

Contents

Native Positions

For most of its residents, New Haven, Connecticut, is a patchwork of clearly delineated neighborhoods that can veer quite suddenly from the abjectly poor to the fabulously wealthy. Largely divided along lines of black and white, these groups often regard each other with mutual fear and suspicion. One day as I was walking through a white, middle-class area toward Newhallville, the predominantly African American neighborhood that is the focus of this book, I ran into a woman who had been a classmate of mine in the fourth grade. The daughter of a Yale professor, she was now a banker living and practicing in Germany. When she learned that I was on my way to Newhallville, she made a stunning admission. For years, her father had driven her through Newhallville in the mornings on the way to school, and for her it had always been a frightening neighborhood that they moved through swiftly, with the doors locked and windows closed. Her admission was that she still had nightmares about driving through that neighborhood; she was ashamed about the symbolic terror the place still held for her, at least in her dreams. Several weeks later, as a winter evening was descending on the 'Ville, a Newhallville woman asked me where I was walking to. I told her I was headed over the hill—into the neighborhood where I had run into my childhood friend. "You walk over there?" she asked with incredulity. "It's dangerous in that neighborhood! There's never any people around!"

Most middle-class white people might be surprised to think that a poor, black woman would think of their quiet, tree-lined neighborhood as dangerous. Of course, perhaps the woman meant dangerous for someone like her—that a black woman walking in a white neighborhood alone at night is suspect. However, the woman was telling me to watch out for myself, and despite my being bundled up in the latest fashion among black kids in the early 1990s—a Starter down coat—no one was likely to mistake me for a kid from the 'Ville. Despite the dangers present in Newhallville—the drive-by shootings, the drug gangs, the break-ins— Newhallville is a neighborhood where most times of the day people are sitting on their stoops, looking out their windows, or scanning the sidewalks as they drive their cars. It is a neighborhood where people on the street are visible, watched, and often not only recognized but also protected. In contrast, in New Haven's middle-class neighborhoods, people are rarely on the street and certainly do not sit on their porches all afternoon watching people pass by or peek out their curtains to keep an eye on what's going on. What this woman was saying to me was that because no one is watching, really, in the middle-class neighborhood, no one is watching out for a lone woman walking home at night either. Anything could happen. In Newhallville, even though it seemed like a more dangerous neighborhood, this was less likely simply because so many people were always around and looking out.

E. E. Evans-Pritchard's classic ethnography *The Nuer* contains a diagram entitled "Nuer Socio-Spatial Categories." Looking something like a semicircular rainbow, the diagram depicts these sociospatial categories as a series of nested hemispheres. The smallest sociospatial category, "the hut," sits at the center of these, surrounded by layers of increasing size and scope until, finally, the largest and most overarching category is reached: "the government operating from various centers." Although this rendering of an indigenous worldview includes no mention of the anthropologist (the implication being that the anthropologist is not part of the native world), in practice most ethnographers are directly or indirectly visitors from "the government operating from various centers." (In Evans-Pritchard's case, this was literally true, since he had been hired by the British colonial government in Sudan to learn about the Nuer, their lives, and political organization.) Generated in an era when the lines between native and anthropologist could be clearly drawn and conceptualized, Evans-Pritchard's layered scheme of categories, with its formal purity and graphic clarity, might be seen to represent modernist anthropology more generally. Today, with the insistence on multivocality, on the changing and flexible nature of identity, and with the increasing slippage between anthropologist and native, the hope and confidence embodied in the diagram seem overly simplistic as a representation of complex, changing worlds.

The neatly stacked, discrete sociospatial categories of the Evans-Pritchard diagram came to mind as I began reflecting upon the research and fieldwork that are this book's foundation. Conducting fieldwork in New Haven, Connecticut, where I grew up, I was both anthropologist and native, both a local resident and a representative of the "government operating from various centers" (courtesy of a grant from the National Science Foundation). There were several of Evans-Pritchard's sociospatial categories in which I operated at once, as did those I knew in Newhallville, the neighborhood where I conducted my research. As a result, there was no clear or delineated way to characterize some pure native point of view, or an anthropological one. Even in naming this a work of native anthropology, such a label only applied from certain vantage points. The fact that I grew up in New Haven did not make me a native of my field site, a poor and working-class black neighborhood very different from the middle-class, predominantly white neighborhoods where I spent my childhood. However, having grown up in middle-class white neighborhoods does not mean that I had a privileged childhood, and I am not white; my status as a "native" of such a privileged place is shaky. I went home to do my fieldwork, but I did not do an ethnography of my own home, except in the most general sense.

This book is primarily about the world of ten-year-old poor and working-class black children in Newhallville, and their entanglements with the world of consumption. While it is a world that has been little described and poorly understood by those outside of it, I do not believe that there is much benefit in speaking about or thinking of that world as being cut off and isolated, as being "another" America. Since childhood, I have been astounded by the kind of racial and social segregation that can be seen in New Haven, a city that appears to be divvied up into disparate, mutually unintelligible worlds. At the same time, I have been suspicious about the degree to which these worlds truly are strangers to each other and wondered about the frequency with which borders are actually crossed. Certainly, my own crossing into the world of Newhallville allowed me to experience personally the degree to which the separateness between communities in New Haven is a collectively maintained social barrier, but one that is not so impossible to traverse.

To a degree, my own journey into and involvement with the world in which these children live and grow is pertinent to the ethnography that follows. It is not, however, the primary object of my attention. My aim in prefacing this book with a discussion of my own positioning is to get these issues out of the way so that they do not distract or confuse readers later on. In the introduction to this book, issues related to doing fieldwork at home are sketched out; they are addressed more fully in the book's afterword. For those interested in knowing more about these aspects of the work before diving into the ethnographic material, I suggest going to the final chapter first. I have not placed this material earlier in the book, however, because it seems to me that as it is, it takes almost too long to get to the lives of the children who are the focus of this work.

Children and childhood have been marginalized in ethnographic inquiry. In particular, the lives and worlds of children have rarely been viewed as profound enough, complex enough, or important enough to support serious social theory or political economy. A growing number of scholars have begun the important work of critically investigating childhood in ways that do not reproduce the paternalism (or maternalism) that has plagued much previous research, placing the lives and worlds of children at the center of social, historical, and political processes. In these new perspectives children are viewed as knowing historical subjects. As people whose lives have implications that go beyond a personal, small sphere, children are more than receivers of care and sustenance, consumers of food and resources: they are, like their adult and adolescent counterparts, active participants in the complex processes that make up daily life and global politics. This book does not engage in a detailed discussion of theoretical issues surrounding the theorization of children and childhood, although I view such questions to be of great importance.[1] Rather, in basing this ethnography on children while engaging questions of political economy, social justice, and social inequality, my belief is that the relevance of children's lives to these important arenas—and the ways in which we think about them—is made clear.

Acknowledgments

Back in the days when "cut and paste" meant scissors and tape, I remember watching my mother and stepfather spend hours, and sometimes all night, in frenzied editing sessions, putting together last-minute pasteups, making calls to track down references and sources. On the opposite coast, in California, I remember looking over my father's shoulder as he spent hour upon disciplined hour hammering out manuscripts for books, essays, plays. Having a novelist and playwright for a father, an editor for a mother, and a stepfather who was a writer and contributing editor for *Life* magazine, I have never expected writing to be easy. And it isn't. My parents—Suzanne Abrams, Frank Chin, and Brad Darrach—have each in their own way infused me with an appreciation for the power of language, how to use it, play with it, mold it, and when to toss it out. I am grateful to them for their example of how to undertake the discipline of writing, and how to experience it as one of life's necessities, however painful the endeavor.

At City University of New York Graduate Center, I was privileged to work with professors who understood what I was after and who helped me get to the heart of things. My advisor, Delmos Jones, was, in his quiet way, my surest guide and sounding board. Vincent Crapanzano, as an ever-present voice in my head, was my constant interlocutor, whether he knew it or not, and remains so. Cindi Katz helped me enter the world of children, in both practical and scholarly ways, and has been my shining example of how to take kids seriously while having fun. The ongoing support from and discussions I have had with John Sherry have been invaluable to this book and my growth as a scholar. After I had admired Russell Belk from afar for years, he provided a maniacally detailed set of comments for this book for which I am especially grateful. Josiah Heyman also generously and copiously commented on an earlier draft.

Many others have commented on parts of the manuscript, and their responses often spurred me into territory I might otherwise have neglected. Among these, Arlene Dávila, Maureen O'Dougherty, Susan Seizer, Jeff Tobin, and Mary Weismantel have been invaluable friends and critics through this process. At the University of Minnesota Press, my editor, Carrie Mullen, has been an unflagging source of hope and energy and has championed this book tirelessly.

Financial support from a number of sources made the research possible and later supported the writing of this book. Grants from the Wenner Gren Foundation for Anthropological Research and from the National Science Foundation allowed me to devote nearly two years to full-time research. The Kenneth and Mamie Phipps Clark fellowship from the CUNY graduate center gave me time to write and allowed me the memorable experience of meeting Dr. Clark himself. Despite the advice of my advisor, I took a job at Occidental College before my dissertation had been completed, and I must also thank my colleagues and the college for their support and patience. Teaching full time while finishing a dissertation is an easy recipe for disaster, and without their assistance and forbearance I might be telling a much sadder tale today. In particular, David Axeen, dean of faculty, has always graciously and generously provided me with time and/or funds to move this project to completion. The support of the Hermione Brown Fund at the college has generously paid for indexing, reproduction of photos, and photo permissions.

Occidental College is lucky in attracting interesting, bright, and engaging students. Katy Spencer is one of them, and her work during the final stages of manuscript preparation was invaluable. I must also thank Jennifer Petersen, whose interest in "rabble-rousing" has kept a social justice agenda constantly in front of me, and who in the last days of writing kept me supplied with healthful treats and a critical reader's eye.

All anthropologists owe their greatest debt, of course, to the people whose generosity and patience make our work and writing possible. My most important thank-yous must go to the children, families, teachers, and others in New Haven who endured my questions, made me welcome in homes and classrooms, and who still often enter my dreams— Tionna, Natalia, Asia, Teyvon, Cherelle, and the rest, you know who you are, although I cannot thank you here using your real names. Diane Garber, at the New Haven school system's central office, smoothed the way and pointed me in the right direction. The Hosen family slipped me information, fed and housed me, made crucial introductions, and saved my life more than once.

Finally, my husband, Robert Gardner, has the most inexhaustible fund of patience and goodwill of anyone I have ever known. I cannot imagine anyone else who could have lived through my making a book and a baby within a few months of each other, and have done so with such grace and love.

Consumption in Context

Natalia and Asia Do Barbie

New Haven, Connecticut, is known for its sweltering summers, and on this July afternoon in 1992 the swelter was prodigious. Hot, gluey air was slowly being stirred by an unenthusiastic breeze in Newhallville, a neighborhood populated by working-class and poor African Americans. The day wore on, and the air stilled. The sky became clogged with soggy, gray clouds. In the living room of ten-year-old Natalia's home, I was talking with her and her cousin Asia (also ten years old) when a suddenly invigorated wind began to twist the leaves off trees and the sky erupted downward, dumping down rain in drops the size of marbles, overpowering our voices with thunder. The girls rushed out of the house to sit on Natalia's stoop, braving the rain and lightning, hopping about like gazelles when the thunder made the houses shake. A thrill! Excitement! I spied a frazzle-haired Barbie doll beneath Natalia's seat and, holding my tape recorder, asked the girls to tell me about Barbie. Natalia held the doll's head under the drain spout to wash her face. With the thunder jolting them periodically from their chairs, Natalia and Asia delivered a dialogue keenly expressing their sense of cultural and social location:

ASIA: You never see a fat Barbie. You never see a pregnant Barbie. What about those things? They should make a Barbie that can have a baby.

NATALIA: Yeah . . . and make a fat Barbie. So when we play Barbie . . . you could be a fat Barbie.

ASIA: Okay. What I was saying that Barbie . . . how can I say this? They make her like a stereotype. Barbie is a stereotype. When you think of Barbie you don't think of fat Barbie . . . you don't think of pregnant Barbie. You never, ever . . . think of an abused Barbie.

A few minutes later, Natalia announced into the tape recorder: "I would like to say that Barbie is dope. But y'all probably don't know what that means so I will say that Barbie is *nice!*" Asia commandeered the tape recorder and took on an Oprah-like persona. Pretending to address an invisible, nationwide television audience, she announced, "The *[dramatic pause]* Streets *[dramatic pause]* of Newhallville *[dramatic pause]* . . . Next on the *Asia Show,*" intoning her words with the same overblown, mock solemnity pioneered on daytime talk shows.

Natalia and Asia's critique is about Barbie, but it is aimed at an imaginary national television audience. The forms of distance recognized by these girls in their dialogue—distance from commodities like Barbie, distance from the projected media audience, and distance from me—are central to their experience of the world of consumption and to their experiences of the world in general. As Natalia and Asia played at being talk-show hosts, they demonstrated an understanding that the primary consumers of media and the images it produces are neither generated in places like Newhallville nor aimed at people who live there. Natalia recognizes that audiences beyond the immediate vicinity literally do not speak her language, and she roughly translates the richly evocative "dope" with its hip and funky connotations as the equivalent of the word "nice," a word saturated with notions of propriety, acceptability, and adherence to the norm. Asia's stance as she addresses this audience is critical, playful, and ironic all at once. She knows that the audience for *Oprah* (or the *Asia Show*) is not interested in "the streets of Newhallville" as they exist and how their residents experience them, but rather audiences want to see and hear about "The *[dramatic pause]* Streets *[dramatic pause]* of Newhallville *[dramatic pause]* . . ." Just as the imagined television audience does not speak their language, Barbie does not represent a future to which Natalia or Asia can seriously or even imaginatively aspire. The specific alternatives these girls pose for Barbie address imperatives particular to their own lives: they wonder why there is no Barbie that is fat, or pregnant, or abused—a Barbie bearing the signs of being the kind of kid who might be living in Newhallville and having a life more rather than less like their own. Natalia and Asia's questions and observations are not just about Barbie. As poor black girls in a consumer world that does not extend full citizenship to them, what they are questioning goes beyond a single toy. They understand that in the consumer sphere normalcy is represented by the white middle class. In such a world, poor consumers are not only an oxymoron but an active threat to a cultural apparatus that is predicated upon the ability to buy.

This ethnography explores the consumer lives of poor and working-class minority children living in New Haven, Connecticut, a medium-sized New England city. Although the culture of consumption has been written about extensively, the breadth and complexity of consumption *within* contemporary industrialized societies has not yet seen much attention, particularly among anthropologists. In looking at the consumer lives of poor and working-class, racial-minority children, this work aims not only to explore and illustrate the ways in which contemporary commodity consumption is internally differentiated, but also to highlight an aspect of contemporary consumption that often has been overlooked: its role as a medium through which social inequalities—most notably of race, class, and gender—are formed, experienced, imposed, and resisted (Belk 1995; Carrier and Heyman 1997).

The question of the relationship between social inequality and consumption is important now because class, gender, sexuality, and race are often portrayed in popular forums as being consumer choices of individuals rather than being shaped in any important way by economics, history, or politics. The historical experiences of African Americans pose especially strong challenges to these notions: slavery and segregation, for example, have shaped the ways African Americans have engaged with the consumer sphere from the outset, both in terms of limiting their ability to consume and in constructing enslaved people as objects of the consumer desire of others. These processes, which were enforced from without as well as experienced from within, have profoundly influenced the consumption practices and beliefs not only of African Americans but of the "mainstream" as well—albeit in different ways. Tying the small details of children's daily activities, such as visiting the neighborhood store or the downtown mall, to ongoing structural processes illustrates that the context in which children engage with consumption shapes both the choices available to them and the choices that they make. In other words, the context of consumption matters, and matters quite a bit. In Newhallville girls walking to the neighborhood store fear rape, not racism. In contrast, at the mall they combat the perception that they are shoplifters because they are black, while fantasizing elaborately about romantic encounters.[1] Even popular media images of crazed and brand-addicted "inner city" youth willing to kill for the items they want are commodities that circulate among people and are consumed by them; as a belief that shapes not only the behavior of many toward these children, but also children's perceptions of themselves, this myth embodies contemporary consumption at its most ephemerally complex.

Karl Marx's oft-cited observation emphasized that people make their own history, but under "circumstances directly found, given and transmitted from the past" (Marx [1852] 1963). These kids undertake consumption under the same circumstances that shape all other aspects of their lives: wrenching economic change, rising social unrest, transformation of urban landscapes, all in an atmosphere of intensifying racism. Class, race, and gender differences in consumption cannot be attributed simply to neutralizing notions of product preferences or shopping habits, individual likes and dislikes. Rather, these differences may instead be viewed as being in large part expressions of or responses to structural oppression, which is itself often created and enforced through consumer channels.

In ethnographically documenting the ways in which Newhallville children engage with the realm of consumption, this work aims to show that social inequality cannot be reduced to a lifestyle choice, although individual choices—good and bad—are vital. When Asia speaks of "The [dramatic pause] Streets [dramatic pause] of Newhallville [dramatic pause] . . ." she draws upon popular imagery that portrays those streets as rife with vice, crime, and dissolution. In invoking these imaginary streets, Asia underscores the function of these stereotypes as a sort of social currency. Some people may "buy into" being on welfare, others "buy into" ideas about what it means to be on welfare, dealing drugs, poor, black, and so on.

Over the past century, each new generation has entered a new consumer world where the forms and avenues for consumption and commodification have multiplied exponentially. The twentieth century saw rapid and dramatic changes in the realms of private and public life that became subject to commodification, fetishization, and marketing. In Japan, for instance, it is possible for lonely businessmen to "rent" a family, complete with children who will sit down to dinner and have "family" conversation. For children like those in this study, born in the United States in the mid-1980s, the incursions made by commodity processes into their lives were more complete, compelling, and in some instances more pernicious than ever before. These children had been targeted as consumers since before birth; the 1980s saw a burgeoning of child-oriented commodities from the experiential (Gymboree and Chuck E. Cheese) to the Barbification or Teenage Mutant Ninja Turtle–ization of just about any product imaginable, including toiletries, linens, clothes, school supplies, foods, dishes, wallpaper, and furniture. The potential for a nearly seamless presence of commodities in any contemporary child's activity, space, or thought is the direct result of changing production and marketing practices, coupled with important developments (some would argue devolutions) of federal policy. These conditions are faced by nearly all children in the contemporary United States, for whom the commodity may no longer be an invasion of life but has become the stuff of life itself. The pervasive presence of the market in children's lives does not eliminate the possibility of confronting or resisting it, but the confrontation (or accommodation) plays out in specific ways among Newhallville kids who, because they are neither middle class nor white, are faced with especially difficult dilemmas.

In Newhallville children are made aware early on of the nuts and bolts of daily living in a way that is less common among middle-class families. Rather than being shielded from mysteries like rent, grocery budgets, and the cost of clothes, kids are often told exactly how much their needs cost the family and are expected at a young age to use their own money to buy socks, underwear, and other necessities. With many of their families experiencing daily difficulties in providing regular meals, these children also learn early on that their own indulgence can mean that someone close to them must do without. From divvying up the milk to figuring out where to sleep there is an emphasis on sharing and mutual obligation that can be onerous and demanding.

The consumer world in which these children operate is one where even the illusionary choices offered by the market are often out of reach: black kids who are kicked out of the mall for wearing their hats backward cannot get lost in the "commodity hall of mirrors" on offer there. Consumption in Newhallville is deeply social, emphasizing sharing, reciprocity, and mutual obligation. These demands and expectations are not always, or even mostly, put forth in an atmosphere of joyous communalism or a Dickensian sort of honorable and jolly poverty: sharing, reciprocity, and mutual obligation are often extracted from people rather than offered by them. This is especially so for children, who may find themselves in the position of being a resource to be shared with others or a burden to be passed from one person to another. Children are encouraged or required to participate actively in complex social and kinship networks through their various consumption activities, whether eating, making purchases, asking for clothes, school supplies, toys, or treats. In Newhallville, children's flights of fancy are continually brought to earth, and theirs is a consumer experience where desire is fettered by material deprivation and social demands. These are ties that can bind, chafe, and cut, but they are also ties that hold their world together.

After two years of field research in Newhallville my primary conclusion was that the monumental pathology commonly perceived to be overrunning our "inner cities" was not exactly monumental in Newhallville and, while present to some degree, was certainly only a small portion of what consumption was about for local kids. What did I see if it was not what we "know" is going on? The children in this study engage with the consumer world by talking about Barbie as well as by playing with her; by wanting an item, and not just possessing it; by knowing lyrics to commercial jingles without ever having laid eyes or hands on the object itself. Their engagements with the consumer world, at the material, ideological, personal, and communal levels, are continually constrained by family, friends, neighborhood, and larger social entities of city, state, and nation and the global economy. Children's consumer lives not only speak of these connections between themselves and the world at large but also embody them. The issue is not so simple as the invasion of children's worlds by masterminds of marketing: it is a long way from the corporate headquarters of Disney to the dining room. Despite the fact that mass-produced items are on their face all alike, it is the context in which they are used and understood by particular children that makes them meaningful.

In Newhallville the pressures of fantasy worlds projected by television, advertising, and the downtown mall collide with the profoundly antifantasy experience of being both economically strapped and black in the United States. From the outside, this mixture of consumer culture and poverty has long been viewed as dangerously combustible, resulting in crazed pathological consumers who kill for sneakers and are addicted to brands. Such destructive images are based more on fiction than they are on fact, and it is impossible to understand these children's lives as consumers or as people through a filter of these assumptions. I do not propose to replace such stereotypes with their opposite: an image of the poor as noble and giving and at one with their deprivation. Rather, in insisting that the stereotypes at both ends of the spectrum are flawed, my aim is to describe a more complex and contradictory terrain.

Thinking about Consumption

Watching ads on TV. Throwing your TV away. Fantasizing about a car or game or house or coat. Making budgets and clipping coupons. Glancing in a store window on the way to a meeting. Buying a pack of gum at a gas station. Playing with a toy. Riding a bus. Visiting a thrift shop. Doling out portions of baked beans to your children. Scavenging dumpsters for cans and food. Displaying a collection of teacups or plastic horses or trophies. Trying on makeup samples in a department store. Contemplating your favorite sportcoat. Shoplifting. Talking with your best friend about which strollers are best. The consumption process is not limited only to the active: shopping and making purchases. Rather, it includes engagement with a diverse range of materials, images, and ideas.

Like production, consumption is part of all societies, but contemporary commodity consumption is most often the subject of inquiry and critique. I make this point in part to underscore the fact that much consumption theory deals with a historically specific form of consumption, one dependent upon industrialization, mass production, commodity exchange, mass media, and, usually, capitalism. While contemporary commodity consumption is widely accepted as having first arisen in western society (Belk 1988), it is today far from being an exclusively western cultural form, as the growing anthropological literature can attest.[2] That said, there is no question that, although not distinctive to it, commodity consumption is a central feature of life in the United States; it is so important that Grant McCracken proposed that consumption has become the basis for American culture and society (1988). This does not mean, however, that American consumer culture can be considered to be uniform in either its form or content; the same diversity that typifies American cultures (immigrant, ethnic, racially marked, gendered) is also embedded in consumer lives in the United States. That is, while American culture is a consumer culture, it does not follow that consumer culture is inherently American.

Both Carl Nightingale (1993) and Alex Kotlowitz (1999) have suggested that poor African American children share mainstream American values precisely *because* they are deeply engaged in consumer culture. Like nearly all children in the United States, African American children are deeply engaged in consumer culture, but their engagement with consumption is not what makes them American. In conflating consumer culture with American culture these authors miss the point that consumer culture is diverse internally as well as globally.[3] The idea of consumer culture employed by Nightingale and Kotlowitz also centers on the desire for brand-name and status items, reducing consumption to its most ideologically charged aspects—aspects that are highly contested across class, gender, and racial lines. These desires should not be understood as being peculiarly "American" in any case: as Daniel Miller (1995b) writes, "none of us [is] a model of real consumption."[4] McCracken's proposal about consumption and culture in America suggests something much more than consumption-as-status-brands: in contemporary society everything is potentially commoditized and our lives are enmeshed with consumption not only through brand-name and status items, but also through the myriad other commodities bought and sold today, both tangible and intangible.

The question is not so much whether poor African American children can be demonstrated to share mainstream values because they desire to consume status goods, an assertion made further problematic in that it implies that the rest of black kids' lives are somehow un-American. Understanding the consumption of kids like those I knew in Newhallville requires a broad inquiry into their consumer lives that goes beyond a particular class of commodities and plumbs the connections between individual children, families, neighborhood, state, and nation. Moreover, I do not consider "mainstream" U.S. consumer orientations a norm against which these children's patterns ought to be measured or compared, a position that privileges middle-class taste and values, contributing to a dynamic in which "blacks are condemned and negatively stereotyped for engaging in activities that white people undertake without a second thought" (Austin 1994a, 225). Rather, I explicitly explore contemporary consumption as a sphere of inequality where differences in consumption are the result of processes beyond that of the accretion of individual desire. The consumer world I describe in this work is not one where both the poor and the middle class find spiritual togetherness in longing for the same things, nor is it one where the same items have similar "social biographies" (Kopytoff 1986) once they leave the store shelves.

While unwilling to take an unabashedly celebratory position regarding consumer culture, neither am I willing to condemn it as utterly dehumanizing. Both positions have been argued and explored in important streams of scholarship. Contemporary commodity consumption has been portrayed as creating false needs, substituting form for substance, and lulling the masses into illusory satisfactions. In the influential work of the Frankfurt school, scholars' passionate indictments of mass consumption were spurred by the conviction that true human freedom and potential were fatally compromised when people settled for what the profit-oriented capitalists were willing to provide them as wish and dream fulfillment (Adorno 1993; Marcuse 1964).[5] Such theorists as Jean Baudrillard have focused on the "system of objects" constituted in the consumer world, similarly viewing this world as dehumanizing (1981, 1986, 1988). For Baudrillard, contemporary consumer society has produced an endless whirlpool of communicating signs and simulacra, ephemera masquerading as reality, where people are sucked in as mere bystanders to the show. Certainly, when confronting a blank-faced toddler (or teenager, adult, or elderly person) who is glued to the television, Baudrillard hardly seems all wrong. There is no doubt that the realms of advertising, television, and marketing have transformed the roles of symbols and signs in contemporary cultures. As Wolfgang Haug (1986) asserts, sign value *is* use value.

Concerned primarily with the political and economic processes shaping consumer society, these theories as to how and why actual people engage in the consumer world are based primarily on guesswork rather than fieldwork.[6] In portraying the dynamic as largely being from the top down, with consumers being relatively passive recipients of products and services concocted by self-interested providers, this view tends to underestimate the range of ways in which people can and do interact with the world of consumption. In response to this perspective a number of works do not condemn mass culture and consumption as hopelessly uniform but instead view it as capable of being refashioned or resisted at the individual or popular level. Early investigations into resistance in the consumer sphere, such as those by John Fiske (1989) and Dick Hebdige (1979), focused on consumers who were often seen to be able to turn the juggernaut of mass culture to their own purposes. Seen as an antidote to the pessimistic view represented by the Frankfurt school, these works have also been criticized for romanticizing the scope and effectiveness of such resistance (Abu-Lughod 1990; Miller, Jackson, Thrift, Holbrook, and Rowlands 1998; Sholle 1990).

With consumption so firmly embedded in daily life, it becomes increasingly difficult to argue that it consists only of falsities and illusions that, if stripped away, would leave people able to pay attention to their "true" needs.[7] As Timothy Burke writes in his historical examination of the role of toiletries—hair grease, skin creams, deodorant—in modern Zimbabwe, a need is no less real for having been historically generated (1996, 216). Constrained by class, economy, racism, and gender, consumption is deeply embedded in social relations that people certainly do attempt to reshape, but they do not do so freely. As James Carrier and Josiah Heyman (1997) note, contemporary consumption is well within the realm of political economy. It is also a cultural arena in which issues of power, hegemony, and ideology confront each other *and* a medium through which these confrontations are mediated (Rutz and Orlove 1988).

Barbie can serve as an example here. There are cases of feminist activists undertaking guerrilla warfare and switching talking Barbie voice-boxes with those of G.I. Joe (Rand 1995, 159); a woman who has undergone dozens of surgeries in order to actually become a living Barbie (Lord 1994); a man who both enacts and soothes his grief over his partner's death from AIDS by creating huge and complex Barbie people-scapes in his home (Stern 1998); and, as Asia and Natalia noted at this chapter's outset, children who vocally challenge the validity of the world Barbie inhabits and represents. These few selected examples of the ways in which some people have used Barbie in their own lives is more than suggestive of the range of consumer engagements possible with mass-produced commodities. But one could hardly argue that making G.I. Joe say such Barbie-esque phrases as "Sometimes math is hard" is likely to change any girl's experience in an actual math class (unless perhaps she brought that G.I. Joe with her into the classroom). Similarly, while I offer an appreciation and even a celebration of Asia and Natalia's critique of Barbie, I remain unconvinced that their awareness of Barbie's faults— from their point of view—will lead to substantive change in the larger social problems upon which their awareness alights.

As ethnographers have moved into examining consumers as well as such industries as advertising, television, and marketing, it has become increasingly evident that consumption is at once a hegemonic force deserving of condemnation and a realm in which people exercise considerable power and creativity. In an ethnography of shopping among residents in a North London neighborhood, Miller explores the way in which shopping can be used for a variety of social purposes, among them expressing love for kin, playing out courtship, attempting to educate children, or giving oneself a "treat" (Miller 1998). In developing a theory of shopping that ultimately views this activity as a form of ritual sacrifice, Miller purposefully puts shopping onto traditional anthropological ground, viewing this much-maligned activity as a modern form of ritual within which are contained profound social themes and imperatives. In a very different vein, Arlene Dávila (forthcoming) shows (in the case of the Hispanic marketing industry) the construction of media images, creation of ad campaigns, and the emergence of ethnic markets as a deeply complex political process that cannot be understood simply as the brainchild of scheming advertisers and greedy corporations. Rather, in this case, marketers themselves, as well as the market they seek to define, are mutually shaped by the vagaries of immigration, U.S. racial hierarchies, and the social politics of language. Like Dávila's study of the Hispanic market, my work seeks to understand consumption as embedded in everyday politics, resonating with the larger political economy in which consumer items, images, and opportunities are generated. This explicitly political terrain is fraught with tensions, many arising from the multiple forms of social inequality that permeate most contemporary lives and identities: those of race, class, gender, age, and sexuality.

Consumption and Social Inequality

Much research on the consumer lives of those who are poor and/or minority has been generated within the concepts of "disadvantaged consumers" or the "ghetto market." Interest in these areas was sparked in the late 1960s, precipitated by widespread urban unrest and the 1967 riots in major U.S. cities, including Chicago, Los Angeles, Detroit, and New Haven (Andreasen 1975; Caplovitz 1967; Honeycutt 1975; Sturdivant 1969). Looting—or what Fiske (1994), in an examination of the 1991 Los Angeles riots, calls "radical shopping"—was an important element in these riots, alerting consumer and marketing researchers to the effects of race, class, poverty, and ghettoization on consumers. It could be argued that the problems sparking the riots of 1967 have actually intensified since that time (real wages are down, social welfare budgets are shrinking along with municipal tax rolls, businesses are fleeing "inner city" areas, and so on), yet the interest in the consumer lives of those who are not middle class seems largely to have fizzled. Alan Andreasen charges that "these changing and worsening problems [are] subject to sustained neglect on the part of academic researchers" (1986, 113).

Extant studies document the particular difficulties typically faced by disadvantaged consumers: local stores carrying inferior brands for inflated prices, high incidence of time-payment at usurious rates of interest; poor access to well-stocked supermarkets and pharmacies; an absence of local banks; and a dearth of businesses such as dry cleaners, hardware stores, and the like (Alwitt 1995; Andreasen 1975, 1976, 1986; Honeycutt 1975). These studies document as well the money-management strategies adopted by households where earnings often are not generous enough to cover the cost of rent, food, and transportation, much less such essentials as cleaning supplies, telephone service, school pencils and notebooks, household appliances, clothing, and medical care (Edin 1991; Honeycutt 1975; Okongwu 1996).

Much consumption theory founders on the question of poor consumers because it implicitly assumes that consumers are, first and foremost, middle class. And yet, although poor consumers remain largely unaccounted for, their consumer entanglements are not less real for the lack of scholarly attention. As Regina Austin observes, the kind of bourgeois intellectual attention that tends to be aimed at poor black consumers often takes the form of moralizing and pronouncements of taste (1994b). The not-so-subtle message often seems to be that if only those people would get themselves on track (by wanting the right things, dressing appropriately, buying the right foods), they too could be middle class. And there's the rub—getting on track is not simply an issue of willpower and stick-to-it-iveness. Consumption does not take place in a vacuum-sealed world of signs and symbols, but rather in a messy material world where other processes are also at work. Thus, while this book is expressly concerned with the consumer lives of Newhallville children, I also argue that these consumer lives cannot be understood apart from the political and economic context and the productive milieu. This is not meant to imply that consumption is ultimately reducible to questions of production. The conditions present in the local, national, and even global economies that create landscapes dominated by empty factories, abandoned homes, and empty lots, a social scene with poverty and joblessness on the rise and education on the decline, are conditions that profoundly influence the ways in which these children come to understand themselves and the world in which they live.

Asia and Natalia's comments about Barbie ("nice," not "dope"; why not fat?; why not abused?) were generated less than two blocks away from the rubble of the factory that once employed 12,000 people, across the street from a now burned-out three-story apartment building, facing a road badly patched and potholed and minimally maintained by the city. Their comments and perceptions were not caused by these conditions, but they were surely shaped by them—and would not have meant quite the same thing if uttered by their upper-middle-class peers living in the handsome brick and Tudor mansions a quarter of a mile away in the Prospect Hill neighborhood. While those living in poor urban areas are undoubtedly both isolated and alienated from the communities around them, they are also connected to those places. This was particularly clear in New Haven, where kids from Newhallville regularly left their neighborhood to go to school, go downtown, visit relatives, or go to the supermarket. The role of geographic space in the lives of the urban poor is multidimensional, and a variety of places are important to them beyond the neighborhoods in which they live.

Feminist theorists have emphasized the multiple axes and experiences of subjectivity (Moore 1988; Visweswaran 1994) and, similarly, a number of feminist geographers emphasize that space itself is experienced and constructed in multiple rather than unitary ways (Holcomb 1986; Rose 1984). Feminist geographers have not been alone in conceptualizing geographic spaces as being constructed and contested in multiple ways by relations of class, race, and gender. From the very specifically located work of Neil Smith on New York's Thompkins Square Park (1992) to David Harvey's influential treatises on changes in capitalism and geography (1989), geographers have been building perspectives that focus upon making connections between the individual and a larger political economy and have tended to avoid portraying the "inner city" as a world apart. I find it useful to add the spatial dimension to the inquiry into people's consumer lives because it leads the inquiry away from a tightly focused attention on an individual and a commodity, making larger social processes relevant. Furthermore, incorporating social geography as an element in consumption, and particularly in the consumption of the poor, exposes notions of self-perpetuating poverty as problematic: the processes at work in creating a terrain where downtown is hostile to black and brown shoppers, and where only two major supermarkets lie within the city's boundaries impinge forcefully on Newhallville residents' lives but are not of their own making. In the section that follows, I turn to a description of that world, focusing especially on Newhallville.

Newhallville

Newhallville has long been a working-class neighborhood, but since the 1950s the residents have become increasingly impoverished. By the 1990s the once ethnically and economically diverse community now had a 91.7 percent minority population and a poverty rate approaching 30 percent. Often referred to as "the 'Ville," Newhallville has a reputation for being a tough, if not downright dangerous place to be. Nowhere is this perception more strong than it is in the upper-middle-class, predominantly white neighborhoods lying adjacent to the 'Ville. Despite the proximity to the wealthiest parts of town, Newhallville is characterized by multiple forms of isolation—geographic, social, economic, commercial—and yet is intimately tied to the rest of the nation and globe in each of these ways. Kids like Natalia and Asia are aware of these connections, and this awareness can be seen most clearly in the area of consumerism and popular culture. These kids see and know about nearly all the same TV programs, stores, and goods that most other American kids do. Their relationships to these commodities, and to the process of consumption itself, are distinctive and characterized by complex and contradictory circumstances that often leave children like Natalia and Asia living in what is sometimes referred to as "the other America," that is, the one that is economically strapped and populated by racial minorities.

Connecticut is an especially dramatic study in social and economic contrasts between these two Americas: in 1990 it was the wealthiest of the fifty states in terms of per capita income, while also being home to three of the poorest cities in the nation. Located eighty miles northeast of New York City on the shore of Long Island Sound, New Haven is a medium-sized city of about 130,000. As the home of the prestigious Yale University, one aspect of New Haven's image is of a gracious New England town, with a central green, a proud colonial history, old money, and a Yankee sense of both thrift and possibility. The Grove Street Cemetery, where such historically important Americans as Eli Whitney are buried, is filled with crumbling brownstone grave markers from the 1600s and earlier. As the inventor of the cotton gin, Eli Whitney is a figure who also connects the former slave economy of the South with later migrations of African Americans north, into cities like New Haven and neighborhoods like Newhallville.

Since its founding, New Haven had been as much a bustling manufacturing town as it was a seat of learning. By midcentury local companies were producing guns and other munitions, tires, beer, paper, caskets, apparel, and bagels, and for decades New Haven had handily (though not always happily) accommodated a wide variety of migrants and immigrants. The years surrounding the two world wars were especially productive, as much of New Haven's factory output centered around munitions. The manufacturing boom peaked in the 1950s, and since then the city's population has shrunk by 20,000. Today two local hospitals and the university are the largest employers along with retail stores, utilities, and restaurants (New Haven Downtown Council 1992). As in many parts of the once-industrial Northeast, the shift from manufacturing to service economy has entailed severe social readjustment. In 1980 New Haven was the seventh poorest city of its size in the United States (U.S. Bureau of the Census 1980); for cities over 100,000, New Haven ranked first in the nation in infant mortality in 1994 (Reguero and Crane 1994).[8] The city also possesses a hefty illegal drug trade, a nearly bankrupt shopping mall, a struggling downtown area, and deeply troubled public schools. As is often the case, economic differences tend to overlap with racial differences, and the poorest areas of the city are populated primarily by blacks and Latinos, most of whom are from Puerto Rico. However, New Haven's residential segregation is hardly the result of such social processes as individual preference; that is, saying that "blacks [or Puerto Ricans, or whites, or the Irish] like to live together" cannot entirely or even primarily account for the on-the-ground situation. Rather, residential patterns can be seen as the not-wholly surprising outcome of programmatic urban restructuring undertaken by successive New Haven political administrations and city agencies. Thus, while such communities as Newhallville are effectively isolated from the rest of the city in multiple ways, this isolation has been accomplished to a great degree through processes that originate outside the community. Paradoxically, then, it is the very processes working to isolate areas like Newhallville that also tie these locations into the larger region. Residential segregation is a case in point.

Already well under way in the first half of this century, residential segregation was given a big boost in the years during which New Haven undertook extensive urban redevelopment. It was also during this period, roughly the late 1950s through the mid-1970s, that the local economy made the difficult shift from manufacturing to service. The combined pressure of these two major events proved especially disruptive for the black community. In the United States urban renewal often has come hand in hand with the decimation of black residential neighborhoods, and the ghettoization of Newhallville has resulted in no small measure from a combination of such projects and programs. One of the most important sources of funds was the federally supported "Model Cities" program: New Haven had emerged as the nation's model "model city" by the time the Great Society years were in full swing (Dahl 1961; Fainstein and Fainstein 1974). Robert Dahl, in his classic study of political organization and participation in New Haven, writes:

> By the end of 1958, New Haven had spent more federal funds per capita for planning its redevelopment projects than any of the country's largest cities, more than any other city in New England, and more than any other city of comparable size except one. Only one city in the country, the nation's capital, had received more per person in capital grants. . . . By 1959 much of the center of [New Haven] was razed to the ground. (1961, 121–22)

From the late 1950s through the early 1970s, over half a billion federal dollars funded urban redevelopment projects to improve economic and living conditions in New Haven. Much of the razing that Dahl notes was accomplished in one of New Haven's oldest and most established neighborhoods of black working-class homeowners. The now infamous

Oak Street Connector was a highway project meant to connect two major interstates. In the 1960s several blocks of houses were torn down in preparation for the highway project. After nearly forty years the project remains unfinished and is unlikely ever to be completed. Urban renewal projects eventually displaced almost 40 percent of New Haven's black population, leveling long-standing communities of houses and homeowners to relocate residents to housing projects owned and administered by city and federal agencies (Minerbrook 1992). The social isolation of neighborhoods such as Newhallville may be seen as an outcome of urban redevelopment, which transported families and neighborhoods away from downtown to more distantly located developments less accessible to jobs and commercial centers. Social factors internal to the black community are undoubtedly responsible to some degree for ongoing social and economic crises, but such internal social factors did not tear down neighborhoods and the social relationships that permeated them.[9]

The history of urban redevelopment in New Haven is only one example of how the city appears to be less and less amenable to its minority population. A city-wide property reassessment hiked 1992 residential property taxes about 40 percent. This was the first step in a five-year tax increase due to raise payments an average of 238 percent (Yarrow 1992). This development came as a blow to many Newhallville residents, who had hoped with the election of John Daniels, the city's first black mayor, that they would have closer and less contentious ties with city hall than had previously been the case. The great-grandmother of one child I knew did feel at home enough with Daniels (whom she remembered as a young man) to call him up herself and give him a piece of her mind about her ballooning tax bill, but the newfound ability to personally blow off steam with the mayor yielded little in terms of material benefits. These recent economic changes have changed the Newhallville landscape dramatically, and abandoned buildings have begun to multiply at an alarming rate. They can be found on almost every block in the neighborhood, fallout from bankruptcies and the vagaries of absentee landlords who control nearly two-thirds of the area's housing units (U.S. Department of Commerce 1993).

Newhallville's tree-lined streets are flanked by two- and three-story frame houses and at first glance the area seems unlikely to have garnered its reputation as one of the poorest and most problem-ridden areas of the city. The neighborhood's median household income in 1990 was $20,569; 26.6 percent of Newhallville residents lived in poverty (U.S. Department of Commerce 1993). The neighborhood's 1990 poverty rate for children aged 5 years and under was 50 percent. These economic extremes are a relatively recent development. Newhallville was for many decades a thriving, multiethnic neighborhood filled with blue-collar workers who owned their homes and worked in nearby factories. These factories set the rhythm of the area, punctuating the day with streams of people going to and from work on one of the three daily shifts. One longtime resident recalled a neighbor whom she had never met, but who used to walk past her house every night, using a shortcut that went through her backyard, whistling on his way to his graveyard-shift job at the Winchester plant.

Inhabited by successive waves of German, Irish, Italian, and African American residents, Newhallville's fortunes have depended largely on those of the Winchester Repeating Arms plant. Employing 12,000 during the World War II years, by the late 1970s that number was only about 1,400 (City of New Haven 1982). Only 475 people worked at Winchester in 1992. Today, Newhallville residents work as home health aides, nursing assistants, nurses, janitors, teachers, police officers, and firefighters, among other things. While these jobs often offer some benefits and security, they just as often do not, and rarely do any of these forms of employment rival that which was once offered at the factory in terms of pay, regularity, and security. Moreover, when factories were major employers, it was possible to land a well-paying job with only a high school diploma. Many service-sector jobs require not only a high school diploma but additional, specialized education or training, and Newhallville residents must now be more highly educated and enter the workforce later than in the past. These are also jobs that typically demand or create a highly feminized workforce. Despite these changing labor force demands, public schools have been increasingly troubled, with high schools graduating in some cases less than half of any incoming class.

During the past several years, the city has been engaged in transforming the former site of the Winchester plant into an industrial park. This success has been tentative at best (City of New Haven Blue Ribbon Commission 1990); at the time of my research the facility was unfinished and only partly occupied. In an ironic twist, one of the most visible occupants of Science Park is the New Haven Family Alliance, a nonprofit organization devoted to helping dysfunctional families and troubled youth. During my fieldwork neighborhood residents had to ask security guards for permission to enter the former site of their (or their parents') employment in order to visit an organization whose purpose is to help families deal with stress and behaviors related to their poverty and underemployment.

The site of the now nearly defunct Winchester plant powerfully embodies the changing nature of New Haven in the experience of Newhallville residents. Not only have successive waves of redevelopment shut the residents out, except as the recipients of social services related to dysfunction, but the gated and guarded borders are also a reminder that they are to some extent shut in as well. One Newhallville resident, a youth of about eighteen years, had a deeply apocalyptic view of New Haven and described in great detail a plan—supposedly a secret pact between Yale University and the city administration—to cut off electricity, water, and food delivery to black neighborhoods should race riots ever occur. As he said, "They'll starve us out." Whether or not such a plan exists is to some degree irrelevant in the face of the widely held belief that such a plan has, indeed, been laid.

The Study

Over the course of nearly two years, I conducted participant observation in homes, schools, and neighborhoods and also engaged in more directed research such as taking children on shopping trips. What I saw repeatedly underscored that for these children consumption entails the negotiation of intimate and complex terrains of obligation, reciprocity, need, and desire. Fantasy was, of course, a significant dimension of children's consumer lives, as the discussion between Asia and Natalia shows, and children's consumption lives were not solely focused on tactical maneuvers within household networks. The overall tenor of these children's consumer lives, however, emphasized self-control, realistic assessment of personal and family resources, and contributions to the household—especially to mothers and grandmothers.

The research centers around the twenty-two children who were members of Lucy Aslan's fifth-grade classroom in 1991–92. My initial introduction to Newhallville came through the Shelton Avenue School, and I discuss the implications and complexities of this in the book's final chapter. The spring before I began intensive work with Lucy Aslan's class, I offered a class through the afterschool program, working with a small group of children to develop and conduct a local study asking adults "what life was like in this neighborhood when you were young." This allowed me to get familiar both with the school and the community, and, perhaps most important, established me as someone parents could trust (the study is discussed more fully in the afterword). It was during this time that I met Tionna, Natalia, and Asia,[10] around whom much of this ethnography centers, and over the course of the summer I spent hours and hours following them through a variety of activities: exploring downtown, walking through the neighborhood, going to local stores, just hanging out in their houses or on their stoops. In the fall I spent time in the classroom, sometimes helping children with their reading or math, other times simply observing. I went on field trips, attended afterschool rehearsals, school fairs, class parties. On one hellish day I actually served as the substitute teacher. While it didn't help me manage the chaos at the time, the degree to which the kids refused to accept me in the authoritative role of classroom teacher was comforting later. If this group of children is described as a "sample" they do not constitute a random group; nevertheless, the children and their families were representative of that neighborhood, which was both economically diverse and complex (see appendix A). Households ranged in size from the two people in Terry's home to the six people in Ricky's and Tarelle's homes. Households were headed by single mothers (11), mother and father (4), married grandparents (3), aunts (2), a single grandmother (1), and a great-grandmother (1). Nine of the families lived in homes they owned; six families used a Section 8 voucher to pay their rent, but among these two were renting apartments in homes owned by another resident family member.[11] Six of the households had no car of their own. Several of the grandparents and great-grandparents were retired from jobs as firefighters, cafeteria workers, and janitors. Stephen's parents earned a combined income they estimated at $90,000 a year, and this family was far and away the most financially well off of those I knew; families on state and federal aid (fully half of those discussed here) rarely had much extra money at all. The others worked in jobs as diverse as seamstress, building maintenance, group home supervisor, home health aide, mechanic. Life was not necessarily much easier for these working folk than it was for those on aid: Natalia's grandfather told me that his pension and his wife's work as a domestic worker provided them and their two resident grandchildren an income of $18,000 yearly.

As families grew more familiar with me I was able to attend celebrations, accompany mothers on grocery shopping trips, conduct a small number of inventories of children's rooms, and go on special outings—shopping trips in Jamaica, Queens, or trips to amusement parks. Children were included in some of these activities, but not all. Getting a wider sense of the full consumer engagement of families and households was important for situating the knowledge and experience of the children I knew and also gave me a chance to talk with caretakers about their perspectives on their children and their children's activities, wants, and problems.

Three girls—Tionna, Natalia, and Asia—are at the core of what follows in the succeeding chapters. Over the course of my time in Newhallville I came to know these girls and their families best. Tionna's great-grandmother, Ella, had been her primary caretaker since birth. Tionna's grandmother, Celia, was also living in the same household. The family was neither especially well off nor especially poor in comparison to other Newhallville residents: Ella owned the family's home, paying for the mortgage, property taxes, insurance, heat, and utilities on her retirement income. After working for more than forty years in the cafeteria of the local hospital, Ella retired at age seventy due to knee trouble. Celia, Ella's daughter, was in her early fifties and received state aid for her own and Tionna's support.

Tionna was nine years old when I met her. She was tall for her age, with a sweet, intelligent face that she could transform into a mask of baleful reproach in an instant. Her gait was shambling and slightly off-balance, as if she were being pulled to the side by some sort of weight or absence. And there was a large absence in her life: the year before we met Tionna's mother had been shot and killed in an incident that was rumored to have been drug related. One afternoon early in my fieldwork, I walked Tionna home after school and she told me of her mother's death in a matter-of-fact, almost distant manner, saying, "My mother said she'd be there for my birthday but things didn't work out like that." She was the only child in the study to have lost a parent to a violent death, yet her situation was not unique: many of the others had lost brothers, uncles, or other close relatives in a similar manner, or to AIDS or the penal system.

Natalia was one of Tionna's close friends. Whereas Tionna still had her baby fat, Natalia had the stick-thin figure of a girl who has just shot into puberty. She lived around the corner from Tionna with her older brother and her maternal grandparents. Natalia's mother lived only a few blocks away, with her boyfriend, and Natalia moved back and forth between these two homes. She had a particular talent for managing to be away from her grandparents' home when it was time to go to church—where her grandmother was pastor and her grandfather a deacon—on Sunday mornings and Thursday evenings. Natalia's well-timed absences contributed to her reputation for being a little wild and unmanageable. She was never someone to walk when she could run, and the small frame house her grandparents own often reverberated from the force of Natalia's feet pounding on the stairs as she dashed up to answer the phone or down to get the door.

Natalia's cousin Asia had recently moved in next door. Asia's father had died the year before from heart trouble, and Asia's mother, deeply depressed, gave up the family's home and was unable to work for several months. Asia, her mother, and her brother shared a two-bedroom apartment with Asia's aunt and uncle. Unlike Natalia and Tionna, who attended the local elementary school, Asia went to a parochial school in another neighborhood. She had a dry, ironic sense of humor and often made up tales, telling them to friends with great drama lighting up her round face and almond-shaped eyes.

The three girls spent time together nearly every day, sitting on their stoops, wandering the neighborhood, playing, running errands, and, on occasion, going downtown. Their caretakers all knew and trusted each other, telling me that they were "good people," and when one girl was with the family of the others, caretakers knew they did not have to worry about where the girls were or wait watchfully for them to return home. These girls' friendships, though strong, also seemed to proceed in cycles, with Tionna sometimes complaining about Asia, Natalia complaining about Tionna, Asia complaining about one or the other of the girls. They would take breaks from each other's company, sometimes for weeks at a time, spending time with other kids instead and pointedly ignoring the others. Nevertheless, overall, their friendship endured during the time I lived in New Haven, and I found them in each other's company more often than not.

A Note about Me

In recent years the question of the ethnographer's identity and positioning has become increasingly important in the writing and doing of our work. This ethnography is and is not a piece of "native" anthropology. I grew up in New Haven, but I did not grow up in Newhallville, and in the book's afterword I discuss in greater depth the complexities of going home to do fieldwork. While nearly all of the people I knew and spent time with in Newhallville are black, I am half white and half Chinese. Many might wonder how a half-white, half-Chinese anthropologist can claim to know or understand anything about the lives and worlds of black kids.

As a number of prominent black anthropologists have pointed out, being of the same race as the people you are researching is no guarantee of mutual understanding and can pose obstacles for discovering information (Jones 1970; Williams 1996). Brackette Williams explored in depth her status as a "stranger" in a black community in Alabama; here her "skinfolk," elderly African Americans, did not recognize her as one of them simply on the basis of race. Williams, in turn, was forced to "figure out the politics of racial and other status positionings as these applied to particular persons" in order to do her fieldwork (84). Racial groups are far from homogeneous and factors other than race may facilitate or impede effective fieldwork—even in the hyperracially conscious United States.

In my case, class was probably a more relevant divide than was race. First of all, my racial identity was a subject at times of confusion: people in Newhallville variously thought of me as white, Chinese, black, or just racially indeterminate. (In other settings, I have also been thought to be Puerto Rican, Native American, Peruvian, Haitian, Jamaican, Cuban, and East Indian.) However, there was rarely, if ever, any confusion over my status as a graduate student and future professional. These were both made evident every day not only by my speech but also by my dress. My jeans and unironed t-shirts were tolerated by the kids but viewed as hopelessly tacky. On days where I did dress up—ironing my clothes, choosing my colors carefully, sleeking my hair down with gel and hairspray—they richly rewarded me with praise and smiles. In the beginning, my being a graduate student and also being associated with the local elementary school meant that families responded to me with the kind of reserved deference they showed teachers, social workers, and welfare officials. Throughout my fieldwork I was called "Miss Chin" by all children and most adults, in part because of my affiliation with the school, and in part because in Newhallville this relatively formal form of address is common. Children often explained to others that I was their "teacher" but never directly referred to me in that way, having quickly figured out that I was not a "real" teacher since I rarely enforced any rules above and beyond trying to stop them from running headlong into moving traffic, jumping off roofs, and, in one case, I attempted to put the lid on a raucous striptease in a parking lot. Typically, then, as an anthropologist in these children's world I defied any ready categorization and they used the closest explanation they could muster, albeit one that only partially fit. As my dealings with kids and families became increasingly ad hoc and informal, my relationships became more comfortable and some began to refer to me as a quasi-family member, some even adjusting to address me on a first-name basis.

It would be naïve to claim that these differences did not matter, and, like any ethnographer, had I been someone else there are pieces of information large and small that I might have discovered simply because of who I was (or who people thought I was). The reverse also holds true: much of what people said to me or did with me was the result of our own particular and unique relationship. Still, it is also arrogant to assume that one's own influence is so profound that any conversation, any social event in which an ethnographer is an active participant observer, is so profoundly transformed that it just would not have happened that way in the researcher's absence. If only we were so omnipotent!

Certainly, people's idea of who I was influenced them in their relationships to me, and vice versa. But none of us were wholly reinvented for these encounters, and the community I describe in this book is a true one. I say that this is "a" true version rather than "the" true version and emphasize that truth, like reality, is not singular. This does not mean that reality is up for grabs and everything is subjective; there's a middle ground between some imagined possibility of absolute objectivity and the equally simplistic idea that if absolute objectivity does not exist it is all just a matter of personal opinion. That middle ground is the messy expanse of fact plus meaning, observation plus interpretation, system plus serendipity.

The Plan of the Book

The pervasive theme of this book is that the consumer sphere, by its very nature, is a medium for social inequality. In the next chapter I lay the groundwork for understanding the particular complexities of black consumer engagement in the contemporary United States. The first analytical section locates the consumer experience of blacks historically, examining slavery as a long-term influence on black and white consumption. The second looks at contemporary media depictions of black and minority youth as out of control and dangerous "combat consumers." Together these analyses insist that any understanding of black consumption must be understood in its specific cultural, historical, and political context, one that engages with centuries-old incidents like slavery, as well as symbolic representations of blacks in the consumer world. For readers wishing to enter the world of Newhallville more immediately, I suggest moving directly to chapter 3 and returning to the theoretical material later.

Natalia, Tionna, and Asia, ten-year-olds when this research began, are the three children whose experiences are the linchpin of this work. Chapter 3 provides description and thumbnail analysis of a variety of daily events in their lives—trading lunches at school, a sidewalk cucumber stand, running around the mall, playing with Barbie on a stoop—and illustrates the vitality and richness of these girls' engagements with the consumer sphere. These are placed in the context of family, neighborhood, and city settings, all of which pose certain restraints and possibilities. Parents, for instance, constantly remind children of how much their maintenance and care cost in material and psychic terms; in response, these children consistently limit or curtail their requests for food, clothing, or other items. Narratives about the dangers and problems of being black consumers in a racist (white) world are also an integral part of children's consumption experience; these narratives tell the story of these dangers and problems, while also crafting responses to them. These particular ethnographic details illuminate the inadequacy of current models of consumption, and of children's consumption in particular, for describing and accounting for poor and working-class children of color. Such models are implicitly (and often explicitly) based on the white middle class and thus make patterns such as those seen in Newhallville appear to be distortions or pathologies. The title of the chapter, "What Are You Looking At, You White People?" is a question that Tionna shouted out one day to a passing car, and a question which, in the face of popular stereotypes and biased models, guides the inquiry presented here.

Moving from children's individual lives, chapter 4 traces the history of New Haven and Newhallville, focusing on how changing vistas in employment and production have shaped New Haven and Newhallville as consumer environments for Newhallville kids. Insights from social geography play a critical role in this analysis, which views the space of the city and neighborhood as the result of social and political processes. The role of urban renewal, for instance, was pivotal in creating a city that is segregated racially, economically, educationally, and in employment. This history gives distinct shape to children's consumer experiences in New Haven, where territories are bounded in multiple ways. An analysis of dilemmas faced by Newhallville girls as they shop in local stores is contrasted with their experiences in a downtown shop selling inexpensive jewelry. In Bob's, a local grocery, neither the girls' poverty nor their blackness is an issue; in Claire's, a downtown accessory shop, these define the prickly nature of encounters there.

Children in the study were taken on shopping trips in order to get a detailed, concentrated look at how they shop, what they buy, and where they spend money. The analysis of the shopping trips presented in chapter 5 ethnographically plumbs children's purchases, connecting those items to their lives and social experiences. The shopping trips take on meaning only in the context of the wider culture in which children operate, and their purchases open up pathways into exploring the complex social obligations they continually negotiate. The ethnographic view provided by the shopping trips, however, provides a stark contrast to popular images examined in chapter 2.

In response to a minority consumer market that wields increasingly impressive economic clout, toy companies have begun to produce what are called "ethnically correct dolls" that feature skin tones and facial features said to accurately represent those of children of varying racial backgrounds other than white. Evidence collected among Newhallville children, however, shows that few of these children owned such toys. In chapter 6 I analyze the goals and ideology behind the production of ethnically correct toys, which can be traced back to the shocking realizations of the psychological studies about race and self-perception cited in the Supreme Court's landmark school desegregation decision, *Brown v. Board of Education*. Although ethnically correct dolls are aimed at helping in the formation and maintenance of "self-esteem," the Newhallville evidence raises the question as to what happens to black children who do not possess these dolls? I assert that these children are engaged in what is at least potentially a much more radical project, that of bringing their blonde-haired and blue-eyed dolls into their own worlds, largely in part through the elaborate braiding and beading that is done on these dolls' heads. Similarly, girls attempted to bring me into this world by beading and braiding what they described as my "Barbie-doll hair."[12]

The final chapter of this work reflects on my ongoing involvement in the lives of these children, and the intertwining of my own remembered childhood with the childhoods they are quickly leaving behind. This is further complicated by the fact that I myself grew up in New Haven. These overlappings provide fertile material for raising questions about the nature of contemporary ethnography and for doing ethnography "at home."

2.

The Shadow of Whiteness

When I began to write about Newhallville, there was no ready way to do this because the available words—like the term *inner city*—are not descriptive in the sense that they bring a reality to life. Rather, they take aim at targets: in the words of one Newhallville resident, the term *inner city* is "just another way of saying niggers."[1] Although Newhallville is a mostly minority area and often referred to as "the ghetto" by both residents and outsiders, it is also economically diverse. The coded meaning of such terms as *inner city* and *ghetto* precludes recognition or analysis of such diversity. Similarly, in a culture where black children are assumed to be poor, as they so often are in the United States, little room is left for consideration of the working-class or middle-class black kid, much less a community where children from a variety of social strata live, play, and go to school together. Poverty is often itself portrayed as remarkably flat and unelaborated, but the bald fact of poverty does not, in fact, lead to lives that are all the same.

The problem of talking about consumption in a place like Newhallville is not limited to vocabulary and language. Whether the questions have come from political camps located left, right, or center, they have often been phrased in terms of "What is wrong?" rather than asking "What is happening?" The two questions open up vastly different spaces of inquiry, one beginning from an assumption of problems, the other more open to exploration and surprise. Beginning from an assumption that the worst urban poverty is the best kind of poverty to pay attention to, the public, books, documentaries, Hollywood films, and the nightly news all tend to reaffirm daily the sense that the borders of the world's most wild and untamed lands are contained within our urban landscapes, not outside them. These lands are continually being rediscovered, to the apparent shock of many. Every few years a documentary like *Hoop Dreams* breaks into the public consciousness as if describing a new and unknown tribe. In the late 1960s Jonathan Kozol's descriptions of the ferocity of economic and racial oppression in Boston public schools (Kozol 1967) were a revelatory slap in the face; nearly thirty years later his *Savage Inequalities* (Kozol 1991) surprised and angered the public afresh—and with no apparent sensation of collective déjà vu. These accounts are moving and important, but I am continually mystified by the assertion (most often made by book reviewers, perhaps) that they speak about something we did not know before. The most disheartening examples of this kind of social amnesia are the stunningly similar reports written after the Watts riots of 1968 and the South Central riots of 1992 (Fogelson 1969; Los Angeles Board of Police Commissioners 1992).

From Oscar Lewis's *La Vida* (1966) to Philippe Bourgois's *In Search of Respect* (1995), the ethnography of poverty has tended to focus on harsh material realities and, while highlighting the point that those who live in poverty can think and speak about their situations with great insight, has not often addressed the ways in which those who are economically strapped understand and manipulate the symbolic world around them. This has had the effect of making it appear as if it is primarily the educated (white) middle class that has the tools for critically examining modern consumer culture, and hearkens back to nineteenth-century European beliefs that "primitive man" spent so much time attempting to scrape together some food, clothing, and shelter that "he" had no time to engage in philosophizing, creating religion, making music or art. Thinking about urban or minority poverty as being just an economic problem is a limited perspective. In a society that criminalizes the consumption of urban minority youth, what is needed is not just a questioning of that assumption, but a realistic assessment of what that consumption is. The popular image of minority youth as addicted to brands and indiscriminately willing to kill for status items assumes that they lack sophistication in dealing with the complex symbols, claims, and imagery of marketing and advertising. A quick peek at music videos, or a short listen to just about any popular (much less underground) rap music, shows not only that minority youth know the difference between ad hype and material reality, but that they can manipulate, appropriate, and reformulate this symbolic material with a sharp, critical eye, a music sample, or an ironic gesture.

Regina Austin charges that African American consumers have been widely portrayed in both popular and scholarly literature as "a nation of thieves": what they buy, wear, use, and covet is seen as rooted in or leading to social pathology (1994a,b). While examining the specific forms of consumption that exist among Newhallville children, this work also takes to task the ideology that portrays consumption among those without resources as fundamentally deviant, if not pathological, and views children as future adults rather than as bearers and creators of culture as much as they are also participants in it. In documenting the ways that Newhallville children take part in consumption or are excluded from it, this research lays some of the groundwork necessary for understanding the dynamics of inequality in the consumer sphere. Such inequality arises from and is perpetuated by the political economic processes of which consumption is inevitably a part. The understanding that consumption is a fundamentally social process, and one that operates in and through global systems of provisioning and exchange, is critical to the emergent scholarship on consumption, and social geography has had a decided influence on the development of this understanding (Jackson and Thrift 1995; Miller 1995a; Sherry 1995). Furthermore, the consumer lives of urban black kids are undeniably different from this Euro-American norm in large part, I argue, because of historical factors that have shaped not only black lives but American lives for centuries.

As James Carrier and Josiah Heyman (1997) note, social inequality has rarely been taken up as an important factor in understanding the ways in which consumption operates in people's lives. Theirs is a stunning point, if you stop to think about it, since social inequality—most obviously economic inequality—would seem to be a critical element in shaping consumption horizons. An examination of slavery illustrates the fundamental influence of social inequality in shaping consumption. This focus also helps to situate the specific experience of Newhallville children in the broader African American consumer experience. Taking a long view of consumption in the lives of black Americans illustrates the familiarity of supposedly new dilemmas, while also pointing to structural reasons for consumption orientations that differ markedly from the "mainstream." My argument is not, I must stress, that slavery has been incorporated like some sort of cultural DNA into present-day black culture. For one thing, slavery has had an impact not just upon those who were enslaved but all Americans, one way or another.

Throughout my attention is directed toward both material questions and symbolic elements, particularly popular culture and media portrayals. The second part of this chapter examines some of these contemporary portrayals in detail. Ideas about the "mainstream" have always existed

in tension with and in opposition to the nonmainstream. What is especially evident in looking at consumption is that in both the North and the
South white identity often has been performed and displayed in opposition to ideas about black consumption.[2] Thus, current images of superpredators and the like draw upon a centuries-old fund of images and assumptions that have a long and complex relationship with both white
and black lives. Historical images show a strong affinity to present-day
conceptions of "combat consumers" and help to demonstrate most clearly the ways in which the consumer sphere has been and continues to be
marked as white, since these images are generated primarily in the white
imagination and for white consumption. It is important to dissect these
images in part because despite a concerted effort on the part of social scientists to subvert them with data and theories these works have had little
impact on the frequency with which blacks continue to be portrayed as
poor, and the poor continue to be portrayed as morally corrupt. Together
with the historical legacy entangling black and white consumption, these
portrayals constitute a sort of "shadow of whiteness" that often colors
the way consumption of and by African Americans is understood.

Denied Entry

Slavery, segregation, economic discrimination, and racism have shaped
the tenor of African American life for over two hundred years, and for
most African Americans consumption has a long and ugly association
with the most profound sorts of violence. The weight of this history
bears heavily and directly on contemporary African Americans and has
ensured that their relationship to the consumer realm is complicated in
ways that are just beginning to be investigated. Likewise, the weight of
this history bears heavily on the nonblack buying and manufacturing
public. Subject to fantasizing the "inner city" youthful consumer as a
brand-crazed crackhead (or crack seller) who is willing to kill for sneakers, a flashy gold chain, or a car—what I call "combat consumers"—the
general public often mistakenly assumes its only relationship to these
terrifying youths is as actual or potential victim of their predations. The
relationship of the general public to these imagined consumers is much
more complex than this: as members of a society that has for centuries
systematically constrained the ways in which black consumers engage
with the marketplace (both symbolically and materially), the wider public is implicated in creating the problems it bemoans.

The media consistently exaggerate the proportion of African Americans who are poor, on welfare, or who commit crimes to get coveted

items (Fiske 1994; Gilens 1996); exposure to these media images has been shown to influence white viewers' opinions on public policy (Pan and Kosicki 1996). When, as they so often do, these beliefs then manifest in subtle forms (the clutching of a purse or crossing the street to avoid scary people) or more dramatic forms like imposing curfews, they can be dangerous and damaging. Moreover, the misperceptions about the epidemic rates of poverty and violence, pathological consumption, and problematic families in the "inner city" or the "ghetto" or among the "underclass" are often applied, by extension, to the entire black population. Thus, while these images portray the poorest of the poor, it is not only poor African Americans who suffer from their effects.

New York Times editorial writer Brent Staples describes the effect of other people's fear of him upon his own behavior in a 1994 essay (Staples 1994). Staples went to the University of Chicago in 1973 as a Ph.D. student in psychology. As a 6-foot 1½-inch tall black man in an oversized peacoat, he realized, he looked big and "fearsome." After learning he could calm the fears of others by whistling Vivaldi's "Four Seasons" (an act that indicated something about his cultural capital), something broke inside Staples and, rather than trying to prove he was not a frightening potential criminal, he took the opposite approach:

> I held a special contempt for people who cowered in their cars as they waited for the light to change at 57th and Woodlawn. The intersection was always deserted at night, except for a car or two stuck at the red. Thunk! Thunk! Thunk! They hammered down the door locks when I came into view. Once I had hustled across the street, head down, trying to seem harmless. Now I turned brazenly into the headlights and laughed. Once across, I paced the sidewalk, glaring until the light changed. They'd made me terrifying. Now I'd show them how terrifying I could be.

These same prejudices and assumptions are at work in consumption, and minority consumers must daily face treatment not generally encountered by whites, particularly in retail settings. Recognition of these problems is on the rise but has not yet erased the need for consumers of color to develop strategies akin to whistling "The Four Seasons."

A strong sense that the market, and hence the realm of consumption, is a democratic and color-blind sphere underlies much popular and scholarly discussion of the consumer world; much theory on consumption seems to have accepted the promise implicit in commodity capitalism that class or race need be no barrier to consumption—that money is the main hurdle to be scaled. Marx aptly describes the promise of the market: that money is the ultimate democratizing force, and that as a consumer class status is (potentially, at least) unimportant: "[As] worker . . . as consumer and possessor of exchange values, and that in the form of the *possessor of money*, in the form of money he becomes a simple entry of circulation—one of its infinitely many entries, in which his specificity as a worker is extinguished" (1969, 420–21).

This ability to become "a simple entry of circulation" is a sort of freedom, and it is this idea to which a snubbed customer refers when declaring, "Isn't my money just as good as hers?" Ben Fine, in a review of political economy and consumption (1995), explores the implication of Marx's comment:

> [Marx's] analysis of a generalized commodity-producing society reveals that it does not allow consumption to be read off from other determining economic relations, since quantitative differences in the ability to consume, derived from the distribution of incomes associated with different class positions, have no immediate implications for differentiation in consumption itself. (135)

That is, class standing does not determine what exactly is consumed, though class certainly has implications for income, raising practical barriers to consumption even though formal barriers might not exist. To put it another way, consumption under capitalism is largely mediated by culture, a notion that Pierre Bourdieu has captured in his study, *Distinction* (1984), in which he develops the notion of cultural capital.

Bourdieu examines consumption not as a relatively consensual process, but as one from which some people are actively barred. According to Bourdieu, consumption is partly based in special forms of knowledge and experience that are often acquired through inarticulate, quotidian happenings he terms *habitus*. In discussing his notion of habitus, Bourdieu pays special attention to children: in the habitus the child is socialized to the small gestures and bits of knowledge that allow a person to operate as a member of one's culture or class: how to eat, where to sit, inflection of the voice, what to wear. This knowledge and experience accrues as what Bourdieu calls "cultural capital," a term chosen expressly to communicate the fact that class is not just clothes or education or accent but the result of a tremendous, lifelong acquisition process. As Thorstein Veblen (1912) had noted, class mobility is restricted not only because climbing the ladder is plain hard work, but because people at the top are actively trying to prevent those below them from following too closely.

One of Bourdieu's enduring contributions to the study of consumption is his detailed analysis of the processes through which the apparent homogeneity within groups is shaped. Contrary to popular belief, personal choice and preferences are not the main determinants of individual consumption. Rather, the habitus offers opportunities for "controlled improvisation," and the range of improvisations varies according to one's position in and experience with the habitus (Bourdieu 1977). The acquisition of cultural capital further shapes consumption choice and opportunities. In this context choice is not free but constructed, not endless but bounded. Bourdieu's observation dovetails powerfully with the recognition that the endless proliferation of choice in contemporary consumer society is, in fact, an illusion. In addition to the Frankfurt school critiques discussed earlier, Stuart Ewen (1976, 1988) and Susan Willis (1991) have explored this theme, but without laying out as carefully as has Bourdieu the mechanisms through which even the choices that are *potentially* available present restrictions.

Bourdieu assumes that, given the choice, everyone would choose the same things—that ultimately what members of a given society want is more or less the same. Veblen's earlier account of social differentiation is based on a similar assumption: the upper classes continually change their consumption patterns because members of classes below them continually try to consume what people of the upper classes do. This notion is implicit to the bulk of consumption studies, but Carrier and Heyman find this assumption problematic, writing, "We do not think it is safe to assume that people would consume the same things if they had the money. We can neither neglect the question of whether people have the money, nor the question of how people enact distinctive life trajectories with the money they do have" (1997, 22).

So while Marx's observation that the possession of money can, for a time, erase the appearance of class difference, creating spaces and situations where "specificity as a worker is extinguished," Bourdieu's notions of habitus and cultural capital are helpful in understanding the limits to extinguishing such specificity. Differences in consumption are not simply differences of style determined largely by economic factors or preferences that may be acted upon freely within those economic limits. American society has, for more than two centuries, shaped and limited the consumption of black communities through a combination of structural factors, everyday social practices, and symbolic means.

Marx certainly never intended to imply that the consumer world actually constituted a realm of unbridled freedom as long as one had the price of entry: "Labor cannot emancipate itself in the white skin where in the black skin it is branded" (as quoted in Leiman 1993, 13). Racism and capitalism have been demonstrated to be twinned, and this second statement by Marx adds a complicating factor to the democratic promise of the market, underscoring the ephemeral and illusionary qualities of the possibility it offers (Genovese 1965; Leiman 1993). The laborer with some money to spend in Marx's first quote may be able to "extinguish his specificity as a worker" when entering into the exchange system, but those with branded black skin—to use Marx's words—cannot. Of course, Marx was writing during the time when slavery was still in practice, and part of the meaning of this second comment is that labor cannot possibly hope to free itself while some remain enslaved. What strikes me, however, is the continuing relevance of these two statements, both singly and together.

In the section that follows, I trace some of the ways in which the legacy of slavery has shaped African American consumption in order to illustrate concretely the profoundly political nature of consumption and its forceful presence in shaping people's pasts and futures. The whites who attempted to demonstrate racial privilege through a series of social, legal, and economic apparatuses were profoundly changed— even formed—in the crucible of slavery and, later, segregation.[3] We are not talking here about a relatively benign world full of "choices" where the manufacturing process itself is the most insidious factor. Neither are we speaking of a world in which the opposing teams are consumers (relatively undifferentiated) and manufacturers. Rather, the history of black consumption in America has been one of engineered deprivation, struggle, and violence, as well as innovation, creativity, and, in some cases, transcendence.

Slavery and Consumption

The two hundred years during which the vast majority of blacks in the United States were considered to be commodities rather than persons endowed with civil and legal rights are perhaps the most dramatic example illustrating why the black relationship to consumption in this country is, to put it mildly, unique. As the Antiguan writer Jamaica Kincaid points out in her biting harangue aimed at colonialism in the form of white, middle-class tourists:

> Do you know why people like me are shy about being capitalists? Well, it's because we, for as long as we have known you, *were* capital, like bales of cotton and sacks of sugar. . . . [T]he memory of this is so

strong, the experience so recent, that we can't quite bring ourselves to embrace this idea you think so much of. (1988, 36–37)

Under slavery, bondsmen did not enter the marketplace primarily as consumers; it was they who were consumed. What Kincaid so starkly illuminates is that if one really thinks about the implications of consumption for slaves, Bourdieu's notion of cultural capital, for instance, suddenly takes on some entirely new resonances, and very uncomfortable ones at that. Likewise, an idea like "conspicuous consumption" has some monstrous aspects when the commodities being conspicuously consumed might be human beings. Even though seventeenth- and eighteenth-century America was a long way from constituting the kind of consumer society we have today, the implications of slavery for shaping people's emotional and material relations to the market must have been immense.

Moreover, the plot thickens, as it were, since contemporary commodity capitalism and, with it, modernity are widely viewed to have been built upon the backs of slaves. Plantation organization and labor in particular have been highlighted as precursors to the rationalized labor and internationally integrated economy that typified early industrialism (Genovese 1974; Gilroy 1993; Mintz 1985; Wolf 1982). In the analysis that follows, I examine slavery as a historical process that in its own time shaped consumption by African slaves and their descendants in profound ways. Looking at the domains of housing, personal possessions, clothing, food, and labor, considering slavery and consumption together reveals this process not only as deeply political but as one often violently enforced. Furthermore, this perspective shows that the themes dominating public sphere depictions of black consumption have a long and ugly past, and that many of these themes—like that of the vain and over-dressed "Negro," or of the lazy thief—find their roots in the engineered oppressions and deprivations of slavery.

Contemporary images of the slave plantation portray it, Tara-like, as an enormous white house fronted with Greek columns, surrounded by rolling lawns and filled with beautiful things. In these images the slave quarters are markedly absent but might be imagined in contrast as rude and sparsely furnished hovels. This image described the reality for only a tiny minority of the wealthiest plantations. In a great number of more modest slaveholding plantations and farms, slaves and masters lived together under the same roof, and we as yet know too little of the tensions and contradictions precipitated by this sort of intimacy. In the antebellum years a two-story structure was *itself* a sign of affluence, not often augmented by fine furnishings, china, and silver; slaveholders tended to use their money to buy more land, more stock, and more slaves rather than investing in lavish homes or interior decoration (Fox-Genovese 1988, 106–7). Most of the slaveholding South relied heavily on locally or home-produced products, and consumption was not defined by activities such as shopping, as it is today. Material and technological niceties were few.

That said, even taking into account the sometimes close quarters between slaveholder and slave, or the frequently smallish gap between the big house and slave quarters, slaves were provided with few material comforts. The account of Solomon Northrup provides a particularly ironic description of these material possessions. Northrup was a free Northerner who was kidnapped into slavery for twelve years. He had been an independent farmer and businessman in the years before his abduction and he was used to having his own home, along with the convenience of furniture, dishes, pails and the like. He deeply resented their absence, as this sharply ironic passage shows:

> When a slave, purchased, or kidnapped in the North, is transported to a cabin on Bayou Boeuf, he is furnished with neither knife, nor fork, nor dish, nor kettle, nor any other thing in the shape of crockery, or furniture of any nature or description. He is furnished with a blanket before he reaches there, and wrapping that around him, he can either stand up, or lie down upon the ground, or on a board, if his master has no use for it. He is at liberty to find a gourd in which to keep his meal, or he can eat his corn from the cob, just as he pleases. To ask the master for a knife, or skillet, or any small convenience of the kind, would be answered with a kick, or laughed at as a joke. (Northrup 1968, 148)

Northrup's carefully chosen words are unequivocal in their portrayal of the sphere of consumption as one quite removed from democracy. In fact, this passage is rather remarkable for the way it manages to portray the condition of slavery through a description of the difficulties of basic provisioning faced by slaves. One can almost imagine that Northrup's diatribe here is directed at the self-congratulatory slaveholder describing the luxuries provided bondsmen under his or her "care." The whole passage continually speaks of freedoms and choices that are in fact deprivations and oppressions. With a blanket, but no bed, Northrup says the slave "can either stand up, or lie down upon the ground, or on a board," as if any of these options were appealing. In the next sentence, he elaborates even further, saying, "He is at liberty to find a gourd in which to keep his meal, or he can eat his corn from the cob, just as he pleases," again finding a cutting irony in these supposed freedoms, since what they equally imply is that lacking the gourd, there is nothing in which to store the meal, and lacking a knife, the "choice" is to eat the corn from the cob or not at all.

It was for the most part slaveowners who decided what their human chattel would consume, and to some extent their control extended to when and how food, tools, and leisure could be used. When Northrup arrived at the slave plantation where he worked, his first task was to carve his own axe and hoe handles (121). Thus, even in the pre- or proto-industrial conditions of the plantation South, slaves had little free access to the essential elements of consumption. Their labor and their wages were largely controlled by slaveowners and the marketplace was a sphere most slaves could enter most easily as commodities rather than as purchasers of commodities.

The politics of eating among enslaved populations were nothing if not complex. Slaveholders were obligated to provide rations, which though they have varied according to historical period and geographic area were usually meager—just enough to keep slaves from starving utterly. Most accounts show that typical rations included cornmeal, bacon, and perhaps a bit of salt (e.g., Clifton 1978, xxxiii). With work schedules arduous and long, little time was left for cooking other than making a cornmeal and water mush that might be made into ash cakes, quickly cooked in the morning's or evening's embers. Hoe cakes, similar to ash cakes, were so called because, lacking proper pots and pans, many slaves made their iron hoe blades do double duty as a kind of skillet (and, incidentally, triple duty as a musical instrument). For field hands especially, plantation provisions provided poor nutrition and barely enough calories to support the hard labor of cane cutting, cotton sowing, or rice planting.

Both archaeological work and slave narratives show that rations were almost always supplemented by hunting, scavenging, small garden plots, and occasional pilfering or theft (Genovese 1974; Singleton 1995).[4] This "theft" might be of time, labor, or the food itself. Bondsmen who hunted or fished on land owned by their masters or some other person were, in effect, stealing fish and game. These activities were overlooked, or not, thus establishing a dynamic by which whites could define the consumption of blacks as illegal, or not, depending on convenience. Enduring images of slaves sneaking into henhouses and melon patches have evolved into present-day portrayals of African Americans who, like the infamous welfare queen, are too lazy to work but not too lazy to steal, ready to play dumb but amazingly ingenious at executing a scam.

Despite having severely limited means and opportunity for entering the market independently, either as workers or consumers, many slaves were able to earn money by selling produce, crafts, and their own labor. This was, literally, a sort of Devil's bargain, since frequently slaves were only allowed to do such work on Sundays. White slaveholders could thus conveniently view their slaves' very willingness to work for money on Sundays as a mark of their debased natures, although Solomon Northrup felt slaveholder approbation worth the monetary reward: "However injurious to the morals, it is certainly a blessing to the physical condition of the slave, to be permitted to break the Sabbath. Otherwise, there would be no way to provide himself with any utensils" (1968, 148).

In this situation lies the foundation for some themes regarding black consumption that continue into the present day. Slaveholders and slaves quite obviously had different ideas about what slaves "needed," in terms of food, utensils, and income. Slaveholders reserved for themselves the right to be mortified by the willingness of slaves to work on the Sabbath and thus endanger their heavenly bliss, turning a blind eye to the desires of slaves to have cabin furniture, water pails, pocketknives, or new shoes. In deciding that these people did not need pails, beds, or more than two sets of clothes a year, slaveholders allowed for themselves the right to interpret slaves' needs and desires for these and other "luxuries" as a kind of depravity. Many slaves thought differently, and the importance of purchased possessions has a prominent place in many persons' recollections, as demonstrations of both independence and personhood. Slave needs were defined from the outset as being different from those of slaveholders and, depending on the mood, could be additionally defined as immoral or illegal, a theme that finds resonance in current welfare debates and policies. Food stamps, for example, help to delineate a differing standard for "need" and cannot be used to purchase a number of food items, including brown eggs and cooked carrots; of course, essential nonfood items like dish soap, toilet paper, sponges, or sanitary napkins cannot be bought with food stamps at all.[5]

The work situation of enslaved people created a dynamic of moral judgment similar to the contemporary myths portraying the consumption desires of the poor and materially deprived as being rooted in depravity. Such moral opprobrium did not stop slaveholders from profiting from their slaves' extra work; they often required bondsmen to pay for the privilege of earning money in their spare time. Skilled artisans were especially apt to be able to hire themselves out independently, and male bondsmen had the added advantage of being generally more free to move among local farms and plantations. Women could find ways to earn money, and Harriet Jacobs's grandmother (known as Aunt Marthy) was given permission to bake and put up preserves at night after her regular work was done "provided she would clothe herself and her children from the profits" (Jacobs 1988, 12). In effect, Aunt Marthy had to pay her owners for the privilege of undertaking paid labor. Those who chose to work or sell things on the side without permission risked being punished for "stealing" their own labor, thereby cheating their masters, much as current welfare recipients are "cheating" taxpayers when they engage in otherwise legal income-generating activities like babysitting or doing hair. Despite ample data showing that much welfare compensation simply does not provide adequate income to pay for even basic necessities, the income-generating strategies to which many welfare recipients turn are deemed illegal—even if they would in any other context be unexceptionable (Hill and Stephens 1997). Kathryn Edin (1991) further documents how, like slaveowners before them, individual welfare caseworkers overlook, or not, at their discretion or whim, transgressions of the rules and regulations over both consumption and income generation.

In myriad ways both overt and subtle, the maintenance of the gap between slave and slaveholder depended on visible differences in consumption. These differences were more easily maintained when slaves' access to money and commodities was limited. In public settings, clothing was a crucial marker of status, not just in terms of social standing, but racially as well. Slaveholders also supplied their human chattel with clothing once or twice a year, often distributed at Christmastime. Clothing intended for slaves was rarely, if ever, bought manufactured, though it was common to cut and sew clothing from industrially produced cloth imported from England (Fox-Genovese 1988, 128). Slave dress, not surprisingly, offered little in the way of style, variety, or choice. "How I hated it! It was one of the badges of slavery," exclaims Harriet Jacobs of the linsey-woolsey dress she received each winter (Jacobs 1988, 19–20). In these circumstances, where slaveowners dictated the "fashions" acceptable for slaves and enforced these decisions, a well-dressed slave was to some degree not only an oxymoron but a joke among whites. The joke has been exceptionally long-lived, thriving not only in minstrel shows, but in contemporary films and television, from the extravagantly hatted and furred pimps of the 1970s to the equally decked-out players of the 1990s.

Slaves who aspired to fashion were derided for also aspiring to something they could not, by definition, attain: whiteness.[6] After having learned the shoemaking trade, James L. Smith was put in charge of a shoemaking shop that his master visited once a week to collect the earnings. When the shop earned a great deal, Mr. Smith would "keep some back for myself, as I had worked for it" (Smith, Mars, Grimes, Offley, and Smith 1971, 163). Eventually, having saved fifteen dollars in this manner, Smith (also known as "Brother Payne") bought a piece of cloth and had a fine suit made—to be worn with the watch, chain, and seal he already owned. "I was very proud and loved to dress well," he says, and goes on to recount with relish his reception when he first wore the suit: "It was Brother Payne here, and Brother Payne there; in fact, I was nearly everywhere." The admiration and excitement he received from his peers was not shared by his master's circle:

> [T]he first Sunday that I was arrayed in my new suit, I was passing the court house bounds, when I saw my master and a man named Betts standing near by. Betts caught sight of me; says he: "Lindsey, come here." Not knowing what he wanted I went to him; whereupon he commenced looking first at me, then at my master; then at my master, then at me; finally he said: "Who is master; Lindsey or you, for he dresses better than you do? Does he own you, or do you own him?" (163–64)

The theatricality of Betts's reaction to Brother Payne's fine suit is unmistakable, and his response chastises both Payne for dressing above his station, and his master for not having a firmer hand in Payne's wardrobe—slaves ought to dress like slaves. The play on race is hard to miss since this performance of racial misrecognition hinges on the "fine suit" that Payne was wearing on a Sunday morning on the courthouse steps, not his race as an attribute of his physical body. In a society where racial mixing was common, it became increasingly difficult to identify the "race" of people based on their physical features alone. The degree to which manner of dress was equated with race in nineteenth-century Savannah is made clear in Venture Smith's description:

> I have frequently walked the streets of Savannah in an evening, and being pretty well dressed, (generally having on a good decent suit of clothes,) and having a light complexion, (being at least three parts white,) on meeting the guard, I would walk as bold as I knew how, and as much like a gentleman; they would always give me the wall.

> One time in particular, while walking home late in the evening, I saw two or three of them together. I was afraid, but summoned all my resolution, and marched directly on towards them, not turning to the right hand nor to the left, until I came up to them. They at first did not notice me, being engaged in conversation. I continued on, head up, walked past them and happening to brush one of them a little in passing, they immediately turned off the walk; one of them spoke and said we ask your pardon sir. (95–96)

Had Venture Smith been dark-skinned, such a masquerade would never have worked, but the quality and fashion of his clothes is also key in marking him as at least potentially white, and as actually white in some people's perception. The three men of the guard whom he passes on the sidewalk give him the wall—an act of politeness in itself, since it puts the walker farther away from possible splashes from passing carriages. This act acknowledges the patrol's deference not only to Venture Smith's whiteness, which they have evidently accepted, but what they assume to be his higher social status: they ask his pardon for being in his way.

The direct buying and selling of human beings was, of course, the most hideous form of consumption. And yet, aside from the manifest horrors of the slave-auction house, and of the scenes so often recounted today of husbands and wives being sold apart from each other, or children being torn from their mothers, a particularly awful kind of buying and selling sometimes took place: people buying themselves or family members in order to gain freedom from ownership by whites. We know little today about the interpersonal dynamics that emerged from such purchases, particularly purchases of children by parents, or of parents by children; of husband purchasing wife, or wife purchasing her husband. In his account of his life under slavery, Rev. G. W. Offley describes such transactions taking place among his immediate family:

> My mother was born a slave in the State of Virginia, and sold in the State of Maryland, and there remained until married, and became the mother of three children. She was willed free at the death of her master; her three children were also willed free at the age of twenty-five. But my youngest brother was put on a second will, which was destroyed by the widow and the children, and he was subjected to bondage for life. My father was a free man, and therefore bought him as a slave for life and gave him his freedom at the age of twenty years. He also bought my sister for a term of years, say until she was twenty-five years old. He gave her her freedom at the age of sixteen years. He

bought my grandmother, who was too old to set free, that she might be exempted from hard servitude in her old age. (Smith et al. 1971, 131)

From other portions of this account, it seems that the sister and brother who were purchased by Offley's father were still young enough at the time that a sympathetic auctioneer had "used great deception in making the purchaser believe that the two children would die unless they could have their mother's care, so that father bought them at his own price, as no person bid against him" (132). What is most striking to me about this account is not that Reverend Offley's free father had managed to buy his enslaved children (a feat). Rather, it is that their father apparently retained them in the status of slavery for several years after their purchase, not freeing the girl until age sixteen, the boy when he was twenty. My assertion that Offley's father kept his children in the status of slavery hinges on the auctioneer's having convinced the other prospective buyers that the boy and girl could not survive without their mother's care. The auctioneer could hardly have made these claims effectively about adolescent children in their teens, since slave children as young as four years old were often given considerable responsibilities as nurses, spinners, and field hands. One wonders what kind of family dynamics resulted from this situation and one thing is certain: such dynamics were complex. In this family even freeborn children had brushes with life under slavery. The freeborn Offley was at nine years old put into service with a slaveowner for four years in order to "pay his [father's] house rent" (132).

Many slave accounts contain observations about the complexity of consumption when one of the major commodities is human beings themselves. In one passage Harriet Jacobs recounts her grandmother's determined efforts to try to save enough money to buy her children's freedom. At one point, she has saved three hundred dollars, which her mistress borrows from her and never repays, since such an obligation would never be recognized by the court: "a slave *being* property can *hold* no property" (12). Jacobs continues,

When her mistress died, her son-in-law, Dr. Flint, was appointed executor. When grandmother applied to him for payment, he said the estate was insolvent, and the law prohibited payment. It did not, however, prohibit him from retaining the silver candelabra, which had been purchased with that money. I presume they will be handed down in the family, from generation to generation.

Incidents like this in some ways raise more questions than they answer. To what degree was Jacobs's grandmother compelled to lend the three hundred dollars to her mistress? How did she feel about the transformation of that three hundred dollars from a portion of her child's freedom into a silver candelabra? Jacobs's own sharp comments reveal candidly the ironic cruelty of the situation, and she does not hide her resentment that Dr. Flint's family will be handing down that candelabra from generation to generation, while her own family maintains slavery as its own generational legacy.

What's Wrong with This Picture?
Images of Poverty in the 1980s and 1990s

The material and symbolic constraints on the consumption of African Americans so evident under slavery have not disappeared in the present day—they have only transformed (in some cases barely) and transmogrified, like the process of consumption itself. Disparities of race, class, and gender continue to be enforced and maintained through consumption. In the 1980s, the Michael Douglas character Gordon Gecko declared that "greed is good" in the film *Wall Street,* an apt summary of an economic period that saw an unprecedented widening of the gap between rich and poor in the United States, a gap that has since developed into a chasm of alarming size. At the same time, images of the welfare queen and streetcorner drug dealer have become more ubiquitous. These images purposefully describe a kind of anticonsumer: the welfare mom has amassed several Cadillacs, while the drug dealer loads himself down with ill-gotten gold chains. In other words, they spend money they haven't earned on things they shouldn't have. Unlike the proud "Brother Payne," who in the eyes of a white property owner was more laughable than scary and could be publicly shamed on the courthouse steps, these two figures are the Barbie and Ken from hell: they are morally corrupt consumers, dangerous and threatening. The evidence of their moral corruption is their very consumption. The power of these images cannot be underestimated and they are embraced even, at times, among the communities who are most damaged by them.

As the problems of deindustrialization and the rapid movement of capital either to the American South or overseas accelerated during the late 1970s and 1980s, so did the media hype and hysteria about pathological inner-city dwellers. In response to the increasing variety and with increasing virulence of portrayals of the pathological consumption of blacks and other minorities during the 1980s, social science moved with force and energy into examining the causes and experiences of poverty in economically distressed urban areas, seeking to clarify the structural foundation for persistent poverty. Researchers scrambled to present their arguments in an even-handed, clear-headed manner, arguing that the sudden appearance of hordes of homeless people on the streets of New York was not due to an inexplicable, lemming-like rush of the indigent to live in cardboard boxes placed over hot-air vents, but rather to such economic and social policies as the deinstitutionalization of the mentally ill and destruction of single-resident-occupancy (SRO) housing.

One important tactic has been to undermine popular images indirectly, by presenting analyses that challenge the primary assumptions behind notions of the undeserving poor. The basic argument is that despite the importance of individual choices, poverty is structurally determined by such elements as an increasingly globalized economy, institutionalized racism, unequal provision of goods and services, policymaking, social geography, and a host of other factors not in the control of any given individual, and least of all a poor one living in an urban ghetto. This is not to say that individual decisions can have no impact on either life trajectories or structural factors, but rather to make the point that any framework that gives undue weight to either agency or structure is fundamentally flawed. Social scientists responding in the early 1980s to analyses such as Ken Auletta's *The Underclass* (1982) strove to move the debate away from individual failings and toward changing economies, historical processes, and federal policy (Katz 1993; Susser 1996; Vincent 1993; Wilson 1987).

In the 1980s many social scientists found themselves making up for lost time. As social historian Michael Katz points out (1993), dividing the poor into moral categories has preoccupied policymakers, relief workers, and the public at large almost since the nation's inception, but the social and academic climate in the 1960s and 1970s resulted in ceding the field to conservative voices and analysts when it came to investigating either the causes of poverty or the lives of the poor. These analysts have tended to turn to moral categories that attribute poverty to personal failings— laziness, lack of self-discipline, greed. At two key junctures, works that had been intended to launch powerful critiques of historic, social, and economic factors in the generation and maintenance of poverty were actually widely interpreted to prove that it was the poor themselves who caused their own misery. Oscar Lewis's notion of the "culture of poverty" was a thinly veiled neo-Marxist analysis of cultural factors at work in the daily lives of the poor (Lewis 1966). He posited that the extremes of social inequality evident in slums of cities like New York, San Juan, and Mexico City could only emerge under capitalism, a point that generally has been glossed over in the years since his ideas were originally published. Instead, another of his theoretical claims, that the culture of poverty tends to perpetuate itself, captured the public imagination. Subsequent debates within anthropology have been heated, and Lewis has often been faulted for not more strongly correcting mistaken claims about what his culture of poverty concept implied (see essays in Leacock 1971). Nevertheless, these debates have remained primarily within the academy and have done little to counter the popular understanding of the term, which has come to be synonymous with chronic poverty, apathy, and a generally low-aspiration mindset.

The second key event was the publication of Senator Daniel Patrick Moynihan's *The Negro Family: The Case for National Action* (1965), which, although intended as a rousing call to action for liberal government and policymakers, ultimately proved to be quite the opposite. In arguing that black families were typified by a "tangle of pathology" (in particular, "matriarchy" and single mothers) Moynihan's report laid the groundwork for claims that poverty was the outcome of pathological family forms. Aside from the questionable validity of Moynihan's version of cause and effect, his characterization of certain family forms as pathological was deeply problematic. It has been pointed out that the furor that emerged after Moynihan's report was released prompted many social scientists to shy away from research among the urban poor and especially the "underclass" (Katz 1993, 3–23; Wacquant and Wilson 1989). The result was that few scholars had the studies or data in hand to refute a 1977 article in *Time* magazine that described the underclass as "a large group of people who are more intractable, more socially alien and more hostile than almost anyone had imagined. They are the unreachables" (quoted in Katz 1993, 4). As Asia said, "The Streets [*dramatic pause*] of Newhallville . . ."

Like Katz, William Julius Wilson argues that in the aftermath of the Moynihan report social scientists either shied away from examinations of urban poverty or would only undertake such examination by emphasizing the positive and adaptive aspects of social practices and patterns that from the outside appeared deviant or perverse (Wilson 1987). The most well known of these studies, perhaps, is Carol Stack's *All Our Kin* (1974), an ethnography of poor black families in Michigan. Like other ethnographies of poor urban populations (most of them centered on African Americans), Stack's work was an important corrective to the misinformation in the Moynihan report. These include a number of classics: *Tally's Corner* (Liebow 1967), *Soulside* (Hannerz 1969), and, more recently, *Ain't No Makin' It* (MacLeod 1987). In this last work, Jay MacLeod looks at two groups of male youths, one white, one black, and seeks to understand the perpetuation of poverty not just as being generated from within, via the culture of poverty, but through a more complex process of social reproduction involving institutional and structural factors. Like sociology, anthropology has shown a sustained interest in questions of U.S. urban poverty and social inequality (Gregory 1998; Mullings 1987; Sharff 1998; Susser 1982).

These empirical responses have been tremendously important, but because few have chosen to attack the images themselves head on social science has to some degree allowed these portrayals to continue their circulation unabated (Wilson 1988 is an exception, albeit an unpublished one). Scholarly critiques of the assumptions and ideas behind notions of the undeserving poor or pathological underclass have given relatively little attention to the question of the symbolic aspects of the debate. The field of cultural studies has been an exception, especially the recent work of John Fiske (1993, 1994), who shows how power and disempowerment can be enacted through material and symbolic channels. Moreover, when young people themselves are consulted about their responses to these images and symbols, they can propose options not envisioned by most other observers. When Dierdre Kelly examined symbolic discourses around teenage pregnancy, three of the dominant discourses centered around blaming the girl, blaming the family, or blaming society. Teen mothers themselves, though, asserted that the problem was that the idea of blame *itself* was wrong (Kelly 1996).

Contemporary consumption is, of course, up to its neck in symbolic issues, and some theorists, like Wolfgang Haug (1986) and Jean Baudrillard (1981, 1986, 1988), have gone so far as to argue that symbols are the only issue that remains. While I cannot bring myself to go quite this far, the questions of poverty, racism, and social inequality in the United States today are in large part questions about consumption (who buys what, who possesses what, and how do they get it?), which means that they are questions of symbolic importance as well. It is therefore unsurprising that symbolic imagery has been one of the primary weapons mobilized in attacks on the poor and underclass and that battles have often taken place over the airwaves. As the old advertising adage goes, "sell the sizzle and not the steak."

Gangsta rap, fashion, advertisements, and national newspaper articles saturate broadcast channels and advertising images with innumerable powerful depictions of minority youth as destructive and out-of-control consumers. These ideas are misguided. More important, we need to look closely at some of those representations and explore how they produce and reproduce images of the pathological poor. Fiske (1994) has already shown in an article about the 1992 Los Angeles uprising that the news media selectively excised footage of white looters from newscast coverage, thus further entrenching widely held beliefs about black consumer violence. The close association of violence and consumption in representations of poor minority youth—and, increasingly, killer children—is unmistakable, particularly in the news media. These images are also highly gendered, focusing on the deadly violence of boys on the one hand and the out-of-control materialism of girls on the other. Examining some recent accounts from the *New York Times* shows how the selective use of images already noted by Fiske is typical even of those news publications with reputations for objectivity. These articles, many of them splashed across the front page, are typical of a genre of news story that reports on "combat consumerism," that is, consumption accomplished through violence.

For Gold Earrings and Protection, More Girls Take to Violence

For Aleysha J., the road to crime has been paved with huge gold earrings and name-brand clothes. At Aleysha's high school in the Bronx, popularity comes from looking the part. Aleysha's mother has no money to buy her nice things so the diminutive 15-year-old steals them, an act that she feels makes her equal parts bad girl and liberated woman.

"It's like I don't want to do it, but my friends put a lot of pressure on me," said Aleysha. . . . "Then I see something I want so bad I just take it. The worst time, I pulled a knife on this girl, but I never hurt anybody. I just want things." (Lee 1991)

Aleysha's pathetic plaint, "I just want things," seems to capture the problem succinctly. Because she apparently doesn't have much money, she ends up in what many believe to be an all-too-common situation: "Then I see something I want so bad I just take it." The *New York Times,* along with most urban newspapers, has consistently reported on such stories, which are focused on deadly desires for status items practiced by minority youth who in their most extreme manifestation are now described as the dreaded "superpredators." Stories in this vein began appearing in the early 1980s with news clips about young men shooting and being shot over shearling jackets or Cazal eyeglass frames (the kind worn by Spike Lee as he played the character Mars Blackmon in his film *She's Gotta Have It*). In the 1990s the reported objects of violent desire more often have been status shoes, especially Air Jordans; the 1990s have also seen the emergence of carjackings as another potent form of combat consumerism, all the more threatening because carjacking directly involves cross-class confrontation at its most dramatically brutal.

The structure and content of these accounts are remarkably stable across media and through time and in this way primarily serve to cement dominant and ahistorical narratives about the consumption of the poor rather than to provide any contextually situated insight. Explicitly or implicitly, these narratives consistently portray as pathological the ways in which poor minority youth enter and participate in the consumer sphere. Although dramatic combat consumption is no more representative of minority desires and practices in general than the equally illegal and obscene excesses of, say, Leona Helmsley (who actually served prison time for tax evasion), Ms. Helmsley's behavior is rarely to be taken as representative of the wealthy.[7]

A Boy in Search of Respect Discovers How to Kill

Cynthia Kierstedt's 15-year-old son, big as a linebacker, foolish as a child, was handcuffed to the wall of a Brooklyn police station house. He had just been arrested in the killing of a man who delivered candy bars to bodegas. . . . He later said he had robbed the man so he could buy a pair of Nikes to replace his three-month-old pair. "The sneakers I had was messed up," he said. "I'd walk down the block and people who know me would start laughing."

. . . Shaul was reared by a mother who worked at an office by day and attended college at night, hoping for a better life for herself and her four children. He was a passable student in grade school, but this behavior soured in junior high. He failed eighth grade, and in the long, lonely afternoons and evenings, he hung out with bad-news friends and fell for a girl who had a closet full of Guess jeans and Esprit shirts— and wanted more. (Dugger 1994)

Combat consumer Shaul Linyear had a deadly desire for new sneakers. We have the standard elements for a kid whose values are all out of whack: an overworked single mother whose commitment to a better life paradoxically forces her to neglect her children who must endure "long, lonely afternoons and evenings," "bad-news friends," and, to top it off, a demanding, materialistic girlfriend. Strangely, it is the mother and girlfriend, and not Shaul, who dominate both the text and the photographs accompanying the story. The girlfriend, Tanisha Franklin, is described in obsessive detail that focuses almost exclusively on her consumption preferences and her possessions. The breathless declaration from the early part of the article portrays Shaul as a victim of a girl who might as well be a spider weaving Moynihan's "tangled web of pathology": a lonely boy looking for the love he can't get from his mother, "[he] fell for a girl who had a closet full of Guess jeans and Esprit shirts—and wanted more." Shaul has practically been pushed into this situation by the combined pressures of these two women, one well-meaning but unable to cope, the other self-indulgent and greedy. These highly gendered portrayals are also typical. Women are either overtly materialistic and pushy, or "trying to do the right thing" and utterly at a loss. The objects of their desire tend to be clothes, jewelry, and the like. Men and boys, on the other hand, tend to be portrayed as physically violent, often manipulated by their love interests, and prone to grand gestures like carjacking and robbing stores.

Tanisha is pictured sitting on her bed in her room. The accompanying caption reads, "Lure of money: Tanisha Franklin, 15, in her bedroom with letters written by Shaul from prison and her boxes of Nikes and Reeboks. The two recently broke up." The caption, oddly random in its juxtaposition of money, Tanisha, letters, Nikes and Reeboks, and a breakup, nevertheless manages to communicate the idea that the nature of materialism among the urban poor is, quite simply, sick. Taken together, the picture and accompanying story seem to imply that the real crime being presented is the consumer desires of the unworthy poor; it is this crime that supersedes even Shaul's act of murder in its senselessness, precisely because the murder was spurred on by consumer greed. Tanisha, in particular, is depicted as being a selfish, shallow, and materialistic girl. Her consumption is consistently contrasted with its antisocial outcomes: robbery, breakup of relationships. While Shaul languishes in prison, she remains free, lounging on her bed in a room stacked high with brand-name shoes, dressed in Guess and Esprit clothes. The article goes on: "'I'm like, materialistic,' Tanisha said. 'Everybody tells me that. When I was growing up, my mother dressed me in Guess and stuff. It's her fault.'" Her comments demonstrate her apparent lack of human decency: she seems little troubled by the connection between her ex-boyfriend's crimes and the stolen cash that was used to purchase her "boxes of Nikes and Reeboks." The picture of her reclining on her bed recalls the shameless,

Tanisha in her room. Note that the paper over her head reads "Certificate of Merit." Photograph by Suzanne DeChillo/NYT Pictures; reprinted by permission of The New York Times Company.

insolent, repellent decadence of Manet's Olympia, and Tanisha is depicted as both whore and handmaiden to her consumer desires. The article continues:

> Tanisha's $120 gold dental caps glinted and her huge, gold-hoop earrings swayed as she sat on her bed. Decked out in Esprit shirt, Guess jeans and Timberland boots, she said Shaul was like a best friend to her. Asked where he got the money to buy her $95 Nike Airs, and other gifts, she said, "He was robbing people."

It is hard to doubt that Tanisha is reprehensible and selfish. Indeed, from the article it is hard to conclude otherwise. What is striking is the seamlessness of the characterization, a seamlessness that suggests the picture drawn of Tanisha is constructed so as to eliminate contradictions and complexities in her (or similar) situations. Though the article describes in detail the magazine ads that decorate the wall above her bed, making sure to mention any name brand depicted, the author fails to make any note of a school achievement certificate that is equally prominently displayed on the same wall. One has to wonder why. One wonders, also, whether the particular array of famous models and brand-name advertisements differs significantly from what might be found on any other starstruck teenager's bedroom walls. The doors of girls' dorm rooms at the college where I teach look a lot like the walls of Tanisha's room and are routinely plastered with ads for expensive clothes, popular movies, and hunky stars.

Let's get real here. Tanisha's $120 gold caps might speak of flash and cash, but they represent only about one-twentieth of the cost of the silver or plastic orthodontia adorning the mouths of millions of middle-class teens. Many might argue that my comparison of gold caps and braces misses the most important point—that braces are good because they are "needed" while gold caps are not and are, instead, wasteful or even crass. This argument, however, takes us into the quicksand terrain already visited by Herbert Marcuse (and before him, Bronislaw Malinowski) in attempting to definitively delineate "real" from "fake" needs. Since all people are cultural and social beings, and because needs are shaped and defined by culture, trying to reduce "true" need to food, clothing, shelter, and perhaps basic nurture is utterly inadequate.

What, in fact, makes braces "needed"? Would it actually be possible to quantify the proportion of physiological need for orthodontia in relation to its cosmetic appeal? Moreover, regardless of how much Tanisha or a kid like her might also "need" braces, she is hardly likely to receive them. Why are her shoes stacked up neatly against the wall anyway? It might well be because her closet is currently overflowing with Guess jeans and Esprit sportswear. Perhaps she wants to put all those shoes on display to impress her friends. But on the other hand, does she even have a closet? To continue the reality check, remember that Tanisha lives in a rental apartment in a New York slum, not a fancy condo on the river, or even a modest single-family home in, say, Queens. Her ex-boyfriend is in jail for murder. She wears Guess and Esprit, fashions whose prices top out well below the $200 mark. She does not wear Chanel and Armani, fashions whose prices begin well above the $200 mark. Those $120 gold caps and "huge, gold-hoop earrings" may be the costliest things she owns. The sum total of all of her possessions is probably not even enough to pay for a set of braces.

It is important to the coherence of the article (and the ideology of combat consumerism) that Tanisha does not appear to care about people, but only about things. When asked about where Shaul got his money, she answers with apparent callousness, "He was robbing people." She takes no responsibility for her own desires run amok but blames it on her mother, saying simply, "It's her fault." Though she is poor, she does not appear to be working; though she is broke, her room is filled with brand-name clothes, her body adorned with eminently visible gold jewelry. Brand-name clothes and fancy jewelry are signs of her transgressions. And so, in this way, preferences in fashion, style, and brands become signs of moral behavior. In modern civic spaces such as malls, fashion, style and brand of clothing are the basis on which individuals are singled out for being observed, harassed, or ejected by security personnel (Lewis 1989; "Teen-Age Pall at the Mall" 1993; "Mall Wins Ruling on Limiting Bus Service" 1995; "Wary Mall Bans Backward Caps" 1995). As increasing numbers of cities in the United States attempt to impose curfews on urban youth, the criminalization of an age-class and of its perceived behaviors has moved beyond the public imagination into public policy. More disturbing than the imposition of curfews and other restrictive measures is the dramatic upsurge in legislation designed to prosecute minors as adults, particularly in murder cases: in 1995 alone seven hundred such pieces of legislation were introduced nationwide (Staples 1996).

The much-publicized murder of five-year-old Eric Morse prompted such a piece of legislation. He was thrown to his death from an abandoned fourteenth-floor apartment by a pair of boys who were at the time ten and eleven years old. Eric's older brother Derrick, who was also there, had tried to save his brother, careening down the stairs hoping to catch him at the bottom. The murder, gruesome by any standard, took place in the Ida B. Wells homes, one of Chicago's most notoriously troubled housing projects. Many papers reported that the two boys had tossed Eric to his death for refusing to steal candy for them, a piece of information that made a shocking incident simply monstrous. As it turns out the boys likely had a more complicated reason for "punishing" Eric, one hinging on gang-style revenge, since Eric had tattled on the boys earlier that day (Jones and Newman 1997). Nitpicking over whether the murder was undertaken out of desire for stolen sourballs or some twisted sense of gangsta honor might seem to be beside the point, but it is striking that all news accounts chose to stick to the simplistic— and frankly more hair-raising—explanation that the boys wanted shoplifted candy. It is a detail that highlights the boys' amorality and, rather than the murder being a senseless crime, it becomes something that illustrates the inhuman pathologies thought to be generated by places like the Ida B. Wells. Gangsta honor is at least some kind of moral code; killing a little kid because he won't steal five- and ten-cent candies is completely beyond the pale.

One *New York Times* story described the boys as examples of "the youngest of the bad" and as "potent symbols of fear of a future overrun by cold-hearted child criminals" (Terry 1996). The article profiled the older boy, Tyrone, in these terms: "He failed every subject in the fourth grade, including gym, but was passed into the fifth grade and was repeating it when he was arrested at 11. His father, who taught him how to fight when he was 6 or 7, is in prison for home invasion. The boy frequently ran away from home and slept in abandoned buildings. His I.Q. is 76."

The accretion of detail is similar here to the pastiche of images swirling around Tanisha. Why note that Tyrone had failed gym? What is this supposed to mean—that he was uncooperative, did not attend class, or was perhaps uncoordinated? A sort of sinister connection is made between Tyrone's being taught to fight at "6 or 7" and his father's incarceration, as if one naturally leads to the other. But what boy growing up in a place like the Ida B. Wells wouldn't be taught how to defend himself? What is the relevance of Tyrone's I.Q. to the crime? Finally, the child is described as running away from home, but we are not told why. Perhaps the fact that his mother was a crack addict, a detail not mentioned in the article, had something to do with it.

The article also describes the Ida B. Wells housing projects, where the boys grew up and where Eric Morse died, as a place "where gangs, guns and death at an early age are part of everyday life" (Terry 1996). These hackneyed images are fleshed out considerably in the account by LeAlan Jones and Lloyd Newman, who also investigated the Eric Morse killing (1997). At the time that the two reporters began to gather their information, they themselves were fifteen years old, and had grown up in the same community as Eric Morse and his killers. In their own musings and as they interviewed a wide range of residents, prosecutors, politicians, and relatives, the relevant problems included "gangs, guns and death at an early age," but the picture was rendered complex in a way the mainstream press failed to explore. Jones and Newman's analysis of the problem included elements most often left out of depictions of "cold-hearted child criminals" like Johnny and Tyrone who killed Eric Morse—depictions that are particularly one-sided when the perpetrators are poor and black (Dowdy 1998). What LeAlan Jones and Lloyd Newman describe are two very troubled boys. They were boys who had problems and who caused problems, but in this account they are also viewed as boys who were also worthy of compassion and even love. In speaking with LeAlan Jones, Johnny's special ed teacher said the following:

> Had I been able to hold on to him longer, I could have taught him. He would have opened up more, because at some time all kids open up. Johnny was not the first Johnny I've had. The school system is full of

Johnnys. That same school is full of Johnnys. And I don't know if it fooled other people, but I think Johnny was just putting on a facade, a front. Tough Guy.

LeAlan: Why do you think he had to have that tough guy image?

To survive. To survive. (125)

Tyrone's father, incarcerated for assaulting Tyrone's mother, was also visited by the young reporters. He described hearing about the crime:

> I was in Stateville Penitentiary. We was in lock-down at the time, and it came on the radio at about five o'clock in the morning. And I sat up and just felt that my baby was involved. See, when you're close to someone you get a feeling, and by me and my son being real tight, when I heard it over the radio I just had this premonition. So when we come off lock-down I called his mother and she was crying on the phone. But I already knew. It's just that gut feeling that you have. So me and all my buddies went to the yard, and we all bent down on our right knees and said prayers for my son and the little boy that died. There was about a hundred of us out there. A lot of people loved my son. (Jones and Newman 1997, 128)

In addition, these young reporters continually stress that the problems in the Ida B. Wells are not only generated from within the confines of the ghetto but have been actively manufactured by the society at large. Such connections are not entirely glossed over by the mainstream media, but continue to make their points by highlighting scary pathologies. While the *New York Times* quoted the sentencing judge as saying it is "essential to find out how these two young boys turned out to be killers, to have no respect for human life and no empathy for their victim" (Staples 1996), Jones and Newman didn't seem to think the answer was so hard to find, and at one point quoted the chairman of the Chicago Housing Authority:

> We've got to get back to the point where we don't stack poor people on top of each other. Also, there are no role models: fathers, brothers, sisters that get up and go to work every day and who are doing positive things. We don't have Boy Scouts, Cub Scouts, Little League— almost anything. So when you don't have any alternatives, I don't know why society would be surprised at what happens in public housing today. (106)

Without downplaying the senselessness of the crime and the faults and failings of the two boys, Jones also allows them a measure of humanity:

> Now they're talking about tearing down all the high-rises and putting everyone in low-rise buildings as the solution. True, it's a start. But Tyrone and Johnny could have thrown Eric out of a vacant apartment in the low-rises and he could have fallen and broken his neck. So what are you going to do—make the low-rise homes lower? It's more than just the buildings. You don't know how it is to take a life until you value life itself. Those boys didn't value life. Those boys didn't have too much reason to value life. Now they killed someone and part of them is dead too. (141)

A more recent account of combat consumption is even more disturbing than the Eric Morse killing, primarily because the accused child killers—seven and eight years old—were found to be innocent, but only after many months of police waffling. They had been accused of killing Ryan Harris, an eleven-year-old girl, for her "shiny blue Road Warrior bicycle" (Slater 1998). The police theory was that the boys wanted the bike and so whacked the girl over the head with a rock (in some cases described as a brick), knocked her to the ground, strangled her by putting leaves and grass into her nose and mouth, sexually assaulted her, and, finally, stuffed her panties into her mouth.

While the community from which the children came faced these charges with incredulity (which was duly noted by the press), a feeding frenzy emerged around these supposedly crazed children willing to kill for a bike. Sticking to journalistic ethics and declining to identify the boys, one *Chicago Sun-Times* article instead settled for identifying the specific city blocks on which they lived (Carpenter and Lawrence 1998). In the end, it turned out the girl had been killed by an adult sex offender, identified through DNA analysis of semen he'd left on her clothing—evidence that surfaced only two weeks after the children had been charged with the crime. None of the media accounts traces the police logic in constructing their theory, but I am left wondering how on earth they arrived at the idea that the two little boys had killed a little girl in order to get her bike. The children's confessions, it turns out, had been coerced under technically legal conditions that were nonetheless troubling: there was no parent or legal counsel present with the children as they were questioned and the children were never advised of their rights. Their "confessions" and interviews were neither audio- nor videotaped and thus reconstructed solely through police interrogators' notes.

The ease with which police and much of the public could believe that two little boys would actually kill another child for her bike is frightening, and as in the description of Tyrone, the connection between combat consumerism, murder, and other forms of depravity is easily made. As one editorial mused:

> But after witnessing how vicious some small boys can be when they attack another child, I never would say what a child will not do. After spending time in the Cook County Juvenile Detention Center, where children are awaiting trial on charges as serious as murder and rape of young victims, I dare not say what one child, would not—could not—do to another. (Mitchell 1998)

Mitchell goes on to recount the police version of events: "after one of the boys allegedly struck Ryan with a large rock, they dragged her body into some weeds, molested her with a foreign object and stuck leaves and clothing in her mouth. Afterward they ran off to play." Again, the nightmarish pastiche of details adds to the image of depravity, without adding up to a logical story. If they killed her for the bike, why did they "run off to play" afterward? Was it that the sexual assault made them forget about their original object of desire? Why would seven- and eight-year-old kids who wanted a bike engage in sexual assault in any case? Interestingly, the issue of the blue bike, which had never been found, disappeared entirely as complications emerged in the investigation—including the fact that one of the interrogating officers had previously had "confessions" by minors thrown out of court for being coerced and irregular. The adult sex offender later accused of the crime had at least three prior convictions. The boys' families are suing the city for $100 million.

The understanding that kids like those profiled above are somehow typical combat consumers not only misreads their consumer patterns at material levels but misinterprets the social impact and genesis of these patterns. It is a portrayal tapping a particularly insidious American myth: that the poor are highly susceptible to commodity fetishism, that they are addicted to brands, and that they are willing to acquire expensive things even at the cost of their own (or someone else's) health and/or well-being. Connected to this idea is a whole rat's nest of assumptions about poverty, money, and consumption: that the poor are poor primarily due to their own lack of discipline and self-control; that the poor do not know how to economize or prioritize expenses; and that commitment of the poor to consume somehow ends up costing "us," whether through crime, welfare dependency, teenage motherhood; that these depravities lead to murder, drugs, sex crimes.

Former Speaker of the House Newt Gingrich, with his singular ability to voice what many think but would never actually say in polite company, has provided us with some especially clear examples of this train of thought. When a pregnant woman and her two small children were murdered in Chicago, reportedly because the murderers wanted to steal her unborn baby and sell it on the black market—the ultimate in combat consumerism—Gingrich announced that the crime was "the final culmination of a drug-addicted underclass with no sense of humanity, no sense of the rules of life in which human beings respect each other. Let's talk about what the welfare state has created. . . . Let's talk about the moral decay of the world the left is defending" ("Gingrich Links Slaying of Family to 'Welfare State'" 1995). At the time that Gingrich made his comments, whether the killers were receiving federal or state aid or whether they had problems with drugs was unknown, much less being irrelevant. In fact, as it turns out, it was the victim who was the welfare recipient. One wonders if Gingrich's response, upon learning this, might have been something to the effect that she probably would not have been murdered had she not been mooching off the state.

I would hope that few would conclude, as Gingrich apparently did, that the horrendous Chicago crime could only have been committed by drug-addicted welfare recipients. And yet, Gingrich's potent ideological soup—where lack of morals correlates with low economic status to create monstrous consumer pathologies—bears a strong resemblance to the equally potent (yet incoherent) juxtaposition of images seen in the *New York Times* when describing Shaul's girlfriend Tanisha, the Eric Morse killing, and in the Ryan Harris case. The main problem with the images in the *New York Times* and trains of thought offered by Gingrich is that they are based on cases selected precisely for their shock value. What is needed is a more even-handed, less shock-oriented approach to the details of particular lives and communities, one that addresses contextual issues as being in fact central to the question.

Making Connections

Two more well-known examples embodying the paradoxes inherent in attempting to retrieve a humane understanding of the "inner city" as it is often called, are Carl Nightingale's *On the Edge* (1993) and Philippe Bourgois's *In Search of Respect* (1995). These notable recent efforts are aimed less at hardening our hearts against the swinging gold earring crowd and more at generating a nuanced understanding of the pressures and problems that shape their lives. In both works a focus on poverty and the most distressed urban communities remains. These studies are not theoretically grounded in the study of consumption (they have other overriding concerns), although one can extrapolate from these and other pieces of research just how consumption might be shaped by the conditions of poverty and alienation. Nightingale does pay significant attention to what he calls "American consumer culture," but the theoretical perspective upon which he bases both his analysis of this American consumer culture and the children he describes is not clearly delineated.

Although stressing the structural factors at work in the immiseration of today's urban poor, like most work in this vein, these authors stress the isolation of "inner city" and "underclass" while at the same time seeking to explore the political and economic connections between these places and the larger society. Nightingale and Bourgois attempt to challenge the two-dimensional, highly selective images of urban minority youth (nearly always portrayed as male) by presenting rich ethnographic accounts of the lives of particular people in South Philadelphia and East Harlem. Both authors reject the notion that the problems faced by their subjects arise primarily from individual failings of character, motivation, or self-discipline. Rather, through historical, political, economic, and social analyses, these authors attempt to draw connections between the ghetto neighborhoods where they conducted their research, the nation, and the world at large. Neither do these authors attempt to whitewash the uglier aspects of the often-harsh conditions in which youth live and the ways in which this, in turn, can harden their natures. The main drawback is in many ways their starting place: in the worst ghettos, among the poorest of the poor. These sites effectively allow researchers to look at the reality behind popular images and to counteract them with carefully researched and reasoned accounts, but they have also, in a way, allowed dominant discourse to lay the boundaries of the inquiry. The census defines a ghetto tract as consisting of a population with 40 percent or more living at or below the poverty line. This means, conversely, that potentially a full 60 percent of the population is living above the poverty line, though how far above might be the relevant question. At the very least, the census definition of a ghetto tract indicates that economic diversity might well be the rule, not the exception.

South Philadelphia and East Harlem stand with South Central Los Angeles and Chicago's South Side as the nation's *ur*-ghettos, at the extreme end of poverty: eleven of the fifteen poorest census tracts in the United States are Chicago housing projects (Staples 1996). Such areas are hardly typical urban "inner city" communities—if such a thing can even be seen to exist. Yet it is precisely because they represent such extremes that these communities are heavily studied. Urban poverty has more faces, colors, and permutations than those seen in the nation's most dramatically depressed areas; as some new work is beginning to explore, there are "inner cities" that are predominantly white (Hartigan 1997). Recognition of the existence of such communities requires the decoupling of much-reinforced assumptions about race and class.

Conclusion

Many researchers have insightfully documented why a kid like Shaul Linyear might be impelled to kill for sneakers, but less attention has been focused on the variety of other ways in which kids like this engage with the world of consumption or the world in general: how do they get money? Where do they shop? What do they buy? A prominent—but still small—body of knowledge exists regarding selected aspects of the consumer habits and practices and preferences of impoverished people, generated by the disciplines of marketing and consumer behavior research (Andreasen 1976; Caplovitz 1967; Honeycutt 1975). And yet, Alan Andreasen, one of the most important and groundbreaking authors in this area, has charged the academy at large with a sustained and insupportable lack of interest in the consumption of the poor—whether in empirical documentation or cultural interpretation (Andreasen 1986). Ronald Hill and Debra Stephens (1997), in developing a model of "impoverished-consumer behavior," wonder specifically about the implications of poverty for children and consumption and close their article by writing, "Most children are socialized into the world of consumption by care givers who have limited resources. How do children come to terms with these limitations, and what coping strategies do they employ?" (46).

This brings us back to the discussion of consumption and social inequality with which this chapter began. The political economy of consumption, like Marx's political economy of production, involves attention to a total socially constructed system whose organization has implications at the individual as well as institutional and ideological levels. Rather than being a simple top-down process, where some overarching and amorphous culture of consumption invades the inner city or children's minds, the relationships between children, commodities, and symbols are contradictory, dynamic, and complex. Moreover, the commodities and resources in question are not limited to candy, toys, and sneakers, but include housing stock, public funds, and geographic space. The ways in which urban communities have been reshaped by the differential disposition of collective resources is in part a question of consumption: if consumption includes buying and spending, the use of federal funds to create housing projects and to profoundly reshape the preexisting communities of color is surely in large part a consumer question. The social inequalities of race, economics, and gender are also enacted in these spheres, shaping individuals, institutions, and ideology. Examining the role of children in these processes illuminates something about their own lives, capabilities, and perceptions. But paying attention to the consumption of children does not shed light solely on the limited sphere of childhood experience. Because they are members of society, and because what children do and think has an impact on the world around them, examining consumption through the lens of childhood also opens up an understanding of the entire society of which these children are part.

Despite the massive amount that has been written on distressed urban communities, the vocabulary used to describe and define them is astonishingly limited. Dense, evocative terms like *inner city* now operate as quick descriptors behind which lurk a host of meanings and assumptions that are loaded like a semiautomatic: poor, black, drugs, gangs, violence, Latino, welfare, joblessness. The long history of focused scholarly attention given to Chicago's South Side, for instance, obscures the range of kinds of urban distress that are to be found in American cities (Kotlowitz 1991; Park, Burgess, Duncan, and Wirth 1925; Wilson 1987; Wiseman 1997). Moreover, a common conceptual thread in the majority of these works is the pathologizing of black consumption: an assumption that to enter the "inner city" is to cross the border into Austin's "Nation of Thieves."

Let me close this chapter by telling a story. Most researchers develop a kind of cocktail party one-liner for describing the projects they are working on, and in my case, when people asked me about my research in New Haven, I would answer something like this: "I'm studying the role of consumption in the lives of poor and working-class black children." Here I would more often than not get a knowing look. "Ah," the response would be, "you must have seen a lot of Air Jordans," referring to the legendarily expensive basketball shoes. "Actually, no," I'd answer. "I only saw two pairs of Air Jordans on the kids I worked with." Rather than piquing my acquaintance's interest in what kinds of things I had seen going on in Newhallville, this statement was nearly always met with incredulity. More than once people responded with something to the effect of "There must have been something wrong with your sample."

I admit that such comments were disturbing because of the breezy dismissal of my status as a social scientist and ethnographer. But, more important, these comments also disturb me because so many people seemed to prefer hanging on to ideas about poor black kids that had been gleaned from the pseudo experience provided by the kinds of news stories I have so extensively critiqued in the preceding pages. Like the terms *inner city* and *ghetto,* the "Air Jordans" response to thinking about poor and working-class black children and consumption obscures more about those children than it reveals.

Before moving into the ethnographic material itself, then, I have felt it necessary to explore the complex, twisted skein of ideas that surrounds the question of consumption by African Americans. I am entirely willing to concede that the lives and worlds I describe in the pages that follow cannot be taken as a comprehensive portrait of all children like these; by that same token, however, it must also be so that the legendary crazed combat consumer is not the "real" truth either. Please leave all Air Jordans at the door. The place you are about to enter is not the inner city or the ghetto, but a place called Newhallville.

3.

"What Are You Looking At, You White People?"

In Newhallville children demonstrated early on their capacity for changing the character and limitations of the research as I had envisioned it. Not surprisingly, their questions and concerns were very different from the ones I had come up with in my New York apartment before coming to New Haven, and they proved to be the guiding questions of the work that has emerged. The most crucial question was asked by Tionna one afternoon as she, Natalia, and I stood on a corner just at the neighborhood's border with one of the city's wealthiest areas. Uncomfortable, perhaps, with occupying this border zone, they both got loud and silly, belting out songs that got significantly louder when cars passed by. One of a pair of older ladies in a light-blue sedan turned her head when hearing the commotion. Tionna shouted at her, "What are you looking at, you white people?" As I have suggested in the previous chapter, the question is not so easy to answer. What are we looking at? Is it the people who we observe and examine, or is it our images of them? Would the people we "see" recognize themselves in our visions?[1]

These questions have become increasingly prickly, not just in research among the urban minority poor but in the writing of anthropology more generally. The "natives" we study are ever more adept at manipulating the anthropologist's vision of themselves to their own political and economic advantage. Such is the case with many lowland Amazonian indigenes who, in a move designed to assert their "true" Indian-ness and hence rights to land and sovereignty, routinely exchange their now more usual dress of t-shirts and jeans for feathered headdresses and body paint when addressing government officials and eco-activists (Conklin 1997). This ability to use outsiders' notions of authenticity to advantage adds layers of complexity to the engagement between anthropologist and subject.

When Tionna shouted out her question to the blue-haired white lady in the passing car, part of it was aimed at me as well. Knowing full well what the prevailing stereotypes are in New Haven about young black kids, Tionna brazenly ups the ante by becoming homey-er than thou, exaggerating the very character traits that she knows are most feared, disliked, and disparaged in the white world beyond her neighborhood. "I know what you're thinking," she seemed to say, "and I can be that person, but if you think that's me, you don't know what you're really looking at." The challenge Tionna offered was to see beyond the act, to recognize her performance for what it was, an imitation of stereotypes held by others. The catch is, Tionna could be reasonably sure that only those familiar with her neighborhood as a community would be able to see through the put-on: people passing by in cars going thirty-five miles an hour are hardly likely to get the joke. When speaking about Barbie to an imagined audience, Natalia and Asia confronted the culture gap by adjusting their language so it could be understood by outsiders. In either case, these girls showed a stark and fundamental recognition of a social and geographic world inexorably separated from their own.

Consumption in Everyday Life

Consumption, like culture, poses a basic conundrum: while undertaken by individuals, what it *is* is larger than can be contained within any one person. And yet, while existing beyond any single person, it is only to be found within the actions, behaviors, and beliefs of individuals. Understanding the consumer lives of the children I knew in Newhallville requires moving beyond the borders of the neighborhood or even the city; simultaneously it requires an almost obsessive attention to the tiny details of children's daily lives, from a discussion over eating a donut to shopping in the downtown mall.

Subsequent chapters in this book focus on specific issues such as children's shopping trips and their relationships with ethnically correct dolls. The remainder of this chapter, however, provides a more free-ranging survey of the wider variety of children's consumer lives, from the intimate settings of their homes, to school, neighborhood stores, and downtown. What follows is a series of scenes or vignettes that illustrate important aspects of the ways in which children in Newhallville engage with consumption as a social process. Most are taken from the lives of Tionna, Asia, and Natalia, but the material is not limited to these three children: their classmates, siblings, and friends appear regularly. While arranged more or less temporally, this series of images is not meant to be comprehensive. My intent is to provide a sense of the tremendous range, flexibility, subtlety, and complexity of consumption in the everyday lives of these children: the way in which their social relationships are forged by and through consumption processes, and the ways in which consumption opens up and closes off social territories to them. At the same time, children's own powers of imagination and transformation are central to the form and tenor of these experiences and, though likely to change substantially as they enter their teen years, give some indication that the urban jungle is not what it is often made out to be.

At Home

August 1992. When I arrived for an impromptu visit with Tionna, she came to the door braiding her hair as she walked. Her grandmother, Celia, was in the dim bedroom that they shared, sitting atop the chenille bedspread, and she said she was going to get back into bed as soon as Tionna was done doing her hair. Celia did not feel well and said she'd been running a fever all week. It was time, she said, to do some back-to-school shopping for Tionna; she was hoping that someone would be able to give her a ride out to K-mart. The store was several miles away and, while accessible by bus, the route was inconvenient and time-consuming.

Tionna spied a glazed donut lying on a paper napkin on top of the bureau. "Ma, is that your donut?" Tionna asked her grandmother. "Yes," Celia answered, and Tionna intoned, "I want one . . ." "Well, they're your grandmother's donuts," Celia said (Tionna often calls her grandmother "Ma" and her great-grandmother "Grandma"). "You have to ask her if you can have one." Either Tionna did not want to ask or Celia decided she did not need the whole donut because she quickly called Tionna back and told her she could eat half. "I won't be able to eat the whole thing, anyway," she said gruffly.

In a way, Tionna and Celia made up a separate household that coexisted with Ella in her home. Tionna and Celia shared a room, and a bed as well. When at home, they generally kept to their small room. There was some tension between Celia and Tionna on the one hand and Ella on the other, especially regarding the day-to-day tasks of raising Tionna and maintaining the house. Ella complained that Celia did not want her to have any say-so in Tionna's upbringing but added that Tionna's mother, before her death, had specifically asked Ella to take care of the little girl. Ella complained as well that neither her daughter nor great-granddaughter helped her to keep the house clean, something Ella was no longer able to do as well as she would have liked. These tensions had given rise to a somewhat divided household, one where resources such as space and food seemed to be at times partitioned off, as in the case of Ella's donuts or Celia and Tionna's room. The family rarely ate together; Ella often declared that she was tired of cooking after fifty-odd years in the kitchen. She was overweight besides, and because she had heart trouble she was constantly battling to lose a few pounds, a task made more difficult because of a recent double knee replacement. Dinner was sometimes nothing more than a bowl of cereal—not because the family was too poor or even too disorganized to rustle up something more elaborate, but because none of the three wanted to do the cooking.

Like many of the older generation in Newhallville, Ella had roots in the rural South, where she grew up. Discipline in these families was strict, swift, and physical. Mothers were obeyed unconditionally, and Ella herself had a mother who was deeply imposing. Ella often told the story of her marriage to her husband, now dead. Though she had had a boyfriend before, she didn't love him. After the breakup she'd begun to see the man she would marry, but her mother had long ago decided that Ella was the child who would be her caretaker in her old age. She was, in her mother's view, to remain a spinster. On the day that Ella and her husband-to-be were to secretly wed, Ella told her mother she was going into town to see a film. She put her best dress on. When her mother saw her leaving the house in her best dress she ordered her upstairs to change her clothes. Without protesting, Ella changed her dress and then snuck off to her wedding. It was a thrilling act of defiance, but Ella was so afraid of her mother's reaction to the clandestine marriage that she spent a month continuing to live at home as if nothing had happened.

When Ella talked about "kids today" the theme was likely to be that they had no respect.

> When I was a girl, if my mother said she didn't have it, I didn't get it, and that was it! Today you say, "I don't have it" and they'll go out and get it somewhere else. We used to get five pennies together and we would buy the world with those pennies! "I'll buy a house with this one . . ." That was in the days where gum was one penny a stick. Kids today ask for a dollar! Tionna asks for two or three dollars. "What are you going to do with that much money?" I ask her.

The imperatives of consumption have entered and influenced Newhallville households in a variety of ways. Ella talks about her frustrations in what she sees as younger people's demands for money. Her comments reflect, as well, a sense that kids' desires are out of control.

Today, unlike when Ella was young, a caretaker's unequivocal "no" is not the final word. "Today you say 'I don't have it' and they'll go out and get it somewhere else." This statement reflects sentiments common among the older generation in Newhallville. Focused on children's lack of respect, or their willfulness, or the belief that they would do anything to get what they want if it was not given to them, these statements are loaded with meaning: the world today is in disorder; children are out of control; kids' values are off-kilter. These intergenerational tensions are not endemic only to communities such as Newhallville; common complaints can be found in homes with well-to-do residents as well.

Ella had plenty of support for her point of view. The small house she owned had been burglarized more than once, and items including prized family quilts stolen. She often remarked that only the junk in her life was left and that it was a shame that people felt entitled to help themselves to her possessions. Always a bit house-proud—in her younger days Ella had been a fanatical housekeeper, changing the curtains in the living room and kitchen seasonally, for instance—the continuing degradation of her home (to which she was increasingly confined) ate away at her.

Children are well aware of what their elders and caretakers think. Tionna knew that her great-grandmother thought she was wasteful and greedy about money, but she also knew that today she could not even pretend to buy the world with five pennies as Ella did when she was a child in rural Alabama. It is true that children today in Newhallville are likely to have more and to want more and to feel entitled to more than their parents or grandparents did when they were young. The conflict in Newhallville—and perhaps in society at large—is that children's lack of self-control or values are often blamed for this, without a recognition of the significant pressures at work in children's lives. Advertising and marketing, for instance, target children much more directly and earlier than has ever been the case previously.

In 1984 the Reagan administration eased Federal Communications Commission restrictions on several aspects of programming for and advertising to children on television, paving the way for unprecedented overlap between products and programs and allowing the lines between shows and ads to become more blurred. As a result, many companies have developed cartoon programs that are essentially designed to promote their toys, and the programs are in essence extended commercials interrupted by shorter commercials for the same products. Corporate incursions into children's lives have also taken on forms even more subtle and complex than Saturday morning cartoons with product tie-ins.

Schools have become sites of growing importance for direct appeals to children's buying power. The most important development here is Channel One, a news program complete with commercials that is piped into schools, including those in New Haven. Corporate incursions into the schools are especially problematic since they often take the form of making donations of needed equipment or supplies in exchange for exposing students to commercials, advertising, or prominent logos. Channel One has entered large numbers of schools (many of them public) primarily because it provides schools with video equipment in exchange for having children watch its morning news program complete with advertisements for national brands of sneakers, soft drinks, and snacks.

Children today enter few environments that do not subject them to market pressures, and their relationship to advertising and the market is radically different from that of people only ten or fifteen years older. Despite the pervasiveness of advertisements and marketing pressures, or perhaps because of them, children today are quite often adept at critically analyzing industry attempts to create desires for their products, much more so than their parents or grandparents were when they were young. In Newhallville, where many grandparents remember rural Southern childhoods without electricity or indoor plumbing—let alone televisions or shopping malls—generational gaps are especially great. This dynamic creates enormous tension and conflict, particularly among household members—even over something as apparently insignificant as a glazed donut.

Summer Jobs and Sexual Politics

Tionna did not receive a regular allowance, but Celia, her grandmother, provided her with pocket money when she needed it. Occasionally, if Tionna was going to go downtown with a friend, her grandmother might give her ten dollars to spend. (At around age ten, many Newhallville kids were allowed to go downtown with friends and without adults.) During the summer of 1992 Tionna and Natalia had a job dropping off Natalia's young niece and nephew at the babysitter in the morning and then picking them up again to take them home in the afternoon. Natalia's older brother, the father of the two children, worked in a local hair salon. He gave the girls five dollars a week for doing this chore and they split the money. It seemed to me that aside from the money the girls really enjoyed this job because it meant pushing two babies along in a stroller and being able to boss and take care of these younger children who were about one-and-a-half and two-and-a-half years old.

One day, when we were dropping the two younger children off at their mother's home, a man in his twenties detached himself from a group near the house and struck up a conversation with me. Within a few minutes he was asking for my phone number. At that moment Natalia came up behind me and said, "I think I'm ready to go," deftly cutting the interaction short. "He's probably a drug dealer," she said with assurance as we walked away. "He probably rapes little girls," she added.

The girls had just been paid by Natalia's brother, who had given them fifteen dollars, eight for Natalia and seven for Tionna. Natalia said she'd been using the money to help pay for camp. Tionna said she could just spend the money on whatever she wanted. When I asked her what she bought with it, she said, "I don't know. Food." "What kind of food?" "I don't know. Just things to eat!"

The girls began talking about someone who had died, a classmate's grandmother. Their friend had missed a few days of school and when she had come back was acting short-tempered and "babyish." The conversation turned to what would happen if various people in the girls' families died. "If my grandmother died, I'd stay with my great-grandmother," Tionna said matter of factly, "and if she died I'd have to find my way to Augusta, Georgia." "Maybe you could stay with me!" Natalia suggested, then went on, "I wouldn't want to go into foster care, because the foster parents sometimes rape the kids." As we continued on our walk, Natalia's sandal came unglued from the sole and she walked along dragging her foot so the sole wouldn't flap against the broken and glass-littered cement.

After a few minutes Tionna said, "I think men go after little kids because they can't talk, they can't say anything, because they're little." Natalia didn't think about this very long. "They go after big kids too," she replied with sureness. "And women too."

Natalia's vision of the lifelong threat of rape, and the matter-of-fact way in which she delivers this vision, is chilling. The girls' heightened awareness of sexual danger, evident in their everyday conversations about men "who rape little girls" and the way these men exploit young children "because they can't say anything because they're little," surfaced again and again, in varying forms, during the time I spent with them.

These girls find many ways to speak about their fears and frustrations and, as will be seen later in this chapter, the consumer sphere is one medium they turn to this purpose. The consumer lives of these and other Newhallville girls are entwined with their emergent sexual awareness in multiple ways and serve as a way for them to articulate a sense of sexual danger, as well as a wellspring of fantasies about "the man of my dreams," dating, and romance; a later vignette will show how shopping and roving New Haven's downtown doubles as a sort of fishing expedition for "slammin'" boys.

Natalia's use of her babysitting money to help pay for camp was not unusual. The Newhallville children I knew were expected to spend part of their pocket money on things they needed—underwear, socks, barrettes— or to help pay for special activities like camp. In these and other ways, kids are made acutely aware of the costliness of their maintenance and their responsibilities as members of families and the extended kin group. This awareness lays the foundation for an experience of consumption that is deeply social, and where individual needs and desires must always be measured and evaluated in reference to those of others.

Children's sense of endangerment makes them acutely aware of how much they depend on their kin and kin networks, but kids do not always view themselves as the endangered ones; on several occasions, and with seemingly no connection to conversations or events taking place, children spontaneously launched into discussions of what they would do if their mothers died, or if someone was trying to hurt their mother. Children's fierce protectiveness of their mothers was evident in these discussions, which included detailed descriptions of how they would hurt or kill threatening individuals by grabbing guns, knives, or any weapon close at hand. At the same time, children also mentally laid escape routes should their present situations fail them, as did Tionna when she said, "If my grandmother died, I'd stay with my great-grandmother, and if she died I'd have to find my way to Augusta, Georgia." Tionna's assumption seems to be that if both her grandmother and great-grandmother died, she would be alone and faced with the prospect of making her way by herself to Augusta, Georgia, where a number of her great-grandmother's relatives live.

Birthdays

July 17, 1992, was Natalia's tenth birthday, and on that same day her mother moved into a new apartment two blocks from her previous one. Natalia invited me to come to her birthday party. Natalia's mother had bought her an ice-cream cake, and the cake was being stored in the freezer at Natalia's grandparents' house, about four blocks "down the hill" from Natasha's mother's new home. The girls and I walked through the July heat to her grandparents' home to get the cake.

Natalia went into her grandparents' house alone, while Asia, who lives next door, waited with Tionna and me on her shady front porch. Several minutes later Natasha came bursting through her grandparents' front door holding her birthday cake in its box and running full speed. "Asia, can you put this in your freezer?" Natalia asked, her voice at once squeaky and breathless. Natalia's brother, who didn't even like ice-cream cake, had been threatening to take a slice before it was time. Asia took the cake upstairs to her apartment and Natalia went back to her grandfather's house.

She came hurtling out of the house again, followed by her grandfather who was visibly angry. He took her over his knee on the front porch, though he did not seem to spank or hit her. Throughout, Natalia, furious, remained silent. Asia, Tionna, and I watched from the safety of the porch, the girls trying to tell me about Natalia's grandfather. They slipped me tidbits of information from the sides of their mouths, so that Natalia's grandfather, if he happened to look over, would not see them talking. When Natalia was released she joined us on Asia's porch. The ten-year-old birthday girl was a vibrating tower of anger. I asked her how she felt, and her response was to wither me with a burning glance. Asia and Tionna laughed the whole thing off and made fun of Natalia.

We collected the cake and some paper plates and took it to the apartment out of which Natalia's mother was moving. The large, second-floor apartment was nearly empty, holding only a legless couch and clothes in piles. Natalia's mother had not expected her daughter and entourage to arrive there and had already sent the dishes and flatware to the new apartment. We had no forks to eat the cake with, though there was a knife to cut it. Natalia's mother continued packing and moving while the party was going on. She did stop to bring the cake out, and we sang "Happy Birthday" to Natalia in as many keys as there were people. Natalia asked what she should wish for, and her cousin said, "Just wish for a million dollars." We put slices of melting ice-cream cake onto the paper plates and ate them with our hands.

Natalia's party was probably not supposed to be the impromptu, disorganized event it turned out to be. Though Natalia's mother was moving on the day of her daughter's birthday and was mostly unavailable for celebrating, she had gone out of her way to order an $18 birthday cake for Natalia and had picked it up downtown the day before. My guess is that the family had planned a small gathering for that evening, after the move was over, in the home of Natalia's grandparents, where the cake was being stored. Whatever her reasons were—and Natalia never explained, beyond the problem that her brother was threatening to eat the cake before it was time—Natalia took matters into her own hands, removing the cake from her grandparents' home and taking it to her mother's former apartment. While Natalia's mother was unprepared to have the party there, she did not object to what Natalia had done or tell her to go back with the cake to her grandparents' house.

This was the single birthday party I attended during my time in Newhallville; birthday parties were rarely held for these children.[2] Gifts were few as well; Cherie, on her tenth birthday, received three gifts: from her mother, a jumprope and a bingo game (carefully wrapped in brown paper from a grocery bag), and from her grandmother an inexpensive plastic toy. Her father, who lives in another town, was supposed to have taken her to buy school uniforms as a birthday gift but never did. Cherie did not have a birthday party, either with family or friends, though her mother made her a chocolate cake from a mix, which Cherie picked out.

Children I knew in Newhallville did not exchange birthday or holiday gifts with each other (neither did they exchange cards). While these children may not have *expected* birthday parties, this does not mean they did not wish for them. Toward the end of my fieldwork time I had a slumber party for Natalia, and on Tionna's birthday I took her and several friends to the movies. These parties were not my idea, but the result of long, repeated pressure from the girls themselves. While the celebration of a birthday was certainly an important element of these parties, by far the most important ingredient was the celebration itself, which had little birthday-related content. The girls did not talk about the birthday girl's age, though some did give birthday hits, punching her once for each year and once more for good luck. As I found was often the case, the girls asked for very little and demanded even less.

The Cucumber Stand

One hot July afternoon, I found Tionna and her friend Tiffany, who lives two doors away, acting as proprietors of a cucumber stand. They had a table set up in front of Tiffany's house and were selling cucumbers that Tiffany had grown in her backyard. They had piled the cucumbers on paper towels and taped signs to the edge of the table saying, "Cucumbers, fresh and clean," and another stating the price of the large ones as forty cents, small ones a quarter.

Some time later Tionna came out with a quite large cucumber and they tried to figure out what the price should be. Tionna suggested sixty cents.

Tiffany wondered if it should be seventy-five. Then, with authority Tionna announced the price should be fifty cents because then they could split it easier and wouldn't have to wait for some change. Tiffany told me the woman next door had given them a dollar to get their business started. Tiffany's grandmother came by and bought a large cucumber, putting fifty, rather than forty, cents into the pot. The kids would occasionally count the money and divide it into two equal piles, since they were planning to split the money equally. They ended up with each having about a dollar seventy-five.

Later that afternoon, my own next-door neighbor's child—about five years old—set up a lemonade stand on the walkway to her home. The neighborhood where I lived at the time (occupying a spare bedroom in my godparents' home) is populated by Yale professors, doctors, lawyers—well-off professional people, or those, like these neighbors, who are graduate students on their way to professional careers. "I think she does it just so she can meet people," her mother said. The girl had been provided with a large bowl full of change and was charging a sliding scale for the cups of lemonade. A child psychiatrist who lived down the street stopped at the stand and then with no apparent sense of irony began grilling the five-year-old proprietor about her "return on investment" and "reinvestment of capital."

My neighbor's observation about her child's motivation for setting up her lemonade stand—that she wanted "to meet people"—stands in contrast to the psychiatrist's interest in educating the girl in business finance. Tionna and Tiffany likewise had highly social reasons for setting up their cucumber stand. For one, it provided them a legitimate reason to stay outside and talk to people with whom they otherwise would have no reason to communicate. For another, it made them objects of attention—and usually praise. Passersby, even if they did not buy, made comments such as "Isn't that nice!" or "Those are good-looking cucumbers." It offered, of course, the opportunity to make some money, but it is interesting to note that the girls' concern with sharing whatever money they generated seemed to supersede their pursuit of high prices, and they decided to price the largest cucumber at fifty cents rather than seventy-five because it was an amount easily divided between the two. For them, the ease of sharing money equally was more important than maximizing their income.

The cucumber stand is a variation on the classic summertime commercial enterprise for American children, the lemonade stand. Like allowances, these stereotypical childhood engagements with the commercial sphere socialize them into the culture of commerce, the roles, rules, and expectations of buyer and seller. Although they may not yet have mastered the arts of cost-benefit calculation, the girls' understanding of several basic elements is undeniable.

Television

While the girls were minding their cucumber stand I asked Tionna about the television programs she watches. She did her sassy act for a while, saying, "I don't know," in a bratty, challenging way when I'd ask her about shows she watches and when they're on. Eventually, she took the pad from me and started writing them down herself. Her list was not particularly long and included only eleven shows; even during the summer, a period in which she might be expected to watch a lot of television because of increased free time, especially during the day, she included only two daytime shows (see table 3.1).

Table 3.1. Tionna's Television Programs

MTV Raps	daytime	MTV
Video Soul	daytime	BET
Living Color	night 8:30	61
Rachel Gunn, R.N.	night 8 or 9	61
Who's the Boss?	night	20
Bill Cosby	day/night 5 & 6	20
Growing Pains	night	20
Full House	nighttime	?
Family Matters	nighttime	61
TGIF	nighttime	61
Step by Step	nighttime	61

With three televisions in her home, one or more of which was nearly always on, Tionna had plenty of opportunity to watch all kinds of programs. Her great-grandmother had a penchant for daytime talk shows like *Oprah* and *Sally Jessy Raphael* because, as Ella herself said, "I like to watch people being stupid!" Whether Tionna actually watched much television was unclear, and it always seemed to me that she spent a great deal of her free time sleeping. There were programs she liked and watched fairly regularly, all of them evening shows. Like most Newhallville families I knew, Tionna's family imposed few rules on her watching, the primary one being that she had to finish her homework before watching television. The lack of rules did not mean, however, that Tionna was glued to the set four hours a day.[3] She was much more interested in spending time with her friends, usually outside, or often playing when inside. Even when watching TV, Tionna engaged in a variety of activities simultaneously—from braiding her hair (or her dolls' hair) to talking on the phone with friends. This seemed typical of Newhallville kids, who could be found outside playing during daylight hours all through the summer and after school. Part of this may be because many children did not have access to private places within their homes, where their play would not disrupt adults.

School Exchange

Being at school provides children with a wide range of experiences, and important among them is being around lots of other kids all day long. They exchange information about styles and fashions in dance, music, clothes, hair, jewelry, television, and toys; they gossip about each other and each other's families. They engage in complex trading and sharing and even selling interactions, often clandestinely. Early in Tionna's fifth-grade year, her classmate Stephen sparked a gimp craze and sold lengths of the colored plastic cord to most children in the room. At nearly every time of day kids were busily weaving the bright gimp into keychains or necklaces, until Lucy Aslan, their teacher, had to ban it except for certain approved times.

One afternoon, during an art class, Tionna, Cherie and I fell into conversation about what they wanted for Christmas. "What about that ice-cream maker, do you want that?" Cherie asked Tionna. Cherie continued, "My mother said that the one they make now isn't that good. The one they used to have is what they should come out with now." Tionna said in the voice of experience, "I had it, and I made that ice cream with it and it was corny so I took it back." She then started describing another thing she wanted, and though neither she nor Cherie knew the name of it, they both knew what they were talking about. "It's like a book bag," Tionna told me, "but you wear it on the front. You can feel the baby kicking and then you open it and you see if you got twins or triplets or quadruples." "You can feel what it was like when your mother was pregnant?" the art teacher asked them. "Well, not really," Tionna answered.

"So this thing isn't very realistic?" I asked. The kids looked at me rather blankly, wondering, I think, what I was getting at. "I mean, is it really like being pregnant?" "No!" they both shouted. "Why?" I asked them. "Because," answered Tionna, as if she were speaking to the village idiot, "you can unzip it and zip it up again and unzip it and zip it up again and take the baby out and put it in. You can't open up your stomach and take the baby out and put it back and take it out and put it back."

The toy the girls were discussing had been the object of some heated debate in the public arena, as certain toys always are. A sort of pouch worn on the stomach to simulate the look of pregnancy, it contains baby dolls that can be activated to make movements and the wearer can feel the baby moving, as a pregnant woman might. There were fears expressed that kids would get the wrong idea about what pregnancy really is—that it is removable like the pouch, or that giving birth is like opening up a velcro flap. It is possible that such misunderstandings might arise among very young children; Tionna's pointed remarks show she was, however, in no danger of entertaining such a misunderstanding. While she found the toy interesting, and might even have admitted to wanting one, she had no illusions that the strap-on pouch is anything like a real pregnancy.

Throughout the school day these kids, like most children, constantly discuss clothes, toys, and other products. These discussions are not always friendly or nice, and making cutting remarks about other kids' desires, appearance, or possessions seems to be a staple of school life just about everywhere. The Shelton school, like a growing number of schools across the nation, instituted the use of uniforms in an effort to minimize the kind of social jockeying that can emerge around the issue of clothes. Children came to school in white tops and blue bottoms, girls having a choice of jumpers, skirts, or pants.

Throughout the day, as children interacted with each other, spontaneous discussion about what products and programs they liked and why, what is cool, what is "corny," filled the classroom. These discussions are more than materialism, but an especially intense form of social interaction, and often a proving ground. In so doing, children express to each other something of who they are both separately and together. They give each other consumer information, as did Tionna in telling Cherie about taking back the ice-cream maker. They also sometimes supply each other with coveted items—for a price—as Stephen did with the gimp. These interactions reached peak intensity at lunchtime, when children at Shelton school had the greatest freedom of their school day.

School Lunch

Tionna got up from the lunch table, remembering that she had a bag of cookies up in the classroom, and ran up to get them. She came back down with the cookies—a package of chocolate chip, two packages of wafer cookies, and one of Nutter Butters. She had bought them at Bob's (a local corner store) the other day with her grandmother. She said I could have some chocolate chip ones. She also let some other kids have them—handing them out in a casual fashion to those sitting near her. She gave the last three cookies in the pack to Carlos, who was sitting next to me.

Stephen, the boy who sold gimp in the classroom, was also sharing his homemade M&M-studded cookies, giving one to the person next to him and one to Natalia, and then handing me the baggie, which now held only broken pieces and crumbs, telling me I could have the rest. Teyvon, who was eternally hungry, was looking downhearted because nobody had given him any cookies. I took a large crumb for myself from the baggie Stephen had given me, then I gave Teyvon the rest.

Lunchtime was always a period of intense interaction among the kids. Trading portions of school lunch, homemade lunches, or cadging money to buy cookies—which the "lunch ladies" (as the cafeteria workers are called) sold for twenty-five cents for a pack of three—were activities conducted in a fevered pitch that often rivals the trading floor of the New York Stock Exchange.

The intensity of the lunch period was heightened by the fact that this half-hour was the children's only free time during the day. Fear of drug-related violence had led the school's principal to keep students indoors from the first morning bell until afternoon dismissal. There was no recess period—that is, neither indoor nor outdoor playtime—and the gym period, which children attended two or three times a week, was likewise conducted inside. In order to keep the lunchroom chaos to a simmer, classes of children waiting to join the cafeteria line had to sit at their tables with their hands folded on the table and lay their heads down on top of their hands. They were not allowed to talk. Lunch periods were one half-hour long; kids sometimes waited as long as twenty minutes to get their food, which left them with only ten minutes to sit and eat their meal. Sometimes it seemed as if kids had no sooner taken their seats at the table with their lunch tray when the school's security guard began pushing the rolling garbage can past the table telling students to hurry up, finish eating, and throw away their remains.

Exchange episodes, such as the one above with Tionna, Stephen, and the distribution of cookies, took place daily at lunch. Having something to give—and something that other children wanted—invested Tionna and Stephen with great power: they meted out gifts to a select few among the many who were loudly clamoring or quietly eying the treasure. This was sometimes done with an air of careless largesse, as if the receiver was almost invisible; at other times those who received were chosen with elaborate care, and relationships were often cemented or celebrated through exchanges of particularly prized foods.

Another element to the lunchtime exchange scene was the content and quality of the school lunches served. The fifth graders received lunches the same size as first graders and were often still hungry after eating. Most children told me they did not like these lunches in the first place. Meals were sometimes made up of a curious, if not bizarre, combination of items. The day of the cookie exchange lunch consisted of a scoop of tuna salad, a pile of cut-up iceberg lettuce, peanut butter and jelly between graham crackers (this item wrapped in a printed foil so it looked like it might be an ice-cream sandwich, albeit a small one), and a "wafer cookie." That day some kids had muffins on their trays also. The muffins looked as if they might have been left over from breakfast.

Kids very often refused to eat all or part of the lunch served; if they *were* willing to eat part of it (for instance, the peanut butter and jelly on graham crackers) they would barter vigorously to get someone else's portion of that item and "Are you going to eat that?" was a phrase often repeated throughout lunchtime, in concert with "Can I have your milk?" or "Do you want your pizza?" The negotiation of relationships between children lay clear on the face of these interactions and I have seen children pointedly dump uneaten portions of their lunches—coveted by others at their table—into the garbage. As a gesture of rejection, such an action could hardly be more decisive.

It was in these interactions with each other that I saw children's desires most clearly expressed. It was the only situation where kids consistently made requests of other people: they wheedled, begged, and pushed to get what they wanted. This direct expression of their wants may have been made possible, in part, because they were among their own; such begging and pushing was rarely tolerated by their elders. In addition, because the lunch was provided to them by the relatively anonymous school cafeteria, it did not enter their lives already enmeshed in the complicated world of obligation and reciprocity that family meals were likely to embody. These wants, their expression, and the negotiations taking place between children were multifaceted and ranged in emotional tenor from lighthearted and teasing to crabby to plain mean and angry. Despite the range and complexity of all that went on in the lunchroom, I never saw kids get out of hand in regard to trading food, giving it away, or receiving it as a gift. Their desires, so openly expressed, nevertheless remained contained and controlled overall.

Going Downtown

A couple of weeks before Christmas I took Tionna and Natalia shopping. Though the event was engineered by me—I provided the money and opportunity to make the trip—the girls ran the show. A partial account of Tionna and Natalia's trip provides a view of how highly complex an afternoon downtown was for these children. By the time they were ten years old, Tionna and Natalia, like many of their peers, were allowed to go downtown by themselves, and did so regularly.

The second we walked out of Tionna's house, she pulled out a tube of lipstick that belonged to Natalia. They both stopped to put the lipstick on, looking at their faces in the sideview mirrors of parked cars and taking quite a bit of time getting it on just right. None of their caretakers wanted them wearing makeup. As we walked along Prospect Street toward downtown they began making up a song to the tune of "Jingle Bells" that goes like this: "Mario, Mario, raped Barbie all day long / Batman tried to save the day but Luigi got her anyway!" (Luigi and Mario are Nintendo video-game characters.) Then they made up a sort of rap to sing as we walked, a call-and-response chant they traded off singing, "Hey hey, hey hey, I'm walking too fast now I got some cramps, I'm walking too fast so I got some cramps." This changed and evolved into several different variations, all of them loud and interspersed with squawks and giggles.

Entering the mall, the girls spotted a boy from their class and chased after him, calling his name. He was on the escalator going up to the second floor and they were hot on his heels, but they lost sight of him. I suggested going to the food court to make a game plan, but I quickly learned that the game plan was that there was no game plan, except to spot some cute boys and follow them.

Sitting at a table in the second-floor food court, the girls watched closely as three boys wandered through and sat by the windows overlooking the town green. "I dare you to go over and talk to them and I ain't comin'," Tionna said to Natalia. "They ugly!" Natalia shot back. "Well, one is a yellow light," Tionna answered, appraising them. Tionna explained to me that a "green light" is an ugly boy, a "yellow light" is a medium-looking one, and a "red light" is cute.

A man standing near us was wearing a baseball jacket with a complex design embroidered on the back. The jacket caught my eye and I stared at it for several moments. "What are you looking at, Miss Chin?" demanded Natalia. "I was looking at that guy's jacket," I said. She asked me, "What would you do if someone came over here and asked you for a date?" "I'd probably say no," I answered. Tionna jumped in and set the scene, trying to get me into the game. "What if you had been seein' him all around the mall and he'd been seein' you and you had a crush on him and he has a crush on you and he's the man of your dreams!" Natalia continued, "And he comes over and sits down and says, 'Would you like to go on a date with me? Tonight. At eight o'clock.'" I said that since he was the man of my dreams, maybe I'd meet him at a restaurant, but I wouldn't give him my phone number or let him know where my house was. "Why not?" they asked brightly.

In contrast to the girls' assurance that a man we ran across in Newhallville "probably rapes little girls," in the mall setting, their romantic fantasies take wing. Yet on our way to the mall the girls voiced some of their lingering fear about sexual threat in their fractured version of "Jingle Bells." As a commentary on their lives, the song is devastating. It speaks not only of their hopelessness in feeling safe from men—something evident not only in this ditty but from many, many other encounters—but emphasizes as well their sense of threat and even victimization in the consumer sphere. And yet these girls are able to make these materials, mass-produced and middle-America as they may be, speak about the particular issues being faced by them as "inner-city" children. These children instantly recognized that even the dark-skinned Barbies have very little relevance to their own lives. There were some moments where they wrapped themselves in the fantasy life offered by these (and other) toys; at other times, they acted upon or talked about the ways these toys represented to them a foreign, almost imaginary world.

The fantasy life offered by Barbie is akin to the romance fantasy the girls spin for me when they catch me staring at a man's jacket. It is not based in their own daily experience but partakes of a cultural fund of similar scenarios—those found in fairytales, Harlequin romances, and the like. Tionna and Natalia were not alone in creating such romantic fantasies about my life, and how I would fall in love with a man. Cherie also spun a startlingly similar tale for me, where a man took me on a series of increasingly impressive dates, culminating with a flight to New Orleans and a ride in a limousine. It is, I believe, no accident that the girls' fantasy lives took off so buoyantly when at the mall. One of the safest places to be away from home, the mall provides children a space to relax and play in ways they cannot in their own neighborhood.

Malls, of course, have been extensively theorized as spaces designed specifically to facilitate people's consumer fantasy lives (Bauman 1993; Goss 1993; Halton 1992), much in the same way that department stores have been viewed as spaces whose intention (and effect) is to loosen everyday concerns and responsibilities (with sometimes disastrous results) (Leach 1984). In a detailed analysis of the 1991 film *Scenes from a Mall,* Russell Belk and Wendy Bryce (1993) show in often painful detail the way in which one couple's emotional lives are enmeshed with the world of consumption. Although concerned with a fictional pair named Nick and Deborah, Belk and Bryce show through their painstaking, step-by-step discussion the ways in which consumption is put to work in specific lives. The bittersweet role of consumption fantasies in those lives figures prominently. While Belk and Bryce are far from being enthusiastic about the degree to which Nick and Deborah seem to be living their lives exclusively through consumer channels, they avoid characterizing the two as empty automatons who cannot help themselves. Enmeshed in the spectacle of the mall, the two nevertheless seem to be living through moments of passion. The overriding tendency, however (especially among postmodern theories), is to certify mall experiences as essentially surfacey, empty, alienating, fragmented. That is, the fantasies on offer at the mall are fake (as any fantasy must be!) and draw people into a cycle wherein they continually take on and cast off commodities that might fill out their fractured identities.

Despite the mass-produced flavor of the girls' romantic fantasies, it seems specious to dismiss them as merely the trappings of postmodern consumerdom. For one, they indulge in these fantasies specifically within the space of the mall, a space that is for them a protective place very different from their neighborhood. Coming as they do from an area where plenty of girls have children by their early teens, fantasies about romance take on a different quality than they might otherwise. Given the profound constraints these girls faced outside the mall, their physical and emotional freedom inside that space was revelatory: rather than hustling me away from a man because he might rape little girls, it is Natalia who, upon seeing my gaze resting upon a man, encourages me to imagine that we might fall in love.

Christmas

Ella had sworn up and down that she was not going to do anything for Christmas but had broken down and prepared a Christmas dinner of pork shoulder, succotash, cornbread, greens, and sweet potato pie. There was a little Christmas tree set up in the front room, covered with tinsel garlands, lights, and a few ornaments. Tionna's presents lay beneath the tree—a Starla doll, headbands, a pair of underpants, a small Walkman-type tape player, and a little musical keyboard. Tionna was still in her pajamas, hair all stuck out like a night creature of some sort, watching the film *Teen Witch* in Ella's room. Celia was watching a movie in her room.

While I was sitting at the kitchen table with Ella, Tionna came in and pulled the gold hairbow off my head. Ella immediately yelled at Tionna to get off my hair, Celia came out of her room and told Tionna to stop "pickin' at Miss Chin's head," and Ella said that Tionna and Natalia were always in my hair and to stop it. A short while later, Asia and Natalia stopped by. Tionna had done her hair so that it wasn't sticking out anymore. Asia and Natalia stopped in the front room to look at Tionna's presents. Natalia was carrying a Walkman that belonged to her cousin. The three girls lay around in the front room listening to tapes. They also played on Tionna's keyboard. Tionna ran into the kitchen and Ella told her not to run. The other two girls were waiting in the front room. Tionna sort of threw her garbage into the garbage bag, and this riled Ella up. "You stop showin' off now," she hollered. "I'll take that belt to you, you know I will," she said with a raised, threatening voice.

The Christmas season arrives in Newhallville with a drama marked most visibly by the decoration of many houses and yards. Across the street from Tionna's home, a three-story house with a balcony and a porch seems to have a Christmasy touch on every available surface. Fat, plastic snowmen and Santas perch on the porch and balcony rails, augmented by festoons of glittery garlands and blinking lights. The well-manicured house next door is similarly decorated, with the addition of mechanized figures of Santas and snowmen looking out from some of the windows, bowing and waving their arms. One house is itself wrapped up like some giant Christmas gift and is tied with a great shining gold and silver bow. Another features a Nativity scene, each of the three-foot-tall figures glowing with the aid of an internal lightbulb. At night, with all the frantically blinking lights turned on up and down the block, it is like being on some wacky amusement-park ride. A few blocks away, on one of New Haven's richest streets—Prospect—holiday decorations present quite a different image. At one house a single red velvet bow is placed on each of the evergreen bushes that rings the huge, flawless lawn; at another a lone electric candle shines from every window. There is nary a blinking light in evidence.

Newhallville's over-the-top home and yard decorations belie the often modest celebrations taking place inside these homes.[4] The children I knew in Newhallville received few Christmas gifts; these came from immediate family, sometimes aunts, uncles, and godparents as well. The children gave few, if any, gifts, either to friends or family. As Tionna's classmate Carlos commented: "The only thing I don't like about Christmas is they be lying at Christmas. They say 'this is from the kids,' and we didn't buy it for them. They know we broke! They be buying it and say that the kids bought it. They bought it and gave it to them." The children are not the only ones who are broke: Tionna's grandmother began talking in July about beginning to save for her granddaughter's Christmas presents. The presents Tionna received that year could not have cost more than $75 altogether.[5]

By the time I arrived at Tionna's home on Christmas afternoon, the family had separated, each watching television in a different room. Tionna was the only one in her household to have received any gifts. While Tionna looks forward to receiving Christmas presents, she is utterly prepared not to receive anything at all. Christmas day had gotten off to an odd start for her. Tionna told me that she had been bad right before Christmas. When she woke up Christmas morning and ran into the living room to look under the tree, she did not see any presents there. She figured Santa just hadn't left her anything since she'd been misbehaving and decided she might as well go back to bed. When Tionna went back to the bedroom, where she sleeps with her grandmother, Celia asked her why she was coming back in. "Because Santa didn't leave me anything," Tionna answered her. Her grandmother said Santa had brought presents, and so Tionna went back out and found the gifts.

In talking with me about her Christmas in 1991 she told me what she did receive: a Shani doll from her uncle ("I didn't even want it, but then I liked it"), a Barbie knitting machine (which nobody could figure out how to work), a Barbie mobile home, and a Barbie washing machine. The present she had really wanted that year was the Barbie dream house and with a glowing face she described its wondrous features. When I asked why she did not get one Tionna said because her grandmother did not have the money.

Carlos gives his mother his Christmas list in October and she buys his presents a bit at a time. When I asked him what he was getting for Christmas, he wrote a very exact list:

Some GI Joes

Vehicles for GI Joes

Arctic Batman

Batman Jetfoil

Green Beret Rafael

Jetfighter

Carlos knows exactly how much his asked-for gifts cost and where his mother is likely to buy them; none were more than fifteen dollars. Moreover, because his mother buys him what he has written on the list, Carlos knows before Christmas what he will be receiving from her. He continued, later, "I forgot to put X-Men on my Christmas list but I already gave it to my mother. We tell what we want for Christmas and then she makes pretend that she tells Santa Claus and at Christmas Eve she wake up at like two o'clock in the morning and wrap the presents and puts them under the tree and makes believe she didn't do it." Like Carlos, Natalia and her brother Darnell knew well before Christmas what their primary gifts would be: an electronic doll for her and a Super Nintendo game system for him.

Carlos's sharp awareness of the circumstances and origins of his own Christmas gifts and Tionna's willingness to accept that Christmas might not even happen at all for her are not the only aspects of children's experiences of this holiday in Newhallville. Fantasy and longing are also to be found, and one afternoon in the classroom where Natalia and Tionna went to school I was sitting with LaQuisha and Sam while waiting for their reading group to begin. I asked LaQuisha what she wanted for Christmas. She wrote down her Christmas list, adding prices for each at my request:

Money	1,000
Dolls	25
Clothes	500
Magic Potty Baby	20
Food	
Pictures	
Cameras	20
TV	
VCR	

Watch	10
Car	500
Magic jewels [trolls?]	
Talking Baby Alive	
Phone	30
Keyboard	100
Sneakers	50
Computer	200
Watch	10
Super Nintendo	100
Play Doh	10
Sorry	20
Game Gear	100
Atari	100
House	500
Game Boy	100
Coat	30
Book bag	30
Earrings	30
Bracelets	30

When I did an inventory of LaQuisha's room later that year, few, if any, of the gifts she hoped for were in evidence. This is hardly a surprise: the sum total of her gift list adds up to nearly half her family's yearly income—and many of her estimated prices are much too low.

After LaQuisha gave me her list, Sam looked at me and said, "I feel like a child," his face breaking into a grin almost too big to contain. "Why?" I asked. "Because I wrote a letter to Santa Claus." I asked what he asked Santa to give him, and he replied that he wanted a Super Nintendo and a trip to Disney World. "The first time I saw a program on Santa Claus, I believed it," he confided. Both LaQuisha and Sam have Christmas wishes that are destined to remain largely unfulfilled. Neither comes from a household with a large income; Sam's life is further disrupted because his primary caretaker, an aunt, is in and out of jail. Though his Christmas list contained only two items, it is likely he received neither of these.

When kids received much-wished-for gifts, there was little mystery about where they came from or how much they cost. Natalia's main Christmas present in 1992 was a blonde-haired, blue-eyed electronic talking doll that she referred to as her "brat." "It cost sixty dollars," she told me. She also received a pair of gold earrings from her mother's boyfriend. "They were thirty-nine ninety-nine at Caldor's," she told me excitedly. "They were originally a hundred dollars," she added, "but they were on sale. My mommy told me to keep them in the box so I don't lose them."

Children whose Christmas booty was relatively abundant are not absent, however. Tarelle, who has three grown-up brothers, is the baby of the family and the only girl. Her mother works about sixty hours a week as a nurse, and her brothers also have steady jobs. Tarelle is indulged all year long by her family and Christmas is no exception:

1. I got a camera
2. I got a outfit
3. I got some boots
4. I got some sneaks
5. I got a nightgown
6. I got three games
7. and a pouch
8. I got $40.00 from my brother
9. I got $10.00 from my aunt
10. I got $20.00 from my aunt
11. I got some socks and
12. I got $100.00 from my mother
13. and I got a watch

It is not especially surprising that the amount and kind of these children's Christmas gifts are closely tied to levels of family income, and children are aware of the sorts of limits this income imposes upon the scope of their wishes. As a result, Carlos is careful to keep his requests within his mother's budget, while Tionna is perpetually prepared for disappointment. This pattern meshes with the more general pattern of kids in Newhallville being made expressly aware of the costs of their care and maintenance, and a growing awareness (or responsibility) upon children's part to keep their desires in check.

The clearly imposed limits on Christmas wanting and getting did not, however, mean that the holiday was not meaningful to Newhallville kids. The careful elaboration of the exact prices of their presents was often a kind of bragging, as when Natalia pointed out the cost of her gold earrings. It is true, as well, that knowing how long and hard many caretakers had worked in order to get children special gifts—putting items on layaway months ahead, for example—made children feel especially loved and valued.

Babies

Tionna, Natalia, and I were hanging out in my kitchen, and Tionna asked me when I was going to have a baby. Then she caught herself and said, "No, don't have any babies, Miss Chin." "Why?" I asked. "Because then you won't have any time to pay attention to us!" she answered, smiling. "Yeah," Natalia piped up from the chair where she sat next to me. "We'll come over and ring the doorbell and you'll say, 'I'm sorry, you can't come in today, I had to stay up all night taking care of my baby and I'm tired.'" We bandied this idea about for a moment and then Natalia looked me straight in the face and said, "Did you know I had a baby?" She paused for dramatic effect, her face utterly deadpan. "I put it in the dumpster." Another pause.

I started playing along. "What happened?" I asked. "Well, I couldn't keep it because I didn't want my family to know about it," she said. "Besides, I didn't know who the father was. I've been with so many men," she added with a sigh. Natalia had just turned eleven a couple of months ago. "I just kept shooting back all this food so my family would think I was just getting fat," she went on.

"I had a baby, too," Tionna said. "I put it in the garbage. I had all these people's garbage, a whole lot of it, and I put the baby in the bottom of the can and put the garbage on top. Then the garbage men came, and they recycled it! They recycled my baby!"

The baby in the garbage can scenario, much like the "man of my dreams" scenario from our trip to the mall, is one widely available to the girls on television and in the newspapers. Like meeting the man of your dreams, the baby in the garbage can (or garbage chute or dumpster or toilet) does occasionally happen and is not simply an urban legend. It is a stereotype, much like the killer drug dealers who wear Air Jordans and drive Mercedes, propagated in the media out of all proportion to its actual rate of occurrence. Like Barbie, Nintendo, and Nike Air sneakers, these images are mass produced, consumed the way commodities are. Though they are not paid for in currency, these images, when used, do exact a price.

What is affecting is that Natalia launches into this tale after a discussion of the girls' fears of being abandoned by me. The girls well knew of my wish to have a baby, since during group time one day at school when each person had to say what they were afraid of, I had blurted, "I'm afraid I'll never have a baby." What was Natalia saying when she told me her "story"?

Natalia and Tionna's playfulness, in the midst of a serious encounter, should not be discounted, and they enjoyed the pretend aspects of telling the "baby in the garbage can" tale as well as its potential shock value. That this particular tale is one so familiar to them is perhaps what is most upsetting. Moreover, we all knew, even as we played, that there was a possibility that this "story" might one day come true. Not much more than a year later, to my dismay, that is exactly what happened. When Natalia was twelve years old, she became pregnant, delivering a baby girl when she was barely thirteen.

Conclusion

Consumption intersects with every arena of importance in these children's lives: family, friends, school, neighborhood, eating, sexuality, romance, and babies. These are not children, however, who consume in great material quantity. As a social process, medium of knowledge, and realm of experience, consumption does not acquire force in these children's lives because they have, want, or receive great amounts of clothes, food, toys, or money; indeed, they are required in many settings to keep their consumption behavior and desires within clearly delineated boundaries and are tremendously skilled at doing so.

In a variety of forms, consumption is an important medium through which many of these children's everyday social and kin relationships are created and maintained. The piece of glazed donut that Tionna ate was drenched in complex meaning (cultural calories?)—among them conflicts between Tionna's grandmother and great-grandmother over household expenses, upkeep of the apartment, and disagreements over who was responsible for Tionna's upbringing and care. The heated negotiations among children at lunchtime during school days are likewise about much more than whether child A is willing to trade child B a cookie for a bag of potato chips.

Such interactions and negotiations do not take place simply between individuals or among groups of people. They take place in the context of the larger society—one from which many Newhallville residents are, at various levels, both alienated and marginalized; and they take place in particular sites, whether the neighborhood, local stores, the mall, or supermarket. These spaces at once shape children's consumer lives and are consumed by kids as they use and interact with them, often in unexpected ways. The next chapter turns to two major sites where children's consumption takes place: the neighborhood small grocery, and New Haven's downtown mall.

4

Hemmed In and Shut Out

Natalia and Tionna have entered Claire's, an inexpensive accessory and jewelry store on the second floor of the downtown mall. It is early December and the girls are wearing their winter coats unzipped and sagging backward halfway down their arms, the better to ventilate their overheating bodies. They wander throughout the store for more than twenty minutes, touching everything it seems. They pull earrings off display racks to look at them; they paw through bins of sale items—flattened hairbows, bent earhoops, scratched bracelets—holding them up for inspection and at times trying them on. They come upon a section of earrings, necklaces, and rings that are adorned with the distinctive squat bodies, squashy faces, and fluffy hair of Trolls. "They are going too far with that mess now," Natalia remarks, moving on to a display of keychains. Pulling one off the rack, she reads the message printed on the decorative tag in a ringing voice, "If it weren't for boys, I'd quit school." A moment later she remarks, at an equal volume, "That white lady's following us around." She is referring to one of the store's salesclerks, who is indeed keeping a close eye on the girls. Though the clerk has undoubtedly heard this last remark, she registers no response.

While these girls visit downtown shops like Claire's only infrequently, neighborhood grocery stores are an almost daily pit stop. In contrast to the long visits, loud discussion, and sometimes frenetic behavior typical of these girls' visits to Claire's downtown, their visits to these small groceries are remarkably quiet and directed. When Natalia and Tionna bustle into Bob's market one summer afternoon, accompanied by Natalia's cousin Asia, they settle down after a step or two inside the store, speaking to each other quietly. They do not handle the merchandise, most of which is not interesting to them in any case. After scanning the cooler for drinks, and considering the large packages of cookies at the back of the store, they decide to buy candy and gum that Bob keeps in a glass case behind which he is stationed. The girls come up to the counter in a bunch. "Can I have a Twix bar?" Tionna asks. "I want Juicyfruit," says Natalia. "A glazed donut," Asia adds. The girls dig into the deep pockets of their oversized jeans and pull out bills and warm coins. Bob dispenses candy, picks up the money, and counts out change, all the while holding a conversation with another customer. Throughout, Bob has kept as much of an eagle eye on the girls as did the "white lady" at Claire's, but this attention does not elicit comments—or discomfort—from them, either inside the store or later.

Children's experiences in and understanding of these two stores are entwined in multiple ways not only with their consumer activities, but also their identity and experience as social beings. The forms of social inequality that come to bear upon children in different consumption sites are a primary factor in shaping their experience in and understanding of those places; in that process, children also build apprehensions of themselves and the society in which they live. For the Newhallville girls, being black, young, female, and poor is an experience that is at once disparate and fundamentally similar in Claire's and Bob's. This variety of experience is the result of the obvious differences in the stores' merchandise and geographic locations, and from the ways in which these stores, their merchandise, and personnel are enmeshed with the politics and power struggles of daily life. The stores themselves do not create the inequalities of race and gender (for example) or experiences thereof, in a vacuum; Bob's and Claire's are not worlds unto themselves, whose borders end with the square footage identified in the lease or deed. In New Haven state and local policies are profoundly implicated in the formation and maintenance of an urban landscape characterized by various forms of social inequality that are especially evident along lines of race, labor, and economy. Thus, the city and state are also centrally important to children's consumer lives: housing and residential policies, taxation, employment, and education opportunity shape urban geography and social experience, including those taking place in and with relation to Bob's and Claire's.

The Polarization of the Consumer Sphere

Below the surface of a seemingly carefree shopping environment lies an underworld of gang violence, abductions, carjackings, armed robberies, sexual assaults, and crimes against young children. Indeed, in some ways malls represent ideal locations for criminals—vast parking lots and garages, upscale shoppers, victims available day and night, private property with few if any regular police patrols, and a population led to believe that malls represent refuges from inner-city ills. (Everett 1994)

The apocalyptic vision described in the above passage does not seem to be that far off from prevailing attitudes in much of New Haven. As the white middle class has struggled to create residential and commercial "refuges from inner-city ills," it has also helped to create the profound polarization of the consumer sphere that exists for Newhallville residents today, since these refuges must, by their nature, exclude whole classes of people. For Newhallville, the polarization has meant the near-disappearance of local commerce coupled with the development and later redevelopment of upscale downtown shopping districts.

From the perspective of Newhallville, it seems that the city has simultaneously poured resources into undermining local commercial centers while supporting the development of a downtown area that seeks to discourage minority shoppers from spending too much time there. Though the relatively large proportion of black and brown shoppers in the New Haven mall might have something to do with its economic decline, the minority population can be held no more singly accountable for the failing fortunes of the downtown mall than they can for the ghettoization of their neighborhoods. First, in comparison to larger, newer and more architecturally and visually spectacular malls, the New Haven mall—which was built in the 1960s—is run down, offers little variety and, in contradiction of a basic mall dictum, does not even have free parking. More recently constructed malls in nearby towns have made a hefty dent in New Haven's business, and the city has developed several successive plans for redesign of the mall but has been unable to successfully court a strong anchor store.[1] After the closing of Macy's, the mall's anchor store was Conran's, a chain home-furnishings retailer; unfortunately, the company went bankrupt several months later. In 1992 the mall housed no outlets of prominent chains such as Gap, Express, Banana Republic, Pottery Barn, Crate & Barrel—all stores that would attract a more economically varied clientele; instead, discount enterprises—Sam's Dollar Store, and Payless Shoes, for example—are in the majority. The stance of developers, who argue that the mall is doing badly because the atmosphere makes upscale shoppers uncomfortable, is hard to accept completely. Minority shoppers have kept the mall going in recent years, and the stores that remain in business reflect this.

Shops on lower Chapel Street, downtown New Haven.

Development of nearby areas has encouraged the movement of moneyed shoppers away from the mall. A prominent local development company, Schiavone, has considerably perked up the upper Chapel Street area, located two blocks above the mall and directly across from part of the Yale campus. This newly renovated stretch of shops and restaurants is now distinctly upscale, housing downtown's priciest venues. Farther up, the rundown Broadway area was rehabbed in the early 1990s with a $7.5-million federal grant and a $1.9-million contribution from Yale (Charles 1994), siphoning off whatever upscale business remains downtown and relocating it closer to the Yale campus. Lower Chapel, which once housed a large Kresge's store (Kresge's is the predecessor of K-mart), is now home to discount stores and jewelry shops. Nearly all those shopping on lower Chapel are black and Hispanic; while shoppers on upper Chapel and Broadway are racially and ethnically diverse, few are poor or working class. As one person who had grown up in Dixwell, which borders the Broadway shopping area, said, "We used to go down there to look at the people walking funny!" This remark was accompanied by a raucous imitation of the stiff, uptight walk of the middle-class whites or fearful Yale students.

In a city already starkly segregated in its residential areas, downtown is now headed toward a similar segregation. The lower and upper areas of Chapel Street house shopping areas that cater to those coming from lower-income levels on the one hand and upper-income levels on the other. The mall physically occupies the middle ground between the two, and though perceived to be used by an ever-poorer and darker population, people who go there remain relatively diverse in terms of both race and socioeconomic level, especially when compared to the territories on either side. As the physical and perceptual middle ground downtown, the mall is a conflicted site. Many shopkeepers are caught between trying to appeal to the customers they would like to have (middle class and white), and not alienating the customers that they *do* have (young and of color). Others have attempted to capitalize upon the mall's changing demographic mix and have opened stores carrying hip-hop fashions, African folklore and artisanry, or Afrocentric merchandise.

Transformations in the local Newhallville business community have made changes in downtown all the more important in terms of daily living. It has not always been the case that Newhallville's commercial sector contrasted so dramatically with that of downtown. In the 1950s, before major employment and economic changes remade the community more generally, Newhallville housed a wide variety of stores and businesses. There were doctors' and dentists' offices, a hardware store, meat market, pharmacy, grocery stores, a dry cleaner, popcorn supply house, florist, lunch counters, beauty shops, barbers, bars, and liquor stores. Newhallville during that time had a lively commercial sector that, while it did not supply every need of the area, provided many essential goods and services that are no longer locally available. In interviews I conducted with people who had grown up in Newhallville in the late 1950s and early 1960s, their recollections of the stores and businesses in the area generally agreed that nearly twice as many commercial sites existed then as is currently the case. These businesses were significantly more varied than they are today, where liquor stores, bars, and small groceries predominate. The florist is perhaps the longest-standing local establishment, having managed to stay in business in Newhallville for several decades. The overall trend has been the decimation of local commercial activity (table 4.1 summarizes businesses ca. 1960 and 1992). Much of the loss of local business enterprise after the late 1950s is connected to the downsizing of the nearby Winchester factory, and, as expected, those businesses that

Table 4.1. Businesses in Newhallville, ca. 1960 and 1992

Type of Business	ca. 1960	1992
Barber/beauty	6	5
Butcher	1	0
Car repair	1	0
Dentist	1	0
Dry cleaner	1	0
Five-and-dime	1	0
Grocery	10	5
Laundromat	1	1
Liquor store	4	3
Luncheonette	3	1
Nightclub	1	2
Pharmacy	2	1
Shoe repair	1	0
Supermarket	1	0
Total	34	18

catered primarily to factory workers have since foundered. An additional element contributing to the decline of local business is that city-initiated urban redevelopment concerned itself with residential housing and attempted to restructure the city's commercial sector in some cases. In Newhallville a stretch of businesses was razed, supposedly in order to build a new and more appealing business center. This center was never constructed, and in the process the neighborhood lost several important resources, including the local supermarket.

These changes have left Newhallville kids with a local commercial setting that is severely restricted in comparison to past years, and children today enter into a local commercial environment dominated by liquor stores, bars, small groceries, and the illegal drug trade. The added insecurity of the drug economy has transformed the neighborhood significantly, despite a prominently located neighborhood police substation. Children routinely avoid certain streets and corners in an effort to maintain their own security. When they were children, older members of the community were able to engage in a wide range of activities, sanctioned and unsanctioned, related to local businesses. Stephen Taylor Sr., whose son participated in this research, recalled his own hijinks related to the local dairy plant, which used to maintain a store selling cut-price products. In the afternoons he and his friends would ride their bikes to the fence near the dumpster where the man who ran the dairy store would put the containers of out-of-date ice cream. The boys would climb up over the fence, dive into the dumpster, and retrieve the melting ice cream, running back to the fence, often pursued by the angry cries of the store manager. Others recalled being able to buy warm donuts from a nearby bakery on the way to school or running errands for their parents to various local stores.

Today children still run errands to the small groceries that dot the neighborhood, picking up small items that might be needed at home, or more often buying themselves inexpensive drinks and snacks. Because of the shrinkage of local businesses, children have fewer opportunities than in the past to do important family-related chores—picking up the dry cleaning or running to the hardware store. They also have fewer opportunities for engaging in the kind of spontaneous mischief that Stephen Taylor Sr. remembers from his own childhood. Whether or not any or all of these activities may be viewed as desirable, the ultimate result is that the variety of activities now available to children in terms of engaging in the consumer sphere has been transformed. Today small groceries are among the predominant commercial sites remaining in Newhallville and are arguably the most important consumer venue visited and patronized by neighborhood kids.

Local Groceries

When I asked kids where they spent their money in the neighborhood, they'd answer "B and K," or "Bob's," or "Moody's," the main small groceries in the area. But when I asked them what they did there, much in the same way that they often refused to talk about school because it was a "boring" topic of conversation or because "we didn't do anything," Newhallville kids rarely waxed poetic on the subject of Bob's. Their silence was actually significant and shows the degree to which Bob's is part of their daily and hence unremarkable landscape. In contrast kids could, at almost any moment it seemed, launch into vivid descriptions—real or imaginary—of downtown shops and shopping.

Bob's store has two aisles and a refrigerator case. Bob also sells coldcuts and subs, which he makes fresh and to order; there is a grill for

Interior of Bob's store.

making hot items like steak and cheese sandwiches and Jamaican beef patties. There is only one brand of nearly every item: Heinz mustard, Morton salt, Domino sugar, Ragu spaghetti sauce.[2] Much of the shelf space is half filled or simply empty. Bob rules over his small store with a stern, paternalistic benevolence and while dispensing advice about purchases, life, education, and love makes his strict standards for hard work and upright living no secret. While some shopkeepers in the area may occasionally extend credit to customers, letting children who are known to them repay small sums (fifty cents or a dollar) if they are short one day, Bob does not. He does not disdain the food stamps that many of his customers pay him with, but neither does he bend any of the rules—allowing them to make small purchases with stamps worth ten or twenty dollars in order to get cash change in return, for instance.

Bob is often caught between his roles as social network member and entrepreneur. There are two video-game machines at the front of the store. The machines bring in about $300 a week; he gets half. Bob told me that he feels he is doing something to keep kids busy and off the street by having the games there. In the next breath he compared playing these games to having a dope habit. He is not so dedicated to the profit he receives, however, that he is willing to jeopardize his standing in the community. When one boy was stealing money from his mother's purse to come down to Bob's store to play the games, she called Bob and asked him to refuse to let her son near the machines. Storekeepers like Bob have a lot at stake in maintaining the goodwill of residents, and commercial imperatives often take second place to community imperatives, up to a limit. As a result, children can expect Bob's to be—if not a home away from home by any means—a place that is in many respects home-like. Children can occasionally use the phone to call home, and care-takers call the store to see if their children are there. Bob is often asked to keep an eye out for certain kids and to tell them to come home when he spots them. Continuing a tradition that many say was once the norm in Newhallville and the Southern communities from which many of its older residents come, Bob, like many local storekeepers, takes a personal interest in neighborhood children. He knows them by name, he knows their families, and he often knows a generous amount about anyone who enters his store.

One summer afternoon a girl came into the store, having been sent to buy batteries. She was about nine years old, and was also returning a bag of biscuit mix. After saying he didn't usually allow returns, and that he would only do it this one time, Bob asked her about the batteries, saying, "What size?" She didn't know, and so Bob let her use the phone behind the counter to call home. On the phone for a minute or two, uttering half-finished sentences that were being both misunderstood and interrupted at the other end, the girl used her most reasonable voice, saying, "Mom, will you *please* let me speak to Duane?" She repeated this entreaty several times. Meanwhile, Bob was both tending to other customers and directing a steady stream of advice and interrogation to the girl behind him. "What size do you need? Double A? Let me talk to your mother!" "Mom, put Duane on the phone, *please!*" "What size do you need?" "Mom!" Finally, Duane got onto the other end of the line and told the girl to get double A batteries. At $2.95 for a package of two, they were very expensive; Toys-R-Us sells a pack of four for $3.99. Toys-R-Us, however, can only be reached from the highway and is in the next town.

Kids can expect Bob to treat them not with the stylized deference that is characteristic of customer-service interactions downtown, but with a no-nonsense familiarity they see plenty of at home. This allows certain prickly aspects of Bob's enterprise to be submerged in everyone's experience:

for instance, the fact that he lives in a significantly more upscale neighborhood about half a mile away is rarely discussed. Because children's relationships to Bob are shaped most overtly along lines of generation and race, he often appears like an irascible grandparent. Children are not necessarily fans of such treatment, but they surely are used to it and find it unremarkable. It is a relationship that in the context of the general social scene in New Haven, where racial lines are so often starkly drawn and maintained, makes Bob an "us" rather than a "them."

The store's doorjamb and a post stationed at the middle of one of the aisles serve as community bulletin boards. A notice taped to the post at eye level reads: "Three bedroom apartment for rent, section eight accepted." Other announcements include a flyer for a talent show and a photocopy of a photocopy of a letter warning about new types of racism. Children are well aware of Bob's views on everything from a good tomato to gospel singing and are well aware also that they may become the objects of his opinionated banter. It is a stream of opinion with which children are intimately familiar, if, like Bob, their grandparents came up from the Southern states in the 1940s and 1950s. I recorded the following conversation between Bob and an elderly woman resident in my field notes:

> They get on the subject of kids, and how they don't have any manners today. The woman says: "Today when I ask a little boy, 'do you want to go to the store for me?' well, it used to be 'do you have a quarter?' Now it's a dollar!" "Inflation?!" I say. "Kids today just don't have any manners," Bob and his customer tell me. "You got to talk to that baby, even when it's in your stomach," says the woman. "Then they know that voice. And then when the baby's born you got to hold it and kiss it and let them know: 'Mommy loves you.' Then that baby could be, like in the back of the store here, and nobody can get it to quiet down, but the mommy says, 'What's that?' and the baby is quiet because it knows that voice. I used to spank that baby even in my stomach," and she demonstrates by patting her middle vigorously. It doesn't look like a spank to me at all. "I was born depressed," Bob says, "because I was born in a depressing time, 1936. We weren't getting nothing to eat!" "But the babies they still eat the same," the woman interjects. "Not me, my mother couldn't nurse me," Bob answers. "She was nursing the baby of the people who owned the plantation and she didn't have enough for both of us, so I got left out!" "That's right, and up in that house, your mother probably got so angry, she spit in their food, too," the woman says. "She made all their food," Bob goes on. "That's what she did."

Stores like Bob's remain on the whole free from the class and race tensions that characterize Newhallville children's relationships with stores outside the neighborhood. Rather, they are places to discuss and air these tensions, to recount stories that illustrate the ways in which the boundaries of race and class, in particular, are erected and maintained in shops outside the neighborhood. Kids do not enter Bob's on the defensive, expecting him to single them out because they are black, or because they do not have money. Rather, they can expect to enter into an atmosphere that speaks of and to the experience of being black in America, whether to see a notice about racism taped to a post, or to hear a story about conflict between plantation owners and black household servants. Though Newhallville children are reminded of "their place" by Bob as he asserts his right to monitor and control their behavior, he exercises that right from a position that is understood to be located within the community by both children and their parents.

Places like Bob's, most of which are black-owned and -operated in Newhallville (some are owned and operated by Latinos), are not generally regarded by older residents as contributing to the area's downslide, though limited stock and high prices for food staples, household supplies, and tobacco constitute serious shortcomings from the adult consumers' point of view. These issues are much less problematic for children who, when making purchases for themselves, primarily buy snacks and drinks. Not only are these items inexpensive, each costing less than a dollar, but their prices throughout the city are fairly consistent. In contrast, cigarettes downtown cost $1.20 at the time of my research, and $1.60 in Newhallville, where people often would buy a pack and sell single cigarettes for a quarter to offset the expense.

Stores like Bob's are strategically located within a couple of blocks of the neighborhood elementary and junior high schools, and nearly all Newhallville children walk to school. Kids stop in to buy candy, chips, and drinks both on their way to school in the morning and when returning home in the afternoon. My research has shown that children are not often included in the shopping excursions of their caretakers, whether to the supermarket or farther afield; even back-to-school clothes shopping trips rarely include the children (often teenagers) for whom the clothes are being bought. Bob's is the store that children visit most often and with which they have the most familiarity. Children as young as five or six, if they live within a couple of blocks, may go there alone during the day on errands or to buy something for themselves. Certainly by the time children are ten years old, as the children in this study were, they go to local stores at least once or twice a week, if not every day.

It might appear at first that Bob's is a magnet for children because he stocks the candy, chips, and drinks they buy so often. However, many local businesses, such as barber shops, also sell candy and drinks. In addition, at other locations throughout the neighborhood, people sell commercially produced or homemade treats from their homes, dispensing ice cream and candy from their back doors or out their kitchen windows. What makes Bob's different from local barbers or kitchen-window ice-cream shops is that Bob's is a public meeting place for children or can be a group destination for kids. And yet, one of the striking things about children's visits to Bob's is their brevity; Bob does not allow kids to linger either inside the store or on the sidewalk outside. It might seem that Bob's tactics ought to discourage youthful patrons rather than encouraging them to make their purchases in his store. Yet it is Bob's vigilance in preventing people from hanging out around his store that is an important factor in attracting younger children.

In comparison to other local markets, which are similarly stocked and laid out, Bob differs most dramatically in the atmosphere right outside his door. The sidewalks in front of two other local groceries in Newhallville are thronged daily by kids of junior high and high school age, whether school is in session or not. Younger children know that when they go to Bob's they will not have to navigate through a clump of "big kids" who might tease or intimidate them. These other corners have a reputation for being filled with kids who are involved in the illegal drug trade at one level or another; one of these spots is a fairly well-known drug pickup spot for those driving in from the suburbs. The presence of older kids and teenagers, especially when there is actual or potential drug trade in evidence, is threatening for younger children on a number of fronts. The threat for younger children is real: Tarelle, who lives across the street from one such corner, told me of being offered money by older teenagers who were trying to enlist her in street business, where children as young as eight can work as runners or lookouts. Moreover, younger children seek to avoid these spots because they have erupted periodically in violence. In the summer of 1992 a small riot broke out in front of the store across from Tarelle's home, a confrontation between teenagers and the police.

Local groceries like Bob's and B and K have a lively, intimate, almost homey atmosphere. Kids are known by name by store proprietors who not only sell them goods but keep them in line, give them advice, do them favors, and even communicate with their parents about their behavior. The central communal role played by such stores is made vividly clear by the discussion between Bob and one of his older customers—aimed in large part at the children who were in the store at the time—which was an oral narrative focused on themes of slavery and life in the South that have been passed down for generations in this African American community. A similar encounter in a downtown store like Claire's is hard to imagine.

Claire's and the Chapel Square Mall

A small store selling inexpensive jewelry and accessories, Claire's is a favorite destination among Newhallville girls. Racks of earrings are particularly enticing, since the girls are just on the edge of being allowed to wear larger hoop earrings, rather than the small studs and drop earrings caretakers prefer for little girls. They play with the idea of purchasing jewelry they know their caretakers will disapprove, holding up a pair of huge, bamboo patterned "door knocker" earrings while proclaiming, "My grandmother would never let me wear these!" This playful dynamic is a striking contrast to children's subdued demeanor at Bob's. These girls' behavior is not limited to playfulness. Kids are often also markedly loud and provoke or anticipate direct and indirect confrontation with store employees; in some instances kids pointedly ignore salespeople's concerns or loudly talk about them as if they weren't able to hear. Children seemed to view these visits not just as an opportunity for enjoyment and excitement, but as a challenge of sorts as well. One afternoon as we neared Claire's, Asia recounted her most recent experience there: "Last time I was in there the lady was laughing because I didn't have enough money. The other day I went in and I bought all this stuff and the lady said, 'That will be forty dollars.' I pulled out a fifty-dollar bill and said, 'Here.'" Asia demonstrated how she slapped the bill down on the counter, and the look on her face was both self-satisfied and challenging. "I swear I was about to say 'keep the change' until my grandmother came up."

Asia's story captures the pressures many Newhallville kids face in having to assert their right to be in the mall by demonstrating their ability to buy. In Asia's story, when she is at first unable to pay for what she wants, she is sure that the saleslady is laughing at her. As she recounted the incident, the pleasure she took in later being able to present this woman with a fifty-dollar bill was palpable, as was her frustration in not being able to add insult to injury by imperiously directing the woman to keep the change. Despite this experience, however, Asia apparently did not consider the possibility of avoiding Claire's or of refusing to go in again. Rather, she returned there armored with the defiance a fifty-dollar bill afforded her and toting a hefty measure of distrust along as well. This was an encounter she was bound to repeat nearly every time she returned downtown.

Children's experiences in the mall and in stores like Claire's, unlike those in Bob's, are shaped by tensions around issues of race. These tensions, in turn, are conflated with problems related to class. Situations and interactions in which kids like Asia are made to feel inadequate or even nonexistent often make shopping an undertaking fraught with difficulty, and their response is to don their street-tough personas. Such problematic interactions—where black shoppers are assumed to be unable to make purchases, where they are steered toward inferior merchandise, or where they are treated as if giving them attention is a waste of time—are an important kind of received knowledge in Newhallville. Deacon Rose, a member of Natalia's family parish, recounted to me one of these stories from his younger days when he was visiting the segregated South. Deacon Rose was living in Detroit but had gone down to Mississippi to visit "this woman I was liking" and took her downtown to look at dresses. They passed a store that had some nice silk dresses in the window, went in, and began to look at them. The saleswoman, a white lady, came over and said, "I think maybe you'll like these dresses better over here," and showed them some cheaper, cotton dresses. "They're probably more in your price," she said, and Deacon Rose imitated her nasal vowels, raising his voice into a simpering falsetto. He went on: "Well, I said to her, 'I don't want those cotton dresses. I want one of these nice silk ones,' and she said, 'I think you'll like the price of these other ones better.' Now she didn't know that I have twelve hundred dollars in my pocket! I said, 'I like these silk ones and I think I'll take a couple.'" Deacon Rose finished his tale by saying, "I bought the dresses, but I don't think she liked it very much."

Deacon Rose's story has much in common with Asia's tale—the pivotal event is confrontation with a store clerk who assumes (rightly or wrongly) that the black customer has no money. For both Asia and Deacon Rose, these encounters arouse a subsequent feeling of dehumanization. In both stories, this feeling of dehumanization is countered by an ability to brandish money in the salesclerk's face: Asia has a fifty-dollar bill, and Deacon Rose twelve hundred dollars. In both cases, they were able to assert not only did they have the money to buy what they wanted, but they had substantially more than that: they were demonstrably *not* poor, but they were, in fact, relatively loaded. But, as Deacon Rose emphasized at the end of his story, even having the money to buy something may not yield a satisfying conclusion to the story.

The potential for humiliation and dehumanization is ever-present for most black shoppers, and they protect themselves against the toll it can take against them in several ways. One of the most important is dressing up when going downtown to shop: the need to appear respectable to store personnel, to appear to have money in their pockets or purses, and thus to be treated with attention and respect is perhaps more tactical than it is psychological. This effect is more easily accomplished by older people than younger ones, in part because the fashion preferences of minority youth are not only more distinctive and recognizable, but specifically associated with danger. Though within minority neighborhoods it is relatively easy to spot signs and signals that mark individuals as drug dealers or gang members, these signals have proven to be generally unintelligible to the outside community. Security guards in malls, for instance, are given red-flag guidelines about youth fashions that tend to brand *all* minority styles as indicative of potential problems. One such red flag is raised when two or more kids dress alike. Though it is true that such dressing alike is a common gang marker, it is also very common in Newhallville for especially close friends—boys or girls, and sometimes boyfriend-girlfriend pairs—to buy matching outfits. In New Haven's social and political culture, black has come to be equated with poor, and this development has had far-reaching repercussions for Newhallville children's experiences downtown.

On April 1, 1992, a *New Haven Register* headline read, "White Person Slips, Falls! Shoppers Shudder; Is Downtown Safe?" (1992). Looking more closely, it turned out the headline was an April Fool's Day joke published by the *New Haven Advocate,* a local weekly tabloid that emulates the *Village Voice.* The headline and spoof article that followed baldly stated what was more often merely hinted at in the *Register:* that the mall is an unsafe place for white shoppers, and African American kids are the reason why whites feel uncomfortable there. The *Advocate*'s sharp parody of the *New Haven Register* front page encouraged readers to call in and answer the daily "sound-off" question, a regular *Register* feature: "Would anyone except a suicidal moron on drugs shop in downtown New Haven?" The text of the article added further ironic flames to the fire:

> The shopper . . . said he will stick to patronizing suburban malls from now on, "like everybody else around here who's scared to death of the city." . . . Sources say police may call a key suspect in the incident,

identified as Javan Reed, a/k/a Dwayne Black Person, who lives in a black neighborhood where everybody deals drugs, in for questioning. Sources wouldn't say on the record whether Reed a/k/a Person is guilty as hell.

In order to retain white, middle-class, suburban-dwelling shoppers, malls in Connecticut, including New Haven, have been aggressive in taking steps in attempting to reduce the presence of minority youth. Trumbull Shopping Park, another Connecticut mall, fought a legal battle in order to gain the right to ban public transit from making stops on its property on Friday and Saturday nights. Their express reason for making this decision was security problems arising from teenagers—most of whom were minority youth from the nearby city of Bridgeport ("Mall Wins Ruling on Limiting Bus Service" 1995). In the early 1980s New Haven had employed a similar strategy, moving bus stops from directly in front of the mall to relocate them across the street on the town green. This move was not as obstructive as that employed by Trumbull Shopping Park, but involved a considerable increase in discomfort for bus riders and was widely thought to be racially motivated. The original bus stops, located in front of the mall, were placed on a covered walkway open to the street that provided at least some protection from rain and snow. Across the way on the green, two rather small bus shelters hardly provided the same amount of protection from harsh weather conditions.

Regardless of the reasons for which consumers who are older, more affluent, or lighter skinned have abandoned Chapel Square, it is primarily youth and teens (mostly minority) who now constitute the mall's most important market ("A Teen-Age Pall at the Mall" 1993). Shop owners have had to develop subtle means of discouraging young people from spending too much time in the mall's public spaces, while attempting to continue to entice them to spend their money in its commercial venues. These strategies include an increasingly visible uniformed security force and the use of piped music featuring genres thought to be unappealing to undesirable youth. In a variation of what Russell Baker (1992) jokingly called "the Beethoven Defense," the New Haven mall often features songs by the likes of Frank Sinatra. For kids who prefer the driving bass and salty lyrics of urban hip-hop music, the crooning of Sinatra grates on their ears as annoyingly as fingernails across a blackboard. That's the theory anyway.

The Chapel Square mall is not unusual in its attempts to maintain a profile as a safe, communal location that exists in distinct opposition to the chaotic, violent city beyond. The maintenance of this image spurs, in part, the attempts to limit or prevent young people's presence there, since they are perceived by some to threaten the pacific atmosphere. Such consumer community building, the proffering of togetherness through shopping, is most evident in the yearly Christmas spree of conviviality and community events, from the perennially popular picture on Santa's knee to caroling and dance performances. Halloween has also emerged as a time when the mall is supported as a healthy alternative to the New Haven street and all its dangers. This perception of the mall as an alternative to the city itself as a site of communal activity is supported with almost equal enthusiasm by its own publicity efforts and such institutions as the public schools. For several years running, mall shopkeepers have distributed candy and Halloween balloons to hordes of costumed kids who trick-or-treat their way around the two-story concourse on a weekend near October 31.[3] Significantly, this event is designed to appeal to young children and their families (segments of the population that mall management finds amenable), not problematic older children and teens. During my fieldwork, the principal of the school where I conducted research sent a note to each child's family that encouraged caretakers not to allow their children to trick-or-treat door to door. Instead, the memo advised, caretakers should either take children only to family members' homes or go trick-or-treating at the mall.

Exploring the Mall

From the time they are very small, Newhallville children accompany their families—parents, older siblings, cousins, aunts and uncles, grandparents—on downtown shopping excursions. As mentioned before, when Newhallville children are about ten years old they are allowed a new kind of adventure: going downtown unaccompanied by older relatives or friends. Among the children I knew, girls go downtown alone more often than do boys, who at this age still prefer to spend much of their unsupervised time riding bikes in and around the neighborhood.

For these girls, going to the mall alone is a thrilling experience that allows them to be playful in ways that are impossible at home and in the neighborhood. Despite widespread feelings in New Haven that the mall is not a particularly safe or comfortable space to be, the statements and behavior of Newhallville children indicate that for them the mall offers freedoms unavailable elsewhere, while also imposing particular forms of restraint. I was struck by the changes in the girls' demeanor when we went to the mall. The mall space itself seemed to be the sort of safe, protective milieu it was designed to be from these children's point of view, at least in some respects.

Malls are often compared to theme parks such as Disneyland (see essays in Sorkin 1992) in part because, like theme parks, malls feature a carnivalesque atmosphere that is at once both controlled and utopian. Several recent megamalls, such as the Mall of America in Minnesota or West Edmonton Mall in Canada (5.2 million square feet) actually *contain* theme parks, further eliding these two forms that are at once architectural, social, and economic. When Tionna, Natalia, and Asia went to the mall, they often used its spaces as their own kind of personal amusement center, going down the up escalators, and up the down ones, running through public spaces loudly laughing and shouting, tailing cute boys like easy-to-spot, giggly spies. When Macy's was still open, the second-floor breezeway connecting the mall to the department store was a glass-encased tunnel through which they could run, run-walk, gallop, shuffle, or tumble. Macy's itself was a kind of playground, with its three floors, numerous escalators, and accessible displays of electronics, jewelry, and makeup. Excerpts of field notes from a shopping expedition taken shortly before Christmas in 1992 detail some typical activities in which these kids engaged when visiting the mall:

> Asia and Natalia lean over the second-floor railing throwing pennies into the fountain on the mall's main floor below. Bunches of poinsettia plants are set high upon wire pillars that rise up out of the fountain and the brilliant red flowers seem to float in the air. By the edge of the fountain is a cart whose proprietors are selling religious clocks and metal, laser-etched images of saints and reproductions of the Last Supper. Asia and Natalia decide to try to throw a coin down on top of someone's head. They drop some pennies down. The coins miss the unsuspecting person, who is minding the cart with the Last Supper reproductions. The girls come running up to me, jumping, hopping, vibrating with the excitement and danger of what they have done. Then they spot some cute boys and take off in close pursuit. I take off after them.
>
> They have lost the boys and decide to look for them in the Macy's game section one floor up. They go up there, pretending to shop, looking at electronic typewriters. The boys are not there. After a few minutes of playing and fiddling with electronic displays, Natalia says, "Now we got to go boy huntin' again." As we are walking, Asia says, "Miss Chin looks hype. All she got to do is lose the bags." Natalia,

however, announces, "Miss Chin is bad luck." Meaning it's my fault they lost the boys. We are by the escalator and the girls consider going downstairs. "That's where the perfume is," Natalia says. We go up to the third floor again. No boys. "Miss Chin, you're making us lose men!" Natalia wails. We go all the way to the first floor and the girls stop at the Clinique counter for a few minutes, playing with the facial "computer" there. We head back upstairs again, on an escalator, and on the way the girls place coins on the moving rubber rail, calling to me and saying, "We gave the coins a ride!"

In pursuing the boys the thrill is in the chase itself. Exploring different departments in Macy's, playing with electronic typewriters and children's toys, riding the escalators, fiddling with cosmetics displays are fun and exciting for these kids. These activities would be fun for any kids, but what was absent from the surface, at least, of these children's playful meandering was any engagement with most spaces as consumers with money to spend. They played with the typewriters just to play with them, not so that they could think about buying them or even wish that they could have one of their own. The escalators were by far the most exciting and fascinating element, aside from a certain pleasure they seemed to take in knowing they were on the verge of wildness—all the roaming up and down and up and down again—and yet unlikely to suffer any painful consequences.

This was *their* mall: a large, open, interesting, exciting space, full of cute boys, though dotted with inconvenient security guards and disapproving grownups; lined with stores containing fascinating merchandise; punctuated by escalators that lifted them to the mysteries above or lowered them to the unknown below. They were not there only or even primarily to shop, but to explore, to go "boy huntin'" as Natalia said, and to generate a safe yet thrilling excitement. This is perhaps not the use for which Macy's or the mall was designed; like the amusement park, Macy's and the mall presented the girls with a closely monitored—and hence relatively safe—space.

Being at the mall does not place kids in a field of unadulterated freedom, but it does allow some pressures and problems to recede from the forefront of their experiences. Cautious and on guard for dangers posed by men when at home in the neighborhood, Tionna, Natalia, and Asia can revel in being girls at the mall. At home they worry that men might be after them; in the mall they chase boys as if every day were Sadie Hawkins Day. The following are portions of an interaction that took place in the mall's food court:

Asia spies a boy she knows. With ten-year-old bravado, Natalia says that she's going to get up and go over to them. Asia tells her to go ahead. Overcome with the idea, Natalia suddenly decides she can't possibly do it. Asia gets up and goes over to the boys, tells one of them that Natalia likes him. Natalia squirms, moans, giggles, slides under the table and, emerging again, tries to bury herself inside her coat. Asia comes back. I drink my soda and they eat, glancing back at the boys who are sometimes looking our way. The taller boy comes over and says to Natalia that the other boy wants her to go over there. Now she's really dying. She's saying she's too shy, she can't, etc., etc.

Later, after the boys have left, Asia continues giving Natalia a hard time for chickening out. "I don't know his last name so I can't look it up," she says. "I am so mad at you," she continues. "Rashad is going to be pissed!" Rashad is the missing boy. "The only thing you had to do was get up, walk over there and say hello, run back and that's it," Asia said. "Miss Chin," Natalia said, "It's all your fault. I told you you were bad luck." "Right this minute we could be walking with them," Asia said with exaggerated wistfulness, totally fake and somewhat funny. "If I see him I'm going to call him and say wait right there, here she is!" "If you see him," Natalia said, "you're going to start laughing."

From an adult point of view the freedom might appear childlike, even though much of it focuses on boy-girl interactions of a romantically (but not sexually) charged nature. The raucous behavior, the playing around, the *play* is what kids do. However, the girls, at least, also think of these mall outings as a way to begin to explore growing up, not being kids. Later, Tionna explained that at the mall "we try not to act like kids. When we're here, at home, then we act like kids, we play, we play with our dolls." Being able to explore the city and the mall on their own is thus not just an expansion of their horizons as shoppers or individuals, but also a mark of maturity—one intrinsically opposed to the vulnerability of childhood and playing with dolls at home. Children often yearn to be grown up for a whole host of reasons. For Tionna, Natalia, and Asia, one of these might be that feeling of freedom and safety they receive when roaming downtown, a feeling they do not experience on home turf. While Newhallville girls who were visiting the mall independently did not ignore the toy store by any means, it was Claire's that was an inevitable pit stop. Going to this store, where more "grown-up" merchandise such as large hoop earrings and sunglasses could be purchased, was part of not acting like a kid in the mall.

Despite widespread feelings in New Haven that the mall is not a particularly safe or comfortable space to be, the things that these kids say about the mall and the things that they do there indicate that, for them, the mall offers freedoms unavailable elsewhere, while also imposing particular forms of restraint. "Kids come here to stay out of trouble and to shop," said sixteen-year-old Cherie Lee in an interview with the *New York Times* ("A Teen-Age Pall at the Mall" 1993). Yet even as a store like Claire's offers an opportunity for independent, grown-up shopping, it also exposes children to another grown-up experience: being directly confronted with racism.

At the New Haven mall, pointed efforts at constraining the activities and limiting the presence of minority youth permeate the atmosphere. Security guards help to provide the safety kids seek but also ensure that safety in part through an intense monitoring of minority kids. Children are hardly unaware that they are at best only temporarily welcome in most mall spaces—and then only under certain circumstances—and that they are almost if not wholly unwelcome in others. Natalia's sudden and loud announcement in Claire's that "that white lady is following us around" is an acknowledgment of this state of affairs as well as an overt challenge to them. Natalia may have had the gumption to make this challenge because she did, in fact, have a twenty-dollar bill in her pocket. Similarly, Asia's insistent conviction that a salesclerk in Claire's was laughing at her because she had no money could only be defused by returning to the store to brandish money and retrieve her self-confidence.

Under these circumstances, Claire's is a location for Newhallville girls that is chock-full of complexity and conflict, where their race marks them—at least in their own minds—for monitoring and judgment. The loud and often disruptive behavior of Newhallville kids in the mall can be seen, in part, as an assertion of their right not only to be where they are but also their right to exist outside the borders of their neighborhood. These girls' shouts and suspicions point to their growing awareness that to be black in this world, unlike in Newhallville, is to be other, and to be suspect; to be black in Newhallville, however, is to be shut out from places like downtown, and hemmed into a neighborhood with pleasures and dangers of its own.

Conclusion

[R]acial, economic, legal and social disempowerment can be condensed into a glance or a tone of voice. . . . The store is a key site where this multiaxial disempowerment is put into practice. It is where

racial power can be redirected along economic and legal axes. . . .
Store counters are the furniture of capitalism, the equivalent in the
sphere of consumption of the workbench in that of production. (Fiske
1994, 481)

The disparaging glance or tone of voice directed at Newhallville children
in Claire's and in the mall is part and parcel with the social inequality
they experience in other aspects of their lives, and, as John Fiske notes, it
is in stores and across sales counters where minority consumers often
come face to face with social disempowerment that is fundamentally dehumanizing. The tension that these children felt, tension over being observed and judged when off their home turf, was particularly pronounced
in downtown stores but surfaced even on the street the minute they were
over the neighborhood's borderline: remember Tionna's shout at a passing car, "What are you looking at, you white people?" One wonders
what they might have answered.

Tionna's question is very much like Natalia's loud pronouncement
that "that white lady is following us around." Both suggest that in New
Haven whites and blacks view each other through a distorting lens. The
larger structural issues at work in creating neighborhood and downtown
spaces that are themselves implicated in the creation and perpetuation of
social and racial inequality in New Haven suggest that any significant
transformation of these children's experience must also involve fundamental changes in the city's geographic as well as social scene. Nevertheless, small changes in the consumer experiences of children, particularly
downtown, can work to transform what Fiske refers to as the "multiaxial
disempowerment" that can be the result of the transactions taking place
across the store counter, between clerk and customer. It is not the aim of
this chapter to suggest what those changes might be, but rather to suggest the far-reaching implications of children's consumer experiences in
important consumer sites. The focus has been primarily upon places like
Bob's and Claire's, but the primary issues to be addressed, while expressed in these locations, concern society at large. Transforming urban
social spaces requires engagement with and understanding of these larger
social processes.

Both the 1992 uprising in Los Angeles and the growing power and
popularity of figures like Louis Farrakhan attest to the centrality of consumption as a political arena and the store as the battlefield where the
struggle is bound to be waged. In Los Angeles it was to some extent a
festering resentment between local blacks and Korean store owners—

one that mingled understandings of race and class together—that fanned the flames of community outrage over the police beating of Rodney King. Against the backdrop of a changing economy that had left the working class increasingly without work and local businesses without business, the riots were what Fiske calls "loud public speech by those whose voices are normally silenced or confined to their own media" (484). In contrast, Farrakhan speaks publicly, loudly, and often. The organization that he heads, the Nation of Islam, explicitly points to the economic realm as an arena of oppression of blacks and urges its followers to start their own businesses and to patronize stores that are black-owned and -operated. In the words of one minister during a service at a Nation of Islam temple that I attended in Connecticut in August 1992:

> We all got to be teachers of the poor and underprivileged out there. What you going to do, sit here and run around with a puff head and keep it all to yourself? That's what the white man does. The white man just keeps it all to himself. If you sit there and let that happen, you're acting like a slave. You are afraid to go out and take what belongs to us. The honorable Elijah Muhammad said that nothing's going to happen to you. You can go to work and not worry, let God protect you. But he's not going to come out of the sky with a machine gun every time somebody calls you nigger. He's going to come out of you!

This excerpt from this minister's much longer social and spiritual analysis of American society elides the social and cultural with the material and economic. What the "white man just keeps all to himself" is a little unclear—is it knowledge, resources, jobs, money? The vagueness may be intentional and meant to indicate all of the above. Moreover, as is often the case, class and race seem to be given some equivalency in this speech, with blacks being "poor and underprivileged" and the white man having everything.

The different social and consumer experiences available to children in local groceries compared to downtown stores like Claire's are not two halves of a whole. The familial and socially chaotic atmosphere of Bob's does not compensate for the tension and mutual suspicion that characterizes the social scene at Claire's; the array of merchandise at Claire's is not an effective foil for the limited choice and higher cost of shopping in the neighborhood's small groceries. The polarization of children's experiences when downtown versus in neighborhood stores can be directly traced to ongoing historical processes, including the economic decline of the city and region and local policymaking. Children are themselves participant in creating the relationships (or lack thereof) that emerge as they deal with store personnel, clerks, and other customers. Their actions are not reactive or predetermined, and in some cases, kids mobilize their own stereotypes about distrustful store owners even before those store owners can demonstrate their distrust. Kids often begin to exhibit the very kinds of loud and disruptive behavior they know will make people uncomfortable in an attempt at some kind of a social preemptive strike. These attempts at rejecting the power of others over their own lives recall the resistance of the working-class "lads" in Paul Willis's classic account of South London youth (1977). These lads, painfully aware that school officials deemed them worthy of little else than monotonous blue-collar factory work, knew they were capable of more and rejected the school's assessment of themselves by skipping classes, doing poorly in school, and otherwise opting not to work within the system. This strategy, paradoxically, ensured that all they were equipped to do once they graduated was the very unskilled work they wanted to escape. Similarly, for minority kids downtown, the loud and raucous behavior, the antics and running around provide the satisfaction of a symbolic nose-thumbing at the powers-that-be while also convincing store personnel and security that close monitoring and distrust are well founded and should be continued.

This chapter has analyzed some of the contextual factors shaping the ways in which a store is thought about, used, and understood by children like those from Newhallville. Shoppers are not anonymous, historyless individuals when they walk in the door, and stores are not monolithic spaces that, many have argued, affect all who enter in predictable ways (see, for example, Halton 1992; Reece 1986; Williams 1982; Willis 1991). In the confrontation between historically situated people and socially constructed spaces, people are reconstructed as particular people *in that space*. The attempts of malls across the nation to selectively inhibit the access of segments of the population by refusing to allow public transportation to operate on their property is one way in which mall operators recognize differences between shoppers as being of great importance.

Not only are people handled and influenced differentially when within "democratic" commercial spaces like malls, but depending on the particular place, the impact and results of these incidents can vary widely. Newhallville children are different kinds of people when they are in Claire's than when they are at Bob's, and the difference lies in part in the ways in which they engage with the social spaces they occupy. It does not matter much when kids are at Bob's that they might be poor. There is not much to buy, the merchandise changes very little from week to week, and everybody in the neighborhood knows a lot about everybody else in any case. Neither is their blackness an issue at Bob's; it is instead a point of common ground. At Claire's and in the mall, the confluence of poor, working-poor, working-class, and middle-class blacks and whites can at times serve to fuel their fantasies about each other more than anything else, as the *Advocate*'s April Fool's Day front page attempted to illustrate. Being black at Claire's is problematic, but often the excitement of the atmosphere is worth it. Being poor at the mall is not just a quiet matter of how much money one is toting in a purse, pocket, or backpack. For kids like Tionna, Asia, and Natalia, it shapes and directs the form and content of most of their time there, either as a sort of specter haunting others' suspicions about them, or as a painful reality forcing their simultaneous admission that such suspicions are true, while asserting that their status as human beings should not be diminished on the basis of their inability to buy.

5.

Anthropologist Takes Inner-City Children on Shopping Sprees

When I asked Davy if he would like to go on a shopping trip with me, he tilted his head to the side, smiling, and looked at me without speaking for several moments. He seemed to want to speak, but couldn't. We sat, me hunkered up in a fifth-grade-sized chair, my knees knocking up against the underside of a fifth-grade-sized table in the reading corner of Davy's classroom. "Yeah," he said, his almost-changing voice creaky and thin, his tone rising to make his answer sound more like a question. He looked away and then peeked back at me, as if he had a suspicion that I would disappear while his head was turned. "Yeah."

By far, most of my research was conducted in a participant-observer mode in homes, at school, and in the neighborhood. This work was central to documenting and understanding the consumer lives of African American children in New Haven, because it immersed me in children's daily lives. However, I also needed to get a close, concentrated look at these children's spending and shopping, precisely in order to understand how the rest of what I was seeing and doing was enmeshed with aspects of consumption. I knew that hanging around with kids might never get me to the corner store with them, much less into the mall, food court, or some secret consumer site. Here, I decided to construct my own opportunities and take children on shopping trips. My aim was to guarantee that I would be able to watch each child shopping, to see which stores they wanted to go to, to see what they bought, and to watch the process of evaluating merchandise, dealing with other shoppers, and negotiating the particular forms of public space presented by malls and stores. These events were conceived of and designed as a foil to the happenstance of more regular participant observation, controlled and controllable (though not experimental), and, frankly, as a relief from the anxiety of waiting for something obviously significant to happen in the course of the everyday.

The methodology of the shopping trips was simple: I provided the children with twenty dollars each and said they could spend it where they liked, on whatever they liked. I conducted twenty-three shopping trips in all, one of which was incomplete. (Most of the following discussion focuses on twenty completed shopping trips, excluding two excursions with teenage girls.) Taking place toward the end of two years of field research, the trips were not particularly natural in that they did not replicate or even attempt to replicate the kind of experience that kids might have with adults within their own social spheres. As a result, I cannot make the argument that these trips are an indication of how such children really do spend their money when they have it, but the strength of the patterns that do emerge provides a firm basis for understanding some of the social and cultural dynamics at work in these children's lives.[1] The basic facts of the shopping trips did not mesh with children's everyday experiences in any case, since most caretakers did not give their children money and then take kids on a shopping trip where the child was free to dictate just about everything: when and where to shop, when and where to eat, when to leave. As Kiana explained to me in her poetic and whimsical way when I asked her to explain to me how her experience with me was different from her usual shopping excursions:

When you're with a grown-up, boy, it's different. "No, stay here. No, no you wait until I get out of the store." I don't like that. I like it when I go with people who just let me be freely in the store to buy whatever I want to buy.

How was it today?

Terrific. Yeah.

How do you feel?

I feel good. Because usually when I come from shopping I'm tired, but I'm not today because it's different . . . but you see, you let me be freely—so that's how it's different.

In letting Kiana "be freely" I did not represent or exercise the kind of adult authority familiar to these children: I was not a mother, aunt, teacher, or older sibling. My dogged refusal to curb their often rambunctious behavior, despite severe temptation on my part, made me even less credible as a grown-up, if the disapproving looks of shop clerks and other adults were any indicator. Although my initial intention was to trail behind kids, seeing what they did, this plan was thwarted by children's consistent efforts to draw me into social interaction with them. I could not remain apart from the shopping but was almost continually required by children to be an active and opinionated participant. This was, for them, an integral part of the shopping dynamic: social relationships. This discussion I had with Cherie as she wondered whether to buy a cap gun was typical in many ways (though Cherie's wit was particularly quick):

Oooh, $2.99. Should I get it?

You like it?

I'm asking you.

Do you like that?

Kind of.

What would you do with it?

Murder my brother [a mischievous grin].

The children who went shopping represent a varied group of friends, siblings, cousins, and classmates because I found myself being asked to take sisters, cousins, and friends along as well. I viewed these requests as important information in and of itself and in response chose not to insist that children shop individually with me. When they asked me, I allowed them to go in pairs or even small groups. Kids were also remarkably adept at ensuring that I could not refuse these requests, which were usually made by girls. More than once, when I arrived at a girl's house to take her out shopping she would run up to me saying, "My friend [sister, cousin] is staying with me, can she come, too?"

In most cases children were caught up in thinking about family members and caretakers even while shopping alone with me, and these absent people exerted a force on children's shopping trips that was in many respects far more powerful than my own influence.[2] Several kids spoke of having been told by mothers and grandmothers to be sure to buy one thing or another. To my surprise, they never attempted to enlist me in surreptitiously derailing those instructions. Likewise, other children, after having made one practical purchase or another, would remark with great satisfaction and anticipation, "My mommy is going to be so happy that I bought this!" From the outset, then, the effort to understand these children's consumption was not possible if I insisted on considering their choices as being generated out of self-interest and personal desire—the starting point for so much theory on consumption in general and shopping in particular. The process of consumption was for these children based quite overtly on a complex and sometimes convoluted web of social relationships—especially to kin, but also including each other, friends, myself, and those they came into contact with while they shopped, as well as occasional imaginary figures.

Through their shopping excursions, kids were engaging with their families, neighborhoods, city, and culture rather than exiting from those social entanglements. Children used shopping as a way to create relationships and, rather than being self-contained packages of information, the shopping trips were a passage into the entire lives of these children.[3] These shopping trips represent a convergence point of social, cultural, economic, and political processes through which children continually navigate. Understanding them ethnographically requires connecting the purchases to children's larger worlds. Although Davy bought only two items when he went shopping with me, those purchases are revealing when understood in the larger ethnographic context, and in the circumstances of his everyday life.

Shopping Excursions

Davy

There is stark and apparent simplicity to Davy's purchases when presented in tabular form (see table 5.1). The items, their prices, and the place where they were bought are not all that surprising: this was a ten-year-old boy on a shopping spree. But what Davy bought cannot speak on its own about his personal concerns and motivations, or the circumstances and forces shaping them. Why walkie-talkies? Why Toys-R-Us? Understanding the things Davy bought takes us into his life at school, at home, and in New Haven.

Davy had arrived in Lucy Aslan's classroom in the middle of the school year. The oldest of four children, Davy came from a home fraught with difficulties. Sometimes he would come to school and sleep all morning, and when asked what was wrong would answer that his

Table 5.1. Davy's Purchases

Item	Price	Store
1 set walkie-talkies	$12.99	Toys-R-Us
batteries	$ 4.29	Toys-R-Us

mother, who was in her early twenties, had not come home all night and he'd had to take care of his younger siblings, the youngest still in diapers. Money was tight for his family, and though a simple uniform of white shirt and blue pants was required at the school, Davy did not have the proper outfit. A couple of months after Davy joined the class, the classroom aide took him downtown and bought him a basic set of school clothes and a sweater. He came to class the next day wearing his new uniform and beaming broadly. Davy's pleasure in being able to dress both according to the school code and like his classmates was openly visible and reflected his new ability to fit in with everyone else.

Davy was painfully eager to communicate with teachers and other children but seemed not quite to know how, and his end of any conversation was usually monosyllabic. My pictures from the field seemed always to catch him on the edge of things, hands in pockets, tall for his age, leaning in longingly toward a group of kids who were doing something that he was not quite part of. Davy was not at the edges of things because the rest of the class was leaving him out; the other kids really seemed to like him, and several students made special efforts to help him with his math or his reading, both subjects he liked but was struggling with. It just seemed that Davy did not know how to make contact with people or that he was afraid.

On his shopping trip, Davy spent his twenty dollars at Toys-R-Us, a store that he had never visited before. He did not even know the store's name and at the beginning of our trip had asked if we could go shopping "where Ronnie and Kareem went." These two boys were classmates of Davy's and had been talking with him about their trip, which we had done the day before. Once we were in Toys-R-Us, Davy's trip did not take long. He seemed to take little notice of the abundant merchandise and, though he was unfamiliar with the store's layout, he found and quickly settled on his choice: a walkie-talkie set. Together with the batteries the walkie-talkies required, the total cost came to just over twenty dollars (I routinely paid small sums over the twenty dollars if they resulted from sales tax, which many children could not calculate or did not anticipate). The problem was, as we moved along another aisle Davy also found Wolverine, an X-Men action figure, which he had told me before we began shopping he had planned to buy. These action figures were tremendously popular among the boys in the classroom, and most of them had two or three of the most coveted ones. The boys would often congregate together in front of Ronnie's house to play X-Men after school. Though the boys freely lent figures back and forth during these play sessions, Davy did not have a figure of his own. Having Wolverine would have let him enter into these play sessions at a new level, just as being able to come to school in the same uniform his classmates wore allowed him to meld more fully with the group, if even only visually. Although Davy knew the walkie-talkies and batteries would cost all the money he had, he spent several minutes standing in the store aisle, holding Wolverine, the batteries, and the walkie-talkies all together, unable to decide which thing to leave behind. It seemed as if he was hoping if he wished hard enough the prices would magically change. Finally, he reluctantly put Wolverine back on the shelf.

As I stood there watching Davy struggle with this decision, I experienced some of the most painful moments of my research. The Wolverine figure, after all, cost under five dollars. It was hardly expensive, but it was more than Davy could buy. More than being a single moment where he faced frustration and disappointment and had to curb his desire, this boy's dilemma in the Toys-R-Us aisle was also the story of his life. Davy's wants were modest. He did not pine for the $200 Sega Genesis video-game system, but a five-dollar action figure; he did not want flashy and expensive brand-name clothes, but rather a simple school uniform consisting of a white shirt and blue pants. Clothing, sleep, food, and time with his mother all seemed to be hard to come by in Davy's world. Just as the five-dollar Wolverine figure was more than he could afford, it was more than he could expect that his entirely reasonable and limited wants would be fulfilled, since even his basic needs seemed to be inconsistently provided for.

Davy's very first visit to the largest, most prevalent, and most economically successful toy retailer in the world needs to be understood in the context of the circumstances that shaped his life. Although scholars and middle-class observers tend to interpret a lack of contact with consumer culture as a sort of uncontaminated state, a freedom, or a benefit, Davy's limited consumer experience was not a sign of his being sheltered from the venal world of consumerism and hence kept pure in relation to it. That Davy had never before visited what is arguably one of the central sites of childhood experience in the United States is at once a *sign* of exclusion and a *form* of exclusion from one of the wealthiest societies now on the globe. An experience like Davy's is made possible when children and whole communities are multiply isolated, just as its residents are multiply oppressed: socially, economically, educationally, productively, and also in terms of consumption. Toys-R-Us, like any major site of consumption, is thus not a great equalizer, as has been argued, for instance, in the case of the department store (Williams 1982). Davy entered that store bringing his history with him, and his entrance into the mecca of children's consumption did nothing at all to change the objective circumstances of his life experientially or objectively, if even for a few moments. The equality of consumers' money as it enters the shop's till does not extend to the consumers themselves: their particular life experiences and expectations shape their relationships with the store itself, its merchandise, and its personnel.

In the interaction with toys on the shelves, Davy's experience was forged *within* his own life situation, complete with the economic, social, and material difficulties with which he was so consistently confronted. These elements came together in Davy's life in particular ways in relation to Toys-R-Us. Located several freeway miles away from Newhallville and nearly inaccessible by public transportation, this store lay far beyond his reach, given that his family had no car. More to the point, his mother could not afford to buy many toys for her children in any case. Davy's actions and decisions while in Toys-R-Us struck me as being most forcefully aimed at social goals rather than being more blatantly consumerist. It was through watching and thinking about incidents like that with Davy that I became convinced that consumption is at its base a social process, and one that children use in powerful ways to make connections between themselves and the people around them. Davy's decision to buy the walkie-talkies is an especially poignant example of the effort to create social connectedness through the process of consumption, and most Newhallville kids expressed similar desires and intentions as they considered merchandise, compared prices, compiled their purchases, and spent their money. This tendency or potential has been remarked upon by others (Williams 1988; Willis 1991) with a special focus on the utopian elements of children's consumption practices. Without attempting to deny or even downplay the prosocial and utopian elements of these kids' consumption—elements that are too often overlooked—my aim is to explore also the contradictions and the limitations of children's efforts to forge social relationships through consumption. It is not consumption itself that poses the primary obstacle for Newhallville children in these endeavors. Rather, it is social inequality itself, in its many forms and guises, that continually shapes these children's consumption, purchases, motivations, wishes, and fantasies.

Davy, who struggled every day to communicate and to connect verbally with the people around him, had chosen, it seems, the perfect vehicle for allowing him to accomplish what seemed so difficult for him. The walkie-talkies were a toy that required another person in order to be enjoyed, and a toy that required him to speak in order to play with them. The walkie-talkies seemed to suit his particular dilemma perfectly: they were a vehicle that allowed him to talk to people but at the same time did not require him to be too close in order to make contact. Davy told me when I asked that he planned to use the walkie-talkies with his little brother, and this detail is also important. Davy had chosen a toy that by its very nature needed to be shared, not just because he wanted to connect and communicate with others; although he was the only child in his family to be taken on a shopping trip, he wanted to come home with something his other siblings could enjoy with him. Davy's choice of toy and playmates can be seen to fit in with his already established caretaking role in relationship to his younger siblings. His projected choice of playmates was not inevitable, and he did not really have to choose his little brother—he could have planned to use the walkie-talkies with his friends Ronnie and Kareem, for instance.

Even the Wolverine figure that he yearned for gives more insight on the nature of Davy's social longings than it helps to understand his material desires, if these things must be considered separately at all. Having his own Wolverine figure would have provided him a way to enter into social relationships with other boys in the neighborhood, as he would have been able to come to the play sessions with a toy of his own and thus level the playing field a bit. The struggle Davy experienced while standing in the Toys-R-Us aisle with only twenty dollars to spend was not focused on a selfish desire to have more stuff. These objects were avenues through which he could attempt to forge more complex, more meaningful, and stronger social relationships with his siblings and with his friends. His struggle was less about whether to buy walkie-talkies or Wolverine than it was deciding which relationships he wanted to foster and strengthen: those with friends, or those with family.

There exists a gap between efforts like Davy's to create and foster relationships with friends and family through consumption, and the ability to successfully accomplish these efforts. For poor and working-class kids, the constraints on access to the material realms of the consumer world are many. Though Davy's choice of merchandise on his shopping trip reveals a multilayered complexity regarding his careful attention to siblings, sharing, caretaking, and building friendships, one wonders what Davy did when the expensive batteries inevitably lost their power. How would he replace the five-dollar batteries? Where could he buy them? Unlike the Wolverine figure he put aside, the walkie-talkies required ongoing purchases in order to keep them going. The continuing effectiveness of his choice—walkie-talkies as a medium of social connection—was also predicated on his continuing ability to consume. Children and adults of all classes are increasingly faced with the dilemma that social participation requires greater and greater levels of consumption, whether of food, services, merchandise, or images. For children who are not only poor or working class, but also racial minorities, this dilemma has especially devastating consequences. Pervasive media images and popular beliefs portraying the consumer engagement of these kids as fundamentally violent and out of control, fueled by greed and drugs, are among the most destructive of these consequences not only because they have a well-demonstrated power to skew perceptions as well as public policy, but also because, like all forms of racist discourse, they are a dehumanizing force.

Shaquita

When I went to pick her up for her shopping trip, Shaquita emerged from her house lurching like a ten-year-old Quasimodo: her small cousin had grabbed hold of her leg and attached herself to it with a toddler's grim determination. Shaquita had to trick the little girl into going back into the house, then lunged out the door, quickly shutting it behind her as the child's wails rose in pitch and volume behind it. We could hear the little girl's shrieks as we crossed the street, and even as we drove away.

The dedication that Shaquita's cousin showed her was not unusual. In her classroom Shaquita was known for her sensitivity and generosity to others and could always be counted on as the one who would comfort or stand by another kid in a crisis. Shaquita's father had been living in California "since I was a little baby," and though he called and sent her cards sometimes, she did not see him. She lived with her older sister and younger brother in her maternal grandparents' home and had been there for about five years, since the time her mother had entered the Army. Out of the Army now, Shaquita's mother lived across town in a city housing project, and the children visited her regularly. "My mother wanted us back," she said, "but my grandmother asked if we could stay there and help her." Her grandmother, a domestic worker, had just received her General Equivalency Diploma that year and the family was still celebrating her achievement. Deeply connected to an extensive kinship network, Shaquita was particularly close to her godmother, who took her on trips "down South," and who often bought her new clothes

Table 5.2. Shaquita's Purchases

Item	Price	Store
1 pair gold-colored slip-ons	$9.99	Payless Shoes
1 pair denim mules	$6.99	Payless Shoes
1 package foam rollers	$2.09	Rite-Aid Drugs
1 bag bubblegum	$ .99	Rite-Aid Drugs

when she needed them. Shaquita's godmother was a member of the church the family attended, and the church played a big part in the family's life.

The first purchase Shaquita made was two pairs of shoes at Payless (see table 5.2). She had originally gone into the shoe store to find herself sneakers for camp but couldn't find any sneakers she liked. She did find a pair of $6.99 denim mules that she liked very much, though, and bought those for herself. As a birthday gift, Shaquita bought her mother a pair of golden slip-ons for $9.99. With the remainder of her twenty dollars she bought a 99-cent bag of bubblegum that she planned to share with her older sister and some hair-rollers made of pink foam for her grandmother for $2.09. Shaquita spent more than half her money on gifts, all for female kin who play central roles in her life.

In her explanation about why she and her siblings continued to live with their grandparents even after their mother had returned from the Army, Shaquita emphasized she was wanted, that their mother had asked to have her children back, but their grandmother wanted to keep them. Shaquita never said much about what she herself preferred to do, but she seemed happy and secure in her grandparents' home, even as she longed for and missed being with her mother. Looking at these gifts in more detail sheds light on the nature of the different relationships that Shaquita had or hoped to have with her mother and grandmother. Shaquita told me before we began our trip that her mother wanted some gold sandals and that she wanted to buy her these for a birthday gift. There is a fantasy aspect to these shoes, with their golden color, and their special-event feel. These qualities dovetail with aspects of Shaquita's actual relationship with her mother, where visits were special events. At $9.99, the shoes cost Shaquita about half of her money, and to some degree this is an indication of the degree to which Shaquita wanted to impress her mother, draw her in, and get close to her. Perhaps, like Dorothy's ruby slippers, the golden shoes are a way for Shaquita to get back to an idealized home.

In comparison to the shoes, the pink foam rollers Shaquita bought her grandmother have a down-to-earth usefulness. Shaquita had good reason to think her grandmother would really be glad she had chosen to buy her rollers, since she and her sister were always "borrowing" them. This choice emerged as well from the detailed knowledge we gain of those we live with—knowledge that is gained from pulling one person's hair off a hair curler in order to use it oneself, using the same toothpaste and soap, from changing each others' sheets. This gift, so eminently practical, is particularly appropriate for a female primary caretaker, who is so often expected to forego luxuries herself in order to provide for those around her. The rollers were in this way a powerful symbolic contrast to the golden shoes, and their practicality attested to the everyday intimacy Shaquita shared with her grandmother as opposed to the more richly imagined relationship she contemplated with her mother. The contrast also "speaks" of the differences between Shaquita's relationship with her mother as an important emotional figure and with her grandmother as primary caretaker.

If the golden shoes helped to create the kind of relationship Shaquita imagined she could have with her mother, the rollers allowed Shaquita to demonstrate that she understood her grandmother's generosity and care by reciprocating it. Shaquita could have decided to solve the roller-shortage problem by buying some for herself; then she would not have had to use her grandmother's anymore. But in doing this she would have been broadcasting an entirely different message than she did by coming home with a gift. If she had said she was buying the new rollers for herself, Shaquita would have asserted not only her right to use her grandmother's things, but also that she felt it was not her responsibility to replace the things she used. Rather than taking this approach, Shaquita chose to make a gesture that could show her understanding of her obligations as a household member, a gesture that showed she was aware of the kinds of things her grandmother needed. With her sister, however, there could be more give and take, and Shaquita bought a 99-cent bag of bubblegum that they could share. In an omission worth noting, Shaquita bought no gifts for the male members of the household, her brother and grandfather. In fact, no child bought a gift for a male friend or relative.

Cherie

Thinking about mothers' wants and needs was an important element in kids' lives, and several children aside from Shaquita bought gifts for their mothers. Cherie spent nearly all of her money ($14.99 to be exact) on a pair of sneakers for her mother (table 5.3). The rest of her money was spent on candy, but she gave most of it away to family members, spending less than five dollars on herself. In Cherie's purchases, once again the deep sense of mutual obligation, and even debt, between family members played a central role. For Cherie, as well as for other kids, these obligations and debts were often at once sustaining and joyful as well as painful, onerous, and highly charged. I sometimes suspected that the lesson imparted to children and imparted by them was a coercive generosity: share or else. These harsher aspects of mutual dependence and obligation were an important part of being connected to family and caring for them, and existed simultaneously with the pleasure and satisfaction children received in participating in their families and households.

Cherie, her newborn brother, and mother Deanna shared an attic apartment in a two-family house owned by Deanna's mother. Though Deanna's sister Lynn, a paramedic, did not live at home, she visited her mother often. Deanna received the bulk of her income from state and federal programs and there was some tension between Deanna and her sister, stemming, I thought, from Lynn's steady and comfortable income coupled with her status as a jobholder, versus Deanna's reliance on public assistance. Lynn had no children herself and often gave Cherie expensive gifts: a television set, Sega Genesis game system, and a CD player. These gifts fanned the competitive flames between the sisters. These conflicts occasionally erupted into physical confrontations. Deanna had a scar on her thigh where her sister had once bitten her during a violent tussle. "Look! She ruined my pretty legs!" Deanna wailed to me in mock

Table 5.3. Cherie's Purchases

Item	Price	Store
1 pair black leather sneakers	$14.99	Payless Shoes
2 containers "juice bar" gum	$ .69 ea	Kay-Bee Toys
2 bags chocolate coins	$ .69 ea	Kay-Bee Toys
1 dish strawberry frozen yogurt	$ 1.35	Food court

anguish as she showed me the marks. Deanna's relationship with her mother also seemed tense, partly out of jealousy over the close relationship between her mother and Deanna's sister, but tension also seemed to emerge around issues of mutual aid and paying of bills. Deanna's rent was largely paid for with a Section 8 voucher, but Deanna felt that her mother expected her to pay too much of the electricity and gas bill. Deanna also did not have a car and felt that her mother was not generous about taking her to the store for grocery shopping, demanding either money or food stamps as payment for the favor.

Cherie's role in this complex web of material and emotional jockeying seemed to be that of an eager, placating human pinball, quick of wit and quick on her feet, working hard to make everyone around her happy and trying to keep out of the way of flashing tempers. She was not, however, just an insecure little victim, and shared a warm and jokey intimacy with her mother, who did not baby Cherie much, speaking and kidding with her like a pal. Deanna was also watchful and protective of her daughter, and my first encounter with Deanna was really an encounter with her disembodied voice—Cherie was outside trying out a new skateboard and Deanna was watching and directing her every move from an upstairs window. But Deanna was moody and prone to drinking, and Cherie seemed ever watchful of her changing disposition.

Cherie's shopping trip reflects these concerns about mediating actual and potential conflicts between these three imposing women in her life and, most of all, anticipating her mother's wants and needs. Even in the planning stages of her shopping trip, Cherie thought she would buy her mother a pair of sneakers "because I took my mother's sneakers because I needed them for junior police." The junior police was part of a community outreach program designed to improve the touchy relations between police and residents of certain New Haven neighborhoods, among them Newhallville. Kids participating in the program went to special events, had educational and training sessions, and wore uniforms. Black shoes were required with Cherie's uniform, and Deanna had given her own black sneakers to her daughter so that she was fully equipped. Cherie knew that replacing those sneakers with the money from this shopping trip would make her mother very happy, and that it would impress her quite a bit:

You're going to try them on to see if they fit your mom?

Yes. She can fit them. She's going to say, "$14.95, child? What were you thinking?"

Why? Is that a lot?

It's a lot for me these days, she says. But she'll say, "Thank you for getting them."

I bet she will.

I'll get them for my dear old mother. Because six might be too small, she could grow into these.

You think she will?

Okay. I'm buying my mother a pair of shoes, size six and a half. That's all I'm saying.

Cherie's decision to buy her mother new shoes may have been calculated, in part, to fend off any bad feelings Deanna may have been having about having given her own shoes to her daughter and then having to go without herself. Her "dear old mother" was not her only concern, however, and once Cherie had decided to buy one person in her household a gift, she began to wonder what she should get for her grandmother, aunt, and little brother. She bought some small bags of candy for her aunt and grandmother and did not get anything for her brother. (Cherie's joking comments about buying a cap gun to "murder my brother" hinted at a bit of tension and even jealousy she was feeling at his arrival, which may explain her omission.) After we finished shopping, Cherie spent her last couple of dollars on a strawberry frozen yogurt for herself at the mall's food court. Cherie's shopping trip took less than an hour, and its culminating moment was not the purchases themselves but the distribution of the gifts.

When we returned to Cherie's house, it was already dark outside, and we found her mother, grandmother, aunt, and new baby brother in her grandmother's living room. Cherie's grandmother was holding the new baby, who slept in her lap. Cherie's aunt Lynn was off from work that night and sat sprawled in a living room chair, wearing a baseball cap, acid-washed jeans, and a frown. Deanna had just gotten a perm from her mother, who did under-the-table beauty parlor work out of her home. With a towel over her shoulders and conditioner in her hair, Deanna sat on the couch, watching TV with the others.

Cherie could hardly contain her excitement as we came into the house and, beaming intensely, put the package from Payless down on the couch, saying, "Look what I got!" "What's that?" Deanna said in a high, girl-baby voice. Cherie told her mother that it was a present for her, that she bought it for her on her shopping trip. Deanna answered with a simple, "Thank you," and opened up the box, moving to sit on the floor as she began to try on one of the shoes. Her foot did not seem to go in very well. "They don't fit," she said, scrunching her eyebrows down. Cherie stood almost frozen, not believing that this could be true. Deanna pulled her foot out of the shoe and saw that her thick athletic sock was hanging over her toes, bunching up inside the shoe. She readjusted her sock, and tried the shoe again. It was a perfect fit. Deanna was all smiles, and Cherie, with evident relief, began passing out bags of chocolate coins to her grandmother and aunt, the enjoyment of this radiating out of her in all directions.

Interpreting the meaning and importance of children's purchases for themselves, which constituted the great majority of purchases overall, is perhaps even more complicated than unraveling the complexities of gifts. For one, children on the whole did not seem driven by their impulses. Kids often managed to buy an astonishing amount for twenty dollars, and overall they were careful, thoughtful, and critical in their buying. Second, when they bought things for themselves, it was not in most cases appropriate to assume that these purchases were self-centered or selfish. Children's purchases for themselves revealed a profound practicality, and the purchase of "needed" items emerged as a central element of kids' shopping. With her twenty dollars Sheila bought a pair of shoes, one package each of socks and underwear, and a bottle of nail polish. Her mother had told her beforehand to be sure and buy socks and underwear with part of her twenty dollars. Marvella, a fourteen-year-old, bought Clearasil, deodorant, and school notebooks with part of her money. Cherelle came prepared with a list that included items such as "gel for the back of my hair" (which she did not buy) and a hair bow to match her school uniform (which she did buy).

Tanika

Tanika had been wearing her brother's sneakers to gym class since she had outgrown her own a few months before. Buying herself sneakers when she needed them was not only practical, but something she found immensely satisfying. "My mother is going to be so happy that she doesn't have to buy me sneakers now," she crowed on the way home in the car (table 5.4).

Unlike many children in her class, Tanika was not regularly expected to spend part of her own money on things she needed, like socks and underwear. Although Tanika's family was not as economically on the edge as Davy's family, Tanika was keenly aware of the stresses upon her

Table 5.4. Tanika's Purchases

Item	Price	Store
1 pair sneakers	$11.00	Payless Shoes
1 pair glasses	$ 3.99	Claire's Accessories
1 t-shirt	$ 5.99	Foxmoor Clothes
1 vest	$ 7.99	Foxmoor Clothes

parents generated by running a family and working. Both her parents worked, and they owned their two-family home. This was the first time she had bought sneakers for herself, and easing the burden on her mother's demanding array of responsibilities seemed to be a big part of this decision—in addition, of course, to getting herself some shoes that fit properly and that had not previously belonged to her older brother.

So, now is this something you'd normally do—spend money on buying yourself—have you ever bought yourself sneakers before?

No. I just did it for the first time because I knew I needed sneakers and I wanted them real bad. Because I'm tired of wearing my brother's sneakers and they're ugly.

Is there a reason you haven't gotten new sneakers?

Because she [Tanika's mother] ain't got the time because she works. And she gets off at 4:30 and she goes in at 8:00 and she's tired. Then she takes her nap and then she gets up and cooks—then eats and goes back to sleep. So—that's why she don't have time. . . . On Saturday she'll do it because she don't have to work.

Tanika occasionally earned pocket money by going to work with her mother and helping her out as she cleaned offices in a downtown building. Buying the sneakers was, in part, another way of giving her mother some additional help. Tanika's excitement over the shoes really blossomed when she imagined her mother's reaction to the realization that she would not have to take her free time on a Saturday to go downtown shopping. Using purchases to make caretakers happy, and imagining their pleased reactions, was something that many children found deeply satisfying rather than a chore. In this way they often connected themselves to family and kin even through purchases that were for themselves, rather than being gifts.

Ricky

At Toys-R-Us, Ricky carefully amassed an impressive array of items: a container of bubblegum, four bags of marbles, a set of eight markers, a set of eight colored pencils, a three-foot styrofoam glider plane, and a repair kit for bicycle inner tubes (see table 5.5). Unlike many children, Ricky did not buy anything that he really planned to share or use with others. A tremendously intelligent and energetic kid with a wicked sense of humor and an insanely goofy laugh, Ricky had been held back in school and was a few years older than his classmates. His major interest was art, and he continually drew astonishingly accomplished renditions of the Tasmanian Devil and other popular cartoon figures. His family life was crowded and in some ways precarious: earlier in the year he had stolen the proceeds of a classroom art show ($18) to help buy food for his family, and he was repaying his teacher with a small sum once a week. He lived in a three-bedroom apartment with his mother, her boyfriend, and three younger siblings. His mother was expecting another child, and their finances were barely adequate to keep the family housed, fed, and clothed.

Ricky's first and highest priority purchase was an inner tube repair kit. For boys in the neighborhood, bikes were a primary avenue to freedom, and they ranged far and wide through the neighborhood and beyond. His tire had a flat, and he wanted to be mobile again. At $2.49 the tube repair kit left Ricky with plenty of money. He checked the price of an inner tube just to compare. "That tube would have cost me $6.99," he said. "It cost a whole lot more and I would only have one of them!" Instead, he pointed out, he paid less and could repair his inner tube several times with the one kit.

Table 5.5. Ricky's Purchases

Item	Price	Store
1 tube repair kit	$2.49	Toys-R-Us
8 color changing markers	$1.99	Toys-R-Us
8 colored pencils	$1.99	Toys-R-Us
styrofoam glider plane	$3.99	Toys-R-Us
4 bags of marbles	$1.79 ea	Toys-R-Us
1 marble	$ .99	Toys-R-Us
bubblegum	$ .99	Toys-R-Us

Like several other children, Ricky was very clearly focused on getting as much for his money as he possibly could. He loved a Lamborghini model car but realized he would have to buy cement and paint for it. He went so far as to pick all of these things out and carry them around cradled in his arms as we continued up and down the aisles, but he suddenly decided it was too expensive and put everything back. Farther down the aisle, he saw a big styrofoam glider plane. At $3.99 it was about half the price of the model car and certainly gave the impression of getting more for the money, being about three feet long. He decided he wanted to buy art supplies with the remainder of his money. He took a great deal of time evaluating different packages of pens and pencils, their properties, their prices, how many were in a box. He chose things that could be used in more than one way: markers that changed color if treated a certain way, and colored pencils that could be used to do watercolors, too. The marbles were to be added to his marble collection.

Unlike the purchases of many girls, nothing that Ricky bought directly linked him back to his family. This was quite common among boys (except Davy). His purchases remain, like those of most children, practical and well thought out. He wanted to buy the tube repair kit first because he was afraid he would forget if he put it off until later in the trip. One of the most impressive things was Ricky's ability to spread the twenty dollars out so that it satisfied many areas of his interests and activities: the tube repair kit for mobility and peer interaction, the plane for playing, the art supplies for drawing and making things, the marbles to add to an already existing collection.

Teyvon

Teyvon came shopping with me on a Sunday afternoon the day before he was to begin a summer school enrichment program. He spent his entire twenty dollars on an outfit to wear for the first day along with a summer's supply of notebooks, paper, pens, and pencils (table 5.6). Our first stop was Sam's Dollar Store on the downtown mall's first floor. Teyvon, a skinny kid who always seemed to be pushing his large round-rimmed glasses back up to the bridge of his nose, wasted little time and we spent all of five minutes inside Sam's. Spotting a salesperson right away, he went right up to the man saying, "Excuse me, where are the notebooks?" The man pointed them out and Teyvon chose one. "Excuse me," he shouted out in his raspy, piping voice, "where is the notebook paper?" For a total of $5.37, he bought a notebook, one package of pencils, two packages of pens, and two 200-sheet packages of filler paper.

Table 5.6. Teyvon's Purchases

Item	Price	Store
1 10-pack of pencils	$1.00	Sam's Dollar Store
2 10-packs of pens	$1.00 ea.	Sam's Dollar Store
2 packs of notebook paper	$1.00 ea.	Sam's Dollar Store
1 notebook binder	$1.00	Sam's Dollar Store
1 pair shorts	$5.99	SuperBargains
1 Hornets t-shirt	$9.98	Champs Sporting Goods

These purchases of Teyvon's had been carefully planned, and earlier in the week he had scouted potential purchases for his shopping trip, picking out an outfit at a clothing store on lower Chapel Street. We went shopping on a Sunday, however, and when we arrived at the store containing his outfit, it was closed. Teyvon did not want to wait and come back another day and instead quickly regrouped, looking for shorts and a t-shirt in the mall stores that were open. In Champs, a sporting goods store, Teyvon once again made a nearly flawless beeline for the salesman, detoured only by a few moments where he gingerly caressed a gold-colored Michael Jordan basketball. "I'm looking for a t-shirt and I have fourteen dollars and seventy cents," he announced to the salesman, who took us over to a rack full of t-shirts. Spotting one he liked, Teyvon felt around for the price tag: $39.95. He dropped the tag and moved on. "There are some shirts that are on sale over here," the salesman said. This rack was full of t-shirts decorated with team logos. Teyvon wanted a Celtics t-shirt, but none were on sale. He settled for a black shirt with a white, blue and purple design of the Charlotte Hornets for $9.99. As we were waiting at the counter to pay, Teyvon spotted some baseball caps emblazoned with the Bulls logo. The hats were $21.99. "The price must have gone up when they won," he remarked wryly.

At this point, Teyvon had very little money left, and he still needed a pair of shorts to complete his first-day outfit. He was looking for big, baggy shorts that went down over his knobby knees, preferably in purple or blue to match the shirt. We looked all over the mall, but there were no stores there carrying kids' clothes except for a place called SuperBargains. The shorts there did not come in the right colors, but they did come in the right size and the right price. Teyvon decided on a $5.99 pair of black mesh shorts that had a yellow underlining. When he took the shorts up to the counter, the saleswoman began to ring them up at $4.99, but Teyvon stopped her and told her this was the wrong price. She checked the price, and indeed, Teyvon had been right. With the purchase, it turned out, he had his choice of "silly sippers," drink holders in funny shapes like a bunch of grapes or a banana, with a curly straw attached. He chose a dolphin-shaped silly sipper, saying, "I'll give this to my little cousin."

In Teyvon's case, his focus was on buying things he needed; being able to stretch a limited sum of money to cover both a summer's worth of school supplies and a new outfit was something that continued as he got older. In 1993 he had a job working as a counselor at another summer program. When I spoke with his mother, Vanessa, she told me with evident pride that he had spent his first paycheck (about sixty dollars) buying himself a pair of sneakers, groceries for the family, food for the family cat, and had even started a savings account and was squirreling away funds for a car. "And he didn't buy the regular cat food," Vanessa pointed out emphatically, "he bought the seven-dollar cat food!" At the time, Teyvon was thirteen years old.

Shopping Trips in Children's Cultural Worlds

Just looking at shoe purchases is revealing. Seven girls and one boy bought shoes with a portion of their money, and I became such a familiar sight at the downtown Payless store (a discount shoe chain) that when the store employees saw me approach behind a ten-year-old, they would greet me by asking how my research was coming. The shoe purchases embodied both these priorities of efficiency and buying for need: kids spent anywhere from $3.99 to $14.99 on shoes and often managed to buy several additional items with the money that was left over. Namisha bought her shoes, a pair of blue flats with embroidery on top, to wear to church. Alan bought a pair of sturdy shoes for five dollars and boasted about it for the rest of the day.

In contrast to the brand-name crazed consumers who live in the popular imagination, these children, while interested and knowledgeable about status items, showed not the slightest inability to distinguish between an abstract wish for expensive, status goods and the practical realities of purchasing ability. Though kids demonstrated often and in a variety of ways their detailed knowledge of and interest in brands for clothing, sneakers, food, cars, and so on, they showed little or no interest in purchasing branded merchandise during shopping trips. This gap between abstract wishes and concrete actions is too little noted in the literature on the consumption of kids like these. When the gap is noted, it is primarily approached in terms of kids' frustration with not being able to buy what they yearn for. While children do harbor these frustrations, the shopping trips also showed that a concern for status items, brands, and fashion does not exist at a constant level and exerts a fluctuating force in children's consciousness.

Sheila and Tarelle, for example, gave me a long and detailed education on the ins and outs of athletic shoes—which brands, models, and colors are "slammin'" and which aren't. Even once inside Payless, Sheila pointed out to me the various "wannabe" models of sneakers lined up on the shelves:

> Sheila tells me that at Payless they have "wannabe" Reeboks, Nikes. She goes to a bunch of sneakers and holds them up one by one, telling me what kinds of wannabes they are. "These are wannabe Huaraches," she says, holding up a pair of sneakers with a cutout top. "They're by Nike."

Sheila and Tarelle even pointed out the sneakers that Tanika had bought earlier for herself, saying that they looked stupid and that they would never wear them. These attitudes did not stop the girls, however, from each buying a pair of shoes in the store: Sheila bought a pair of multicolored Docksider-type shoes, and Tarelle bought a pair of blue suede clogs. Kids had a keen eye for brands that was undeniable, but it was rivaled by their equally adept eye for bargains.

While on one hand kids would tell me with utter certainty that "everyone" was wearing Air Jordans, and that they really wanted a pair, they would duck into Payless a few minutes later and come out with a ten-dollar pair of shoes or sneakers. I became, upon reflection, very curious about who this supposed "everyone" was since, as I pointed out to Stephen, only two kids at his school actually wore Air Jordans, and he was one of them: this hardly constituted anything approaching "everyone." This was an imaginary "everyone" nonetheless experienced at some level by kids as being real, though not necessarily immediate. This "everyone" is similar to the real but nonexistent amoral and pathological consumer that these kids are so often portrayed as being. In both instances these images possess a powerful influence, one at odds with an on-the-ground situation.

The shopping trips were also striking for what children did not do, even when they were with me, a singularly lenient adult. Family, household, and community dynamics in Newhallville did not foster the kind of wild-child consumer who pitches fits in supermarket aisles and runs amok in Toys-R-Us. A lack of self-control, especially in stores, was not tolerated by the Newhallville caretakers I knew, and when kids pressed their luck by whining, wheedling, or crying they were most often dealt with harshly. As a result kids learned early to keep control. Certain tensions and realities are made visible and present for Newhallville children that for their middle-class counterparts are more often hidden and secret. The cost of being fed, clothed, and cared for is one of these things. Kids in Newhallville are frequently expected to spend part of their allowance, birthday, or Christmas money on buying things for themselves that they need, and their purchases during shopping trips reflect these patterns and expectations. While most kids certainly seemed to be attending to their desires in their shopping, what is most striking is the degree to which practicality on the one hand, and generosity on the other, influenced their shopping trips.

In the presence of caretakers children rarely, if ever, asked for things, whined, or wheedled, and only once during shopping trips did a child attempt such tactics with me. Teyvon, who in the classroom demonstrated world-class cadging abilities, tried his skills out on me during his shopping trip, hounding me to buy him an ice-cream cone. I bought him one, and he later told me he'd just been testing me to see if I'd give in. "You weak!" he crowed, laughingly. More often, rather than Teyvon's calculated exploration of my weak spots, children instead seemed to take care not to impose upon what many saw as my largesse—not only because I was giving them twenty dollars to spend but because I was taking them on an outing and spending time with them when it seemed to them I did not have to. At the outset of each trip I would buy kids a snack and we would sit and chat for a bit. Some children, however, insisted on using a portion of their shopping money, paying for these snacks themselves. As Tarelle said, "I don't want to be spending up all of your money, Miss Chin." Children were extremely careful not to incur debt with me by overtaxing what they saw as my generosity (I usually reminded them they should be thanking the government, not me, for the twenty dollars) and this kind of mental recordkeeping in relation to social and monetary debts was the norm: once Nyzerraye came to visit me at my apartment and got soaked in a sudden downpour. I lent Nyzerraye a pair of socks so that she could have dry feet during her afternoon with me. I told her she could keep them and forgot about it after she went home. A week later, her grandmother sent Nyzerraye back to return the socks, which had been washed, neatly folded, and enclosed in a Ziploc sandwich bag.

Gift-giving was a powerful way for children to strengthen, transform, or maintain relationships with those around them. While Cherie and Shaquita were the only kids to spend more than half of their money on gifts, eight of the twelve girls who came on shopping trips with me bought a gift for someone. In contrast only one boy bought a gift, a small porcelain picture frame decorated with flowers, which he gave to me.[4] This boy was Shaquita's brother and, looking back, I am not surprised that it was this boy who showed this kind of concern—it fits right in with the kinds of priorities and concerns that Shaquita showed in her own shopping trip. The basically gendered aspect of children's gift buying fits in well with expectations at home regarding relationships between friends and family, where the active maintenance of relationships was often managed by girls and women, and the accounting of material and emotional debts brokered by them as well. This is what Michaela di Leonardo has called "the work of kinship" (1987). Though di Leonardo identifies this work as being primarily the province of women, children's purchases here suggest that girls are drawn into this work early: girls bought gifts for their mothers, younger siblings, grandmothers, and, in one case, an infant niece. The purchases showed an intimate understanding of the needs and wants of the people around them and I was especially struck that children seemed to know quite well their mothers' shoe and clothing sizes. This sort of intimate knowledge suggests that children do not regard their caretakers just as the givers of care and resources and as therefore somehow able to provide for all of their own needs as well. Rather, these girls demonstrated the degree to which they understand the very human and real limitations of their caretakers' abilities and recognized their own responsibility for acknowledging or lightening the load. Being able to arrive home after a special outing like the shopping trips with a gift for someone else, especially for a primary caretaker, was a way of demonstrating that kids understood that their membership in the network of kin needed to be active in order to be activated. These gifts were an effort to reciprocate with care and caring and at the same time allowed kids to show that they were competent in meting out material resources in ways that served not only material ends, but social ones as well.

Another aspect in the buying of gifts and its importance for these children was that most of the time kids were not in the position to give gifts of a material kind; the pleasure aroused in children through choosing, buying, and giving gifts should not be taken lightly or discounted. Although I have emphasized above the practical and tactical nature of gift-giving, there was also a distinct and profound gratification that children experienced in being able to give something to someone else. For them, the power to be generous was often a tremendous motivator, not engaged with cynically or out of obligation, but one generating a pleasure and satisfaction unlike that of buying something for themselves. This is not to deny in any way that children found buying things for themselves pleasing and satisfying. Kids loved buying things for themselves, and they did it more often than they bought things for others.

"It would seem that shopping has become about the only area of social action which is defined as clearly not politicized," observes Daniel Miller in an essay entitled "Could Shopping Ever Really Matter?" (1997, 31). What Miller pinpoints in his essay is the long-standing and still influential position of Left-leaning scholars (Right-leaning ones as well) which defines the "mere" act of shopping as vulgar, disconnected from social relations (but somehow not disconnected from political economies), self-referential, surfacey, and inherently apolitical or even antipolitical, a position that he aptly characterizes as "a strange mixture of Marxism with elite criticism of low culture" (44). Just how a socially and culturally organized activity like shopping might be divorced from the social relations of production while remaining firmly rooted in the political economy that has generated it is a question most observers have successfully evaded for decades. More recently, however, the more obvious answer has suggested itself, which is (of course) that shopping cannot be excised from social and cultural relationships, and therefore neither can it be separated from the realm of the political. Miller points out complexities similar to those I have outlined in this chapter in a discussion of the issues surrounding shopping for mundane, everyday items like household disinfectant:

> The atmosphere reflects a gamut of social relations. In one case a daughter-in-law may exact revenge on a dominating mother-in-law by her superior knowledge of changes in the market and constantly implying that her rival's products and choices are out of date or inappropriate. In another context two housewives freely exchange experiences of consumption in order that both should be protected against critical comments from what is regarded as the ignorant but malevolent world of men. The conversion of shopping knowledge into social relations was most evident in intra-female discussion but may become highly emotive when it is others (especially children) of the household complaining that their expectations have been thwarted. (Miller 1998, 41–42)

Miller's assumption that children are passive and/or receptive in this process is as suspect as the claim that shopping is all about self-gratification and purchase of surface identities. Seen through the context of Newhallville children's life circumstances, the picture that emerges from close observation of what these kids bought when they went on shopping trips with me is one that contrasts greatly with the common assumption and assertion that children are primarily responsive, for instance, voicing their "thwarted desires" but not working to actively satisfy those desires, or the desires (or needs) of others. Even more specifically, poor minority children are often seen as acting on desire but little else, and with often antisocial results.

The major defining factor of these kids' engagement with the consumer sphere is social inequality, and it is understanding the ways in which social inequality shapes their lives, including their shopping lives, which renders visible the political aspects of such "vulgar" activity. Thus the politics of shopping for these children operates at the intimate levels of relationships with mothers, siblings, peers, and caretakers, and at the same time is bound up with "larger" political processes: racism, poverty, residential and economic segregation, and gender bias.

6.

Ethnically Correct Dolls:
Toying with the Race Industry

In the late 1980s the toy industry's leading manufacturers—Mattel, Hasbro, and Tyco—began to introduce "ethnically correct" dolls and toys. These toys differed from their precursors in that they were designed with skin tones, hair types, and facial features that were meant to accurately represent a specific ethnic group. Mattel, for instance, introduced its Shani line, three African American dolls, each with a slightly different skin tone and with newly sculpted faces. These faces were purportedly more realistic in their representations of black features than those of other dolls. The Shani dolls provided unequivocal contrast to Mattel's first black doll, "Colored Francie," introduced in 1967. Unlike the Shani dolls, with their variety of facial features and skin tones, Colored Francie came in one color and was literally formed in the same mold as the white Barbies on the shelf. But ethnically correct toys hardly originated with the industry leaders, and their political roots are located in the urban communities of Los Angeles and New York, tied to the civil rights movement, urban riots, and, more recently, to rising nationalist sentiments. At the time that Shani and her compatriots were introduced to the market, ethnically correct toys were not a new idea: minority-owned toy companies had been making such dolls for over twenty years. Early manufacturers of ethnically correct dolls such as Olmec or Shindana had a focused social and political agenda aimed at undermining the racism endemic to an industry that seemed to believe that all baby dolls and Barbies—and, by implication, people—ought to be white. By the early 1990s, however, this agenda seemed to have its greatest potential in its ability to generate profit rather than social change.

Ethnically correct toys have been designed and marketed specifically to reshape a territory dominated by an assumption of whiteness, an assumption embodied most powerfully in the icon of the Barbie doll. While ostensibly part of a progressive social vision, these toys have integrated the toy world while simultaneously more firmly fixing racial boundaries in ways that are surprisingly regressive. This chapter examines the complexities and paradoxes of ethnically correct toys through looking at the toy industry, focusing on Mattel's Shani dolls and Olmec, a manufacturer of ethnically correct toys. These paradoxes can be seen in analysis of the toys themselves but emerge with greater clarity when close attention is paid to the ways in which the children for whom the toys are supposed to mean the most actually play with and think about them. Children's use of and relationships to these toys, as well as the discourses of race, go beyond the packaged messages of manufacturers and challenge popular conceptions of racial boundaries in potentially radical ways.

The primary appeal toymakers offer with their ethnically correct playthings is the idea that such toys can help minority kids to feel more at home in the world through allowing them to play with toys—and especially dolls—that look like them. The statement on Olmec toy packages asserting that "Our children gain a sense of self-importance through toys. So we make them look like them" bears a heavy debt to the revelations that emerged from the groundbreaking "doll studies" conducted by psychologists Kenneth and Mamie Phipps Clark in the late 1930s and early 1940s. These studies used black and white dolls as a way to unearth black children's views about race, asking them to point out, for instance, which doll "looks nice." In a series of devastating publications, the Clark studies revealed that black children often thought the white doll "looks nice" while the black doll "looks bad" (Clark [1955] 1963; Clark and Clark 1939, 1940, 1947, 1950). Despite ongoing debates about problems with the methodology and interpretation, the doll studies remain among the most compelling bodies of data demonstrating the negative effects of racism on black children's self-concept or what is more often now referred to as their self-esteem.[1]

The doll studies gained additional clout when they became associated with the landmark civil rights ruling by the U.S. Supreme Court in *Brown v. The Board of Education of Topeka, Kansas,* the case in which segregated schooling was declared to be unconstitutional. It is a testament to the emotional power of the doll studies that, although they were never directly referenced in the court's decision, it is often asserted that it was these very studies that convinced the Supreme Court justices that segregated schools caused what were then referred to as "Negro children" unconscionable damage.

Makers of ethnically correct dolls attempt to harness the power of

the Clark studies to the moral force of the civil rights movement in producing ethnically correct dolls whose ostensible purpose is to make kids
feel better about themselves as they play with toys that look like them.
Embedded in these toys is a set of assumptions that hearkens back to the
Clark studies, but with a commercial twist: preventing the kind of self-
hatred observed in the Clark studies can be accomplished by having
children play with dolls that resemble themselves. The message that
manufacturers impart to concerned parents is "Buy toys that represent
racial diversity and your children will be empowered as racial beings,
not overpowered by racism."

These products are often described or marketed as multicultural, but
the vision of multiculturalism as it exists in the market seems to rest primarily on market segmentation and the carving out of separate ethnicity-
and race-based niches; in the end many cultures are represented in this
multicultural market, but they do not mix. The paradox is that while the
introduction of ethnically correct dolls has significantly expanded the colors and backgrounds with which dolls and toys may be imbued, this has
been accomplished through the commodification of race and the consumption of racialized commodities. In the process, racial boundaries are
represented as ever more fixed and as increasingly unbreachable. Treat-
ing race and racial identity as a commodity thus has been accompanied
by the emergence of products like ethnically correct dolls whose marketing appeal is based upon problematic ideas about race and ethnicity. In
the realm of childhood, ethnically correct dolls have proven to be a powerful medium through which notions of race have been mass-marketed by
both mainstream and minority manufacturers, without seeing significant
challenge or remolding in either literal or figural terms, except, perhaps,
among children themselves.

In the early 1990s racialized commodities in the form of ethnically correct playthings were poised to take up residence in children's rooms,
imaginations, and hearts, and were generating millions of dollars in rev-
enues. The industry took little interest in just whose rooms, imaginations, and hearts these products lodged, as long as the products were
leaving warehouse and store shelves to lodge somewhere. One thing is
certain: few of these toys were coming home to Newhallville. In this
neighborhood, the presence of these products was uncommon at best. In
a framing of the problem that rested almost exclusively on the recognition and reproduction of racial difference, toymakers assiduously avoid-
ed the problem of class.

For residents of Newhallville, taking part in the benefits offered by market multiculturalism required material and economic resources often beyond their reach. This hardly meant that themes of race and racism were absent from children's toy kits. Newhallville children's commentaries about race and its boundaries did not conform to the limits proposed by toy manufacturers. Looking closely at children's interactions with their toys, and especially in girls' relationships with their dolls—who were often white—children's understanding of the complexities of race in society continually surfaced in acute and perceptive commentaries that took note not just of race but several forms of inequality, including class, gender, and age. These children thought about, used, and spoke about their playthings in ways that directly challenged the assumptions about the fixity of race evident in ethnically correct toys. These children did not appear to view race as a range of solid, immutable categories. Likewise, children's commentaries reveal their understanding that racialized commodities can only incompletely embody the experiences of kids who are racial beings, but also poor, working class, young, ghettoized, and gendered.

In looking at these girls' relationships with their dolls, some thorny issues are raised in relation to the claims and assertions made by producers of ethnically correct dolls about the power of self-esteem through consumption of racial signifiers. Large numbers of girls in Newhallville had white dolls, not ethnically correct ones. In their interactions with these dolls, girls seemed to be engaged in a project whose progressive potential was much greater than the one offered by producers of ethnically correct toys. While toymakers commoditize racial difference but pay little attention to issues of social class, Newhallville girls seemed to have relatively flexible notions about the barriers posed by dolls' skin color, as well as other racial signifiers, especially hair. These girls also did not limit their view of difference or inequality to race but remained keenly aware of class difference. These children's interactions with their dolls reveal their sophisticated but rarely enunciated understanding of the intertwined nature of forms of social inequality.

In Newhallville commodities have become racialized, and the discussion of race has become commodified as well. The complex commentaries on race that I argue take place among Newhallville girls are not speech per se. This is in large part because speaking about race in words has taken on manufactured forms akin to the ethnically correct toy. This process has not curbed the power of race to shape the consciousness of kids, but the modes used to speak about race are often formulaic and constrained by the sound-bite format. Newhallville kids are enormously adept at throwing out sophisticated stock phrases assessing the current state of race relations. I had a memorable comeuppance when Sugar, a twelve-year-old girl, was demonstrating some especially sexually explicit "Jamaican" dance steps. Watching her splayed out on the floor and making graphically detailed humping motions, I blurted, "That's disgusting!" Utterly composed, she shot back, "That's not disgusting, that's my culture."

Sugar's response to my comment instantly and effectively placed our interaction within the arena of racial and cultural difference. Had her grandmother, who was her primary caretaker, witnessed the same demonstration, the conflict was more likely to have been framed in terms of age and authority. (I can imagine it: Sugar's grandmother sees what she is doing and tells Sugar in no uncertain terms that she is to quit it. Sugar is mortified, if only because she is worried about being punished.) At one level, Sugar was well aware that invoking our supposedly fundamental differences was the surest way to shut me up. At another level, however, Sugar attempted to shape the situation so that my only grounds for objection could be along racial and cultural lines, thus denying the possibility that age and authority had anything to do with my relationship with her. Her response seemed to say that my being taken aback by a twelve-year-old barely pubescent girl so enthusiastically bumping and grinding a schoolroom floor could not be made of the same stuff of her grandmother's objections. The sophistication of Sugar's response is at once as shallow as it is deep, and shares this quality with other seemingly off-the-cuff statements that kids in Newhallville would make about race and difference in their worlds.

Statements like Sugar's, while a sign of kids' acuity, are also a kind of diversionary device. Their impressive ability to adroitly disparage or mobilize the social and geographic dividing lines between black and white, the haves and the have-nots, the ghetto and the suburb, or any of the other classic oppositions is diversionary because children's relationships to race and racism are more complex than the sound bites they have so skillfully mastered: to say "that's my culture" is in some ways to say nothing at all, but to say everything as well. This very mastery of the canned observation enables these children to evade the raw and brittle nature of their own racial experience and the racialized territories they traverse. The effectiveness of speech like Sugar's lies as much in its ability to prevent discussion as it does in an ability to promote it.

Despite the constraints posed by sound-bite discussion and racialized commodities, children in Newhallville spoke about their experiences of race in multiple ways, using a vocabulary that included more than just words of mouth. In the case of a number of girls, powerful commentaries on the limits, boundaries, and flexibility of racial categories and racialized experiences emerged when I began to pay attention to their interactions with their dolls. The way that Newhallville girls dealt with and thought about their dolls allowed them to express things that they could not, for a variety of reasons, discuss verbally. One of the fundamental reasons that these girls' observations found expression away from the realm of words and conversation is that the themes and problems they articulated did not fit easily into the dominant models for talking about race. It is precisely because these observations and actings-out remain unarticulated speech in the conventional sense of the term that these girls were able to "say" what they understood in a way that retained the complexity and subtlety of their perceptions. Conversely, however, it is precisely because these observations and actings-out remain unarticulated speech that what these girls were doing is also unlikely to enter public discussions of the topic, even among themselves, much less to enlarge and deepen the astonishingly leaden and concrete vocabulary that used to talk about race in the United States.

The Unbearable Whiteness of Barbie

Welcome to Our World of OLMEC Toys

Almost seven years ago, my son sent shock waves through my body when he said he couldn't be a super hero because he wasn't white.

"What!" I thought. At the tender age of three, my boy was already limiting his fantasies because he thought some dreams didn't come in his skin color.

That was my inspiration to create Sun-Man, the world's greatest super hero. Since then we at OLMEC have expanded into girls and preschool toys. We've got one thing in mind with all our products— let's build self-esteem.

Our children gain a sense of self importance through toys. So we make them look like them.

Now that he's 10, my son's dreams and goals soar. Playing with toys that look like him make him feel good.

I hope you'll buy something from us that will expand your child's dream.

Product packaging, Olmec toys

Stories like the one that Yla Eason has printed onto the packaging of many of her company's products are pervasive among minority toymakers and emphasize the deeply personal motivation behind the corporate entity. Olmec's Sun-Man figure gets his superpowers from the melanin in his skin, and in conceiving of this toy Eason's intention was to upend racial hierarchy by making dark skin a source of power so that her son could no longer assume that "some dreams did not come in his skin color." This statement effectively marries Martin Luther King's civil rights oratory ("I have a dream . . .") with the startling discoveries of the Clark doll studies (the Negro doll is ugly/bad) to provide a powerful argument for the need of dolls that accurately and positively portray blackness.[2] Even the makers of Barbie herself have, in effect, recognized the unbearable whiteness of Barbie as they have begun to manufacture ethnically correct dolls. A more cynical assessment of both Olmec and Mattel, however, might question which is more unbearable: the Eurocentric toy industry that purportedly stifles children's dreams, or the untapped market segments.

The impulse to diversify the social vision that the toy world expresses deserves certain praise, even if undertaken for profit. Close attention needs to be paid to the type of diversity that has developed in the toy industry. While mounting a challenge to whiteness as a norm, the diversity currently under manufacture in the form of "ethnically correct" playthings does not significantly transform the understanding of race, or even racism, as it exists in the United States. Rather, ethnically correct dolls refashion (or refashion-doll) racist discourses without challenging the foundations upon which the notion of race, as a social or biological reality, can be seen to exist at all.

Until companies like Olmec jumpstarted the mass production and marketing of ethnically correct toys, mass-produced black dolls were basically made by pouring brown plastic into the same molds used to make white dolls. This was and continues to be a powerful material manifestation of an assimilationist ethic, one that has been rejected with increasing vehemence by minority groups. The signature aspects of ethnically correct dolls are resculpted faces, skin tones, hair types, and fashions that are meant to reflect a particular group. With their emphasis on the visibility of race as a collection of markers, ethnically correct dolls mask the complexity of race both as a social construct and as a social experience. These toys do celebrate and enshrine difference in a way that preceding black dolls and toys do not, and in ways that are undeniably progressive. However, an unintended outcome of these toys is the reification of an understanding of race that anthropologists, at least, have been working to dismantle since the discipline's early days. The fundamental conflicts between the social agenda of toymakers and the imperatives of business contribute heavily to this tendency to commoditize race while working to create a market for the racialized commodity.

To compete in this notoriously competitive and unstable market, makers of ethnically correct toys must put business first; any social agenda can be accommodated only insofar as it also generates profit. The toy industry is not about fun, it is about competition, marketing, and economic success, generating $17 billion in revenues in 1993. It is an enterprise dependent upon children, who are regarded with both wonder and suspicion by toy executives because—as a group—kids are fickle, unpredictable, and hard to comprehend, especially from the point of view of adulthood. Thousands of new toys are introduced to toy shelves each year, but a toy is considered a success if it lasts any amount of time beyond its introductory season. A toy that lasts five years is a real winner (My Little Pony, Transformers, Teenage Mutant Ninja Turtles), and perennial favorites (Cabbage Patch Kids, G.I. Joe, Barbie) are the foundation upon which toy dynasties are built. A toy that can retain its popularity and its moneymaking ability provides the financial stability needed by toy companies if they are to undertake the huge financial risks required to develop and launch their yearly horde of new products. Bringing a quality toy to production can easily require an investment of several million dollars. These funds go into researching and evaluating play value and safety; sculpting the faces, limbs, or parts of the toy; engineering; setting up assembly line; training of workers to do painstaking hand-painting of details such as eyes and eyelashes; designing of clothing and hairstyles; packaging; marketing and distribution. It's no wonder, then, that socially progressive goals often end up taking a backseat to the priorities imposed by the need to recoup an investment.

The situation is similar in the retailing of toys, where the largest buyers have shrunk to only three: Toys-R-Us, Target, and Wal-Mart. Leading the group by a wide margin, Toys-R-Us is, literally, the buyer that can make or break a toy or a toy manufacturer. The company is so fully in control of the toy market that the Federal Trade Commission has twice in the 1990s investigated the organization on antitrust-related issues. A manufacturer is lucky to get a line picked up by Toys-R-Us and even luckier to avoid having to give the retailer an exclusive. If the line is also picked up by buyers from Target and Wal-Mart, success is almost assured, at least for that year.

For minority toymakers attempting to refashion the racial diversity on the shelves of a large retailer like Toys-R-Us or Target, their task is convincing these eight-hundred-pound gorillas that ethnically correct toys can make money, not that stocking their stores with a multicultural array of toys is the socially progressive thing to do. Toys-R-Us has been very supportive of up-and-coming manufacturers of ethnically correct toys, notably Olmec and Playmates, but this support has a conspicuous connection to sales and profits. Once those profits began to seem solid, large toymakers decided to enter the market, a potential blow to Olmec and a fatal one to Shindana. Hasbro, Kenner, Tyco, and Mattel have significantly greater resources than the smaller, minority-owned companies. During the 1980s Hasbro stock was the best performer not just in the toy business but in the entire market. By the early 1990s Hasbro was the largest toy company in the world, having acquired Playskool and Milton Bradley. In comparison, Olmec's $2.9 million in sales was a drop in the barrel of monkeys. In a move that at once allowed Olmec to retain its corporate identity and Hasbro to demonstrate its progressiveness, the two companies entered into a cooperation agreement, with Hasbro providing Olmec with financial, marketing, and technical assistance while also developing its own lines of ethnically correct toys.

Mattel launched its much-vaunted Shani doll in 1991; during the 1992 Christmas season Toys-R-Us was quietly and cautiously test-marketing ethnically correct dolls in Atlanta and Philadelphia. Toymakers who could not rely on the sell-appeal of the Barbie connection held their collective breath: it was only with the cooperation and backing of Toys-R-Us that they could confidently sink the huge sums required into launching ethnically correct lines of toys and dolls. In February 1993 the numbers looked good enough for *Ebony* magazine to sponsor a special seminar on "Black Toys for Play and Pride" at the New York International Toy Fair. All the major toymakers—Mattel, Hasbro, Kenner, and Tyco— rushed a variety of lines to market, and Toys-R-Us hired the Mingo Group, the nation's largest minority-owned advertising agency, to launch a marketing campaign aimed at African American consumers. With these great successes, these large retailers and producers were touting the ethnically correct doll as a sign of their dedication to democratic values while collectively patting themselves on their backs for the success of this new niche-market.

Unfortunately, a toy shelf stocked with ethnically correct merchandise does not necessarily lead to the same thing in children's toyboxes. This was certainly the case in Newhallville, where only a couple of the children

I knew possessed any of the ethnically correct toys available at the time. The market for ethnically correct toys has been explicitly built upon the buying power of the black middle class; marketing and publicity materials often note the hefty amount of money spent by black consumers on toys—$745.6 million in 1992–93 according to *Ebony* magazine press materials. While this is sound business practice (marketing toys to the poor is unlikely to generate much revenue), it forces manufacturers of ethnically correct toys into an uncomfortable position, arguing on the one hand that these toys are good because they serve an important social function, and on the other that it is not their responsibility to make these products available to economically disadvantaged kids. If ethnically correct toys are primarily about self-esteem, it stands to reason that minority children who are also poor are more likely than their better-off peers to face challenges in creating positive feelings about themselves. It is around the question of poor minority children that the conflicts between social agendas and business realities manifest themselves most dramatically.

For kids in Newhallville, access to the retailers offering these toys was often difficult, if they had it at all. There were no local neighborhood stores where playthings could be purchased, and the downtown mall housed only Kay-Bee, a toy store specializing in manufacturing overruns and discontinued items. Toys-R-Us was located in the next town and all but inaccessible by public transport. In an area where 40 percent of households do not have cars, Toys-R-Us was, for most families, visited only on special occasions. Remember that until he was eleven years old Davy had never visited Toys-R-Us and did not even know what that store was. Similarly Tionna told me her favorite store was the supermarket; Carlos's favorite store was Ames (a discount chain) but, he told me, "they went bankrupt." Though these children often were well informed about the toys they did not have from watching television, they had, on the whole, few illusions about being able to possess them.

In a subtle and unexamined way, then, even minority toymakers have been committed to enhancing the play lives of minority children only as long as these children could buy their products—which involved not only having the money to make the purchase, but having the ability to get to the store where the items could be bought. The breadth of this social agenda is circumscribed by the limits of business and, in a sense, minority entrepreneurs while seeking to multiculturalize the market have been attempting to do so while being fully assimilated into corporate culture. As Yla Eason put it when she spoke at the 1993 *Ebony* event, "The marketing strategy is forming alliances and creating ethnic streams of revenue." Companies like Olmec marry the corporate cachet and know-how of a Harvard MBA (founder Eason has one) with Afrocentric themes and a nationalist program in a strategy that might be called corporate nationalism. Even the company's name points to a corporate nationalist position: the Olmec, a central American culture, have a significant place in Afrocentric scholarship. Ivan Van Sertima has advanced the theory that the massive sculptures attributed to the Olmec are actually monuments to visiting Africans, who traversed the Atlantic ocean in reed boats (Van Sertima 1976). Corporate nationalism, in "creating ethnic streams of revenue," does not challenge the inequities of the market so much as it diverts minority money into its own coffers. In critiquing this strategy, I do not intend to say that it has been either ineffective or unproductive. On the contrary, corporate nationalism has forced larger companies to begin producing their own racialized commodities. Regardless of who is making the money, the effect on the diversity represented in dolls and toys has been undeniably positive. And yet, while manufacturers of ethnically correct toys often point out that kids of color are a growing proportion of the population, they never mention that a significant portion of those minority kids are also poor. The speedy, if as yet incomplete, integration of the shelves of Toys-R-Us has been a major accomplishment of companies like Olmec and an admirable one. However, transforming the population of the store's shelves has not changed the larger context that denies many children access to the store in the first place.

In a critique of the supposedly positive role-model aspects of Mighty Morphin' Power Rangers, Peter McLaren and Janet Morris write, "This statement exhibits the common logical error that many people tend to make: Equality is based on the extent to which females and people of color have the opportunity to adopt the dominant Euro-American ideology" (1997, 120). This observation may also be applied to manufacturers of ethnically correct toys, and especially minority toymakers who utilize the moral force of racial solidarity as a marketing tool. One wonders how much cultural and nationalist concerns have actually transformed these companies' corporate behavior, one that oppresses children like those living in Newhallville regardless of whether a white Barbie or an ethnically correct one is being produced for their consumption. When I asked Yla Eason what her company was doing to make toys available to the large numbers of minority kids who were unlikely to have access to them, she reminded me that her company was a business, not a charitable organization.[3] No one could be expected to run a business that doesn't make enough money to keep itself afloat, and it is unfair to single out minority toymakers for not participating more fully in their stated social agenda. The entire toy industry, not just minority-owned companies, grapples with the tensions generated by being a business that makes money from providing the well-being tools for enjoyable childhoods; the larger companies, such as Hasbro, run their own foundations funding community projects, and the industry as a whole funds several foundations devoted to providing toys, clothes, and services to needy children. Nevertheless, the degree to which business realities are at odds with the claims toward improving self-esteem among minority children has been steeply underplayed. A few months after my exchange with Eason, she was quoted in a leading toy-industry publication as saying, "For us, it's not just a stream of revenue. It's an issue of self-esteem. Our mission is honestly to make black children feel good about themselves, to feel good in the skin they're in" (Shapiro 1993). As long as they can afford it, that is.

Consumption has been examined by several scholars as a profoundly feminized, and thus gendered, activity;[4] looking at ethnically correct toys is one way to understand the ways in which consumption is also an experience that is also deeply "raced" and "classed." For Newhallville kids, the whole sphere of consumption is itself often conceptually "white," other, and suffused with the attendant pain of inequality based on discrimination due to race and economic background. When I asked a group of kids one day to tell me how white people talk, a twelve-year-old boy not only began talking the way he thought white kids did, but moving like them. "Let's go to the mall and buy some rags," he drawled, adopting a clumsy, gangling walk. For him, the mall was the province of white kids, and shopping one of their signature activities. By implication, this world was not one that included kids like himself.

Shani and the Marketing of Blackness

The commodification of race and the introduction of racialized commodities have not erased the color line so much as they have replaced it with lines of color, an array of products intended for minority consumers. The Shani line of dolls introduced by Mattel in 1991 illustrates the way in which ethnically correct dolls solidify racial categories in problematic ways. Developed in consultation with African American psychologist Darlene Powell Hopson, the dolls are designed to represent African American variety. Hopson had advocated that the dolls also have different body types and different hair textures (DuCille 1996, 50), but Mattel rejected these suggestions in the interest of keeping costs down, since modifying molds is extremely cost intensive. Shani dolls come in three shades of skin: light, medium, and dark.

Ironically, in launching the Shani line, Mattel made racial difference concrete in a way it had not before: while all of its previous black dolls were part of the Barbie line (even Nigerian and Jamaican Barbie), the Shani dolls are not technically Barbies. Mattel has designed, produced, and marketed these ethnically correct dolls as a separate line, in effect creating a market segregation between Shani and Barbie dolls, formalizing through commodification the dividing line between black and white. To emphasize the difference between the Barbie and Shani lines, the Shani boxes announce "From the makers of BARBIE!" This statement seems to suggest at least a sort of corporate kinship between the dolls but subtly underlines their basic difference as well, driving the point home that Shani is *not* Barbie. The packaging is not the trademark Barbie pink, but red. Barbie dolls and accessories in their packages lined up on store shelves form what is called "the wall of pink" that can be recognized from long distances inside even the cavernous spaces of Toys-R-Us. Shani dolls, however, do not make up the wall of pink, though they may stand beside it.

The limitations of the market in reproducing ethnic or racial variety have been much commented upon, especially in critical analyses of the Shani dolls (DuCille 1996; Lord 1994). Even Cabbage Patch Kids, whose market appeal derives largely from the much-touted uniqueness of each doll, produce that uniqueness by the random combination of a set group of prefabricated elements. Underlying the millions of "unique" doll faces are a limited number of basic face molds to which are applied a limited number of additional elements including skin tones, freckles, eye colors, and hairstyles.

Compared to Cabbage Patch Kids, the Shani dolls cover a much more limited ethnic diversity. With their three different skin tones Shani dolls are meant to signify different kinds of blackness. The progressive notion that black does not look just one way is not as progressive as it might appear when one looks closely at the Shani dolls, whose facial features seem to get more stereotypically black the darker the doll's skin color: Asha, the light-skinned doll, has the smallest nose and thinnest lips; meanwhile Nichelle, the darkest doll, has lips that are much wider than the outlines of her stamped-on pink lipstick, and her nose is the largest and widest of the Shani dolls. Light as Asha is, she is not so light that there is any danger that she might be able to "pass" as white. Mattel's

From left to right: Nichelle (dark), Shani (medium), Asha (light).

willingness to deliver Shani in more than one skin tone extends only to the point that racial identity remains visibly bounded and uniform. Or does it?

In the mind of at least one Newhallville child, the meaning of the various skin colors was not kinds of blackness, but rather of kinds of racial mixing. When Carlos and I were in Toys-R-Us, after just having completed his shopping trip, I wanted to see if the store stocked ethnically correct dolls. When we saw the Shani dolls, I pointed out to Carlos that they came in three skin tones. As I held one of each color in my hand, Carlos described them to me. "She's African American," he said, pointing to Nichelle, the darkest-skinned doll. "She must be part Indian," he said, referring to Shani—who does have especially high cheekbones. "This one is like Puerto Rican or a light-colored black person," he finished, as he examined Asha. Carlos had hit upon two of the biggest contradictions embodied in these ethnically correct dolls. When he describes Asha as being "Puerto Rican or a light-colored black person" he captures the difficulty in being able to know race simply by looking: just because you look black (or white) does not mean that you are. Race, as

Carlos understands so well, is not established visually, but rather accomplished socially. Further, racial boundaries are fuzzy. They are not, as the division between the red and pink boxes would suggest, visibly obvious and absolute (Barbie *never* comes in one of the red Shani boxes). Although Shani is Mattel's brand-name figurehead for its ethnically correct African American dolls, Carlos describes Nichelle as "African American," and distinguishes her from Shani, who in his view "must be part Indian." Here Carlos seems to know and recognize more about African American heritage than Mattel is willing to admit.

What Carlos has revealed through his observations is this: in depicting kinds of blackness, Mattel has inadvertently roused the specter of miscegenation. There is (of course) no interracial Barbie, no mulatto or quadroon Barbie, no Eurasian Barbie, nor a Barbie that like golf sensation Tiger Woods might be described as "Cablinasian"—Caucasian, black, Indian, and Asian—a mixture not of two races, but several. Tiger Woods's insistence on creating a name for what he is, like Carlos's description of the racial backgrounds of Shani, Asha, and Nichelle, speaks to the inability of our racial categories to capture the finely tuned perceptions of kids, who may not easily accept the notion that blackness in all its diversity is ultimately one real, bounded category. While Mattel has produced a threefold array of representations of blackness, Carlos views these representations as also signifying much more than blackness alone.

Ann DuCille has extensively discussed much of the complex and contradictory nature of Shani dolls (1996). She highlights two central issues: derrière and hair. Both of these features are riddled with multiple racial resonances. According to DuCille's interviews with Shani designers, the dolls are designed to give the illusion of a higher, rounder butt than Barbie's. This has been accomplished, they told her, by pitching Shani's back at a different angle than Barbie's, and changing some of the proportions of her hips. I had heard these and other rumors from students at the college where I teach: "Shani's butt is bigger than the other Barbies' butts," "Shani dolls have bigger breasts than Barbie," "Shani dolls have bigger thighs than Barbie."[5] DuCille rightly wonders why a bigger butt is necessarily an attribute of blackness, tying this obsession to turn-of-the century attempts to scientifically justify racial categories. What does it mean that Mattel would attempt to use the illusion of an enlarged backside to indicate an ethnically correct doll, while maintaining the doll's ability to wear the same clothes as Barbie? And if the larger backside was just an illusion, what was the point, and how could it be a sign of race?

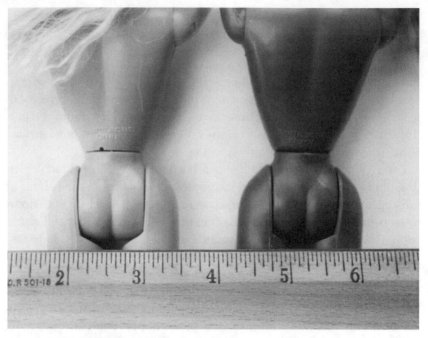

Barbie and Shani from behind.

Deciding I had to see for myself, I pulled my Shani doll off my office bookshelf, stripped her naked, and placed her on my desk next to a naked Barbie doll that had been cruelly mutilated by a colleague's dog (her arms were chewed off and her head had puncture wounds, but the rest was unharmed). I have to say I felt like one of those anthropologists who, wielding a pair of calipers, had set out to codify racial difference in a scientific manner. Try as I might, manipulating the dolls in ways both painful and obscene, I could find no difference between them, even after prying their legs off and smashing their bodies apart in an effort to isolate their butts from the rest of them. As far as I have been able to determine, Shani's bigger butt is an illusion.[6] These ethnically correct dolls demonstrate one of the abiding aspects of racism: that a stolid belief in racial difference can shape people's perceptions so profoundly that they will find difference and make something of it, no matter how imperceptible or irrelevant its physical manifestation might be.

The faces of Shani and Barbie dolls are more visibly different than their behinds, yet still, why these differences could be considered natural indicators of race is perplexing. As a friend of mine remarked acidly,

"They still look like they've had plastic surgery," and even with their lips widened by a millimeter or so the African American faces of the Shani dolls still conform to a white-dominated norm of beauty. The most telling difference between Shani and Barbie is at the base of the neck, where Shani bears a mark that looks a lot like the scar left by a branding iron: © 1990 MATTEL INC. Barbie's head reads simply © MATTEL INC. I am unsure why Shani requires a copyright date and Barbie does not (perhaps Barbie's beauty is timeless?), but this difference has an absolute and clear-cut quality to it that other changes do not. However, Barbie's and Shani's torsos bear nearly identical inscriptions: © MATTEL INC. 1966. (Barbie's torso was made in China, Shani's in Malaysia.) I looked carefully for a butt copyright, but could find none. It seems to me if Mattel's big coup in designing Shani was giving her a distinctively African American face, with its own copyright, the purportedly equally distinctive derrière also deserved a copyright. Because Shani's derrière shows no copyright, I'm inclined to believe that Shani and Barbie are really the same from the neck down. Although DuCille asserts that Shani's legs are shaped differently than Barbie's, their legs bear the same part numbers, which would indicate identical molds.

Literally and figuratively, the differences between Shani and Barbie are primarily from the neck up (witness the copyrights) and these differences are overwhelmingly cosmetic. Race, as embodied in the redesigned faces of the Shani dolls, in addition to becoming a commodity, has become material for corporate proprietary control. Mattel's mix-and-match approach to combining differently copyrighted body parts suggests that some parts are more racialized, more commodified than others. Mattel has copyrighted their ethnically correct African American faces but leaves them to share the same torso Barbie has had since 1966.

As for the hair, the claims for differences in texture did not seem to hold water when I scrutinized the Asha and Nichelle dolls in my office. Like Shani, they had long, silky "Barbie-doll hair," styled in ways similar to those typical of white Barbie dolls: curls for Nichelle and Asha and a crimped style very much like that found on "Totally Hair Barbie" for Shani. In what seems a somewhat half-hearted stab at African-Americanizing this hair, my Beach Dazzle Shani dolls come not with the brush that my white Barbie has but wide-toothed implements that might be hair picks. Aside from facial features and skin tone, blackness seems to be signified more by accessories than anything else, at least in the hair department. DuCille describes the situation in these terms: "In today's toy world, race and ethnicity have fallen into the category of precious ready-to-ware [sic] difference. To be profitable, racial and cultural diversity—global heterogeneity—must be reducible to such common, reproducible denominators as color and costume" (43). The emphasis given to these sorts of markers is part of the commoditization of race and the racialization of commodities.

Among Newhallville children, and among my own African American students at the college where I teach, the phrase "Barbie-doll hair" denotes a specific phenomenon—long, long silky hair. There are at least three types of Barbie-doll hair: the kind that grows out of the heads of "white" girls, the kind implanted to the head of a Barbie doll, and the kind someone can buy at a beauty shop and add on to his or her own. I am loath to pronounce this last type of Barbie-doll hair as incapable of being conceptually black because it is one of the main ingredients of a prodigious range of hairstyles that are nearly impossible to achieve using actual white-girl hair. The problem is more complex than that of long silky hair being an absolute signifier of whiteness: when purchased Barbie-doll hair is used in distinctively black hairstyles, it is not just an exercise in reproducing whiteness upon the heads of black girls. While actual white-girl hair might be appropriate for use in styles that *do* replicate the head of whiteness, it does not serve at all for a whole range of other styles for which the synthetic hair serves beautifully. Some styles call for melting the ends of synthetic hair, which would be a smelly disaster with white-girl hair. While synthetic hair may be metaphorically white, it literally *is* Barbie-doll hair: both are made from the same material, known as Kanekalon (Jones 1990, 290). The now-common joke is when someone asks you if that's "your hair" to respond, "Sure it's mine. I bought it!" This reference alludes not only to plain old race but to good old consumerism, and elides the absolute difference between what is white and what is black. Ultimately, it may be the reference to consumerism that is more important for the girls and women sporting Barbie-doll hair on their heads. Can one reasonably argue, in the face of that kind of statement, that the braid-ins, extensions, or weaves are "really" white rather than black? As with determining Asha's race or Shani's racial mixture, the question is not so easy to answer definitively.

What is black hair or white hair anyway? DuCille seems to assume that black children do not have the kind of silky hair represented by the Barbie doll, essentially drawing a clear line between "black" and "white" hair when she writes, "[F]or black girls the simulated hair on the heads of Shani and black Barbie may suggest more than simple hair play; it may represent a fanciful alternative to what society presents as their own less

attractive, short, kinky, hurts-to-comb hair" (53). I do not wish to suggest that dominant American society has not represented stereotypical
black hair as being everything that DuCille suggests. However, accepting
the stereotypical notion of black hair makes light of the fact that the
"good" and "bad" hair debate would not be possible if black kids did
not have hair that comes not just in tight, nappy curls but also in straight
or curly locks to rival Veronica Lake's famous eye-obscuring cascade.
There are some indications that the absolute line between what constitutes
"black" or "white" hair was originally enforced by white slave-owning
women who, when faced with female slaves who had long, silky hair,
would have it cut off (White and White 1995).[7]

"But what," DuCille wonders "does the transference of flowing fairy-
princess hair onto black dolls mean for the black children for whom
these dolls are supposed to inspire self-esteem?" (51). My guess is, it de-
pends on what you're doing with the flowing fairy-princess hair. Underlying criticisms of Barbie-doll hair is the assumption that one must treat
white hair in certain ways, that is, putting it into styles that are marked
as being white. The assumption seems to be that one must treat this
racialized commodity within the confines of the racial boundaries it is
seen to represent. As Erica Rand has so keenly observed in her book
Barbie's Queer Accessories (1995), people do not necessarily respect the
manufactured identity of Barbie when they deal with her. Rand's book
focuses mostly on the ways in which people's play with Barbie made her
queer in many senses of the word, not the least being in terms of her
sexuality. Similarly, Barbie (or any other doll) can be queered racially as
well. Certainly, in Newhallville, kids do not seem to respect these boundaries, at least when it comes to dolls' heads. After seeing what it is that
these kids do with their white dolls, one might rephrase DuCille's question: what does the transference of intricate braids and cornrows onto
white dolls mean for the black children for whom these dolls are thought
to inspire lack of self-esteem?

Braids and the Blonde Doll

I have a photograph of Cherelle's younger sister, Clarice, sitting on the
front steps of their porch, next to her younger brother Joey. Joey seems to
look out from the photo (at me) with a skeptical, almost belligerent
glower. He holds a plastic toy in his hand as if to display it to me, the way
you might display a weapon. Clarice, more at ease, has a doll snuggled
on her lap. Against the dark color of Clarice's t-shirt, the doll's light skin
and blonde hair are blazingly white. The front section of the doll's long,

Joey and Clarice on their stoop.

silky hair is done up in braids, each held at the end with a small plastic barrette. Like the doll, Clarice has her hair in braids and, like the doll, the end of each braid is secured with a small plastic barrette.

The first thing one might notice about Clarice and her doll is that Clarice is black and her doll is white. But Clarice and her doll are also wearing their hair in almost identical ways. Several other Newhallville girls had dolls that, while white or white-like (One brown-skinned doll had platinum blond hair.) had distinctly un-white hairdos. What happens when you put a "black" hairstyle on a "white" head? When white baby dolls with cascades of long blonde hair have got that hair heavy with beads and foil, or tucked up into a braid-upon-braid 'do, what has happened to the boundary between white and black?

One obvious development is a sort of appropriation: the image that jumps to mind is Bo Derek in the movie *10*, jogging along a Caribbean beach in slow motion, her hair braided and beaded, a vapid smile on her face, her sleek Barbie-doll body the main plot element in the film. Derek's hairstyle sparked a sort of beachside cottage industry in the Caribbean, where (native) women and children scour vacation spots persistently trying to recruit people to get their hair braided as a sort of souvenir. What is happening between Newhallville kids and their dolls is not, however, directly analogous to what happens to kids on vacation in St. Croix.

The context in which heads get done matters tremendously, and so while perhaps overtly similar, these situations are not analogous primarily because the power relationships and conceptual boundaries between white and black are destabilized as Newhallville girls braid their dolls' hair. This destabilization is delicate, fleeting even, and is likely to have little social impact beyond the realm of these children's own personal spheres. In this way, what kids are doing with dolls is limited much as I have asserted that the self-esteem angle is also limited. Such destabilization is not even likely to have any real or lasting impact on these kids' living relationships with either white people or the idea of whiteness. It is worth noting, and worth analyzing, because what these girls are doing subtly works away at the constricted and constricting notions of the clarity of race that continue to dominate current discourse on the subject. It is a form of racial integration that for the most part has been unimagined by adult activists, scholars, politicians, or toy manufacturers. One of the primary differences between this precarious, temporary destabilization and the self-esteem work made possible by ethnically correct dolls is that the former is (as yet) not a commodity, though it is worked out on and through commodities.

In what way can the similar hairdos of Clarice and her doll seem like a challenge to the fixity of racial identity? Clarice, like a number of other girls I knew in Newhallville, does not appear to assume that just because her doll is white she must treat her that way. When deciding to do her hair, she gives her very white, very blonde, and very blue-eyed doll a hairstyle that is worn by young black girls. She does not put her doll's hair into a ponytail, or brush it over and over again just for the pleasure of feeling the brush traveling the long strands. Clarice was not alone in this: other girls' dolls had beads in their hair, braids held at the end with twists of tinfoil, and series of braids that were themselves braided together. In some sense, by doing this, the girls bring their dolls into their own worlds, and whiteness here is not absolutely defined by skin and hair, but by style and way of life. The complexities of racial reference and racial politics have been much discussed in the case of black hair simulating the look of whiteness; yet what these girls are creating is quite the opposite— white hair that looks black.

If one accepts that racial divisions are absolute and unbridgeable, what these girls are doing with their dolls makes little sense. Why put a black hairstyle on a white doll? And yet, if these dolls belong to these black girls, and live in the worlds they inhabit, how inflexibly white are they? Remember Asia and Natalia's ruminations on Barbie. Their comments most urgently pointed out that the main difference between them and the doll could be summarized with a nod to race, but really rested on the way they lived, the way they spoke. They wondered why there was no fat Barbie, no abused Barbie, no pregnant Barbie, and these criticisms apply as much to Shani as they do to any white dolls. What these girls are doing seems to recognize in multiple ways the socially constructed nature of race, the ambiguity of a racialized existence, and the flexibility of racialized expression: it is not always or only the color of their dolls that makes them hard to relate to or identify with. Their attention focuses both on appearance (hairstyle) and social factors. More than the bald recognition of racial difference, it is the social factors that seem to delineate the chasm for these girls between a doll to whom they can relate and in whom they can see themselves versus one who represents a whole world to which they cannot belong. Moreover, what these girls are doing emphasizes that they do not need to buy racial difference, or even to buy dolls that look like them; they can create dolls that look like them in fundamental ways through their own imaginative and material work.

The argument for the ethnically correct doll is often reduced to the maxim that children play better and feel better about themselves when they have dolls and toys that look like them. This assumption limits itself quite overtly to visual indicators of race and carefully evades questions of social difference and inequality that relate to class, economy, or region. For Newhallville kids, though, the equation was not quite so simple. They did not seem to accept wholesale the notion that they could not relate to dolls that were apparently a different race from themselves on that basis alone. Moreover, their interactions with these dolls do not seem to indicate that in giving attention—or even love—to white dolls that they are rejecting their own blackness as worthy of respect, attention, or love. Quite the contrary, in fact. These girls seem to be working in very complex and subtle ways to transform whiteness, to bring their white dolls into the existence they know and understand. They are not in these instances working to enter some fantasy world inhabited by Barbie and all her bourgeois accouterments, represented best of all, perhaps, by Barbie's dream house. These efforts bend notions of race without threatening to break them, but in this very bending demonstrate that the fixed ideas about racial difference that permeate ethnically

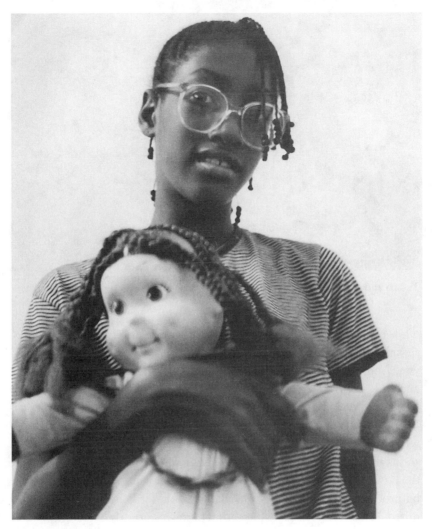

Shaquita and her doll.

correct toys as well as much public discussion are really more flexible than they may seem.

The girls' refusal to accept racial boundaries as absolute and unbridgeable spilled over into my relationships with them, since from the very beginning they were fascinated with my own waist-length "Barbie-doll hair." As I grew to know the girls better, they began to get their hands in my hair, styling it in ways that made me look better to them,

Tionna and Natalia with Tionna's doll.

while also demonstrating their nearness to me both physically and emotionally. Rather than my practical buns and messy ponytails, they'd yank and gel and twist my hair into sleek topknots with long, twirling curls just in front of each ear, or part my hair into five or six sections and braid each one. One rainy afternoon Nyzerraye spent five hours meticulously putting my hair into over sixty braids, their ends sealed closed with bits of aluminum foil that made a scratchy, musical sound when I shook my head. These girls were changing my head around on days like this, and when they had finished their creations and sent me into the bathroom to look at their work, it seemed that it wasn't quite me in the mirror. Their work of transformation here was not to rearrange my race or racial identity in some biological sense; nevertheless, they were working to make me more like them just as they did with their dolls.

Dolls and the Discussion of Race

Implicitly or explicitly, most contemporary discussions about dolls and race make reference to the landmark studies conducted in the 1930s and 1940s by the psychologists Kenneth B. Clark and Mamie Phipps Clark (Clark and Clark 1947, 1950). Although the Clarks used a number of techniques in their investigations, it is the doll studies that are invariably mentioned as their most striking work. In the doll studies, which were designed to understand the development of racial self-concept of Negro[8] children, the child was presented a white doll and a black doll, identical in every way except their color. Each child was asked a series of questions, including items such as "Which doll is the nicest?" The results were startling then and remain so now. The majority of Negro children preferred white dolls, thinking that they were "nicer" and "prettier," while they often pointed out the Negro doll as being "bad" or "ugly." By implication, the Clarks argued, this is just what Negro children thought of themselves: that they were bad and ugly. What the Clarks described as a poor self-image could easily be magnified, in their view, to self-hatred, underachievement, juvenile delinquency, and a host of other social ills and pathologies. The Clarks' conclusion was that although children's self-images needed adjustment and change, the key to effecting such change lay in transforming the society in which these children lived and grew, since that was the ultimate source of these attitudes.

Drafted into service in NAACP test cases against segregation in American society, Kenneth Clark testified in the lower courts as to the effects of segregation on school children. Clark argued that in a largely segregated society, different groups responded not to each other, but to inaccurate and lopsided stereotypes. Because whites lived primarily in their own insular society, as did Negroes in theirs, these inaccurate stereotypes remained largely unexamined. In such a situation, the Clarks emphasized, rapprochement was impossible. Moreover, they insisted black children were damaged by such a state of affairs, but white children suffered as well, since their own sense of well-being was dependent on being able to point to a whole race who were, by definition, more inadequate than they in any endeavor.

The event that really catapulted the Clarks' studies into the American popular consciousness was a footnote in the Supreme Court's celebrated case *Brown v. Board of Education*. The members of the Supreme Court had used Kenneth Clark's comprehensive survey of social science literature on the effects of prejudice on children "as a factual basis on which to rest its conclusion that segregation of white and Negro school children was a deprivation of the equal protection of the laws commanded by the Fourteenth Amendment" (Clark [1955] 1963, 143). Although the doll studies were never directly referenced in the *Brown* decision, and although the Clarks themselves felt that other methods (such as the coloring test) provided more nuanced information about the complexities of children's racial self-concept, it is the doll studies that continue to be remembered as the Clarks' connection to the watershed opinion.

With the *Brown* decision, the notion that separate and equal were compatible notions under the constitution was soundly rejected; the decision was one of the major turning points in the civil rights movement and held great promise, or so it seemed. Today, the doors that the *Brown* decision promised to open seem to be rusting on their hinges, and despite the illegality of government-supported segregation, public school systems across the nation have been largely unsuccessful at integration. In 1992 a suit was filed against the Hartford, Connecticut, schools arguing that the state had allowed a de facto segregation of school populations to arise, and that this could not be tolerated under the *Brown* decision. In the Connecticut governor's State of the State speech early in 1993, Lowell Weicker announced statewide restructuring of school bureaucracy, hoping to head off a court takeover of Connecticut schools. His speech all but acknowledged that the de facto segregation did indeed exist:

> Eighty percent of the state's minority students live in 18 urban school districts. Hartford public schools have a 92 percent minority population. Bridgeport is 86 percent, New Haven's 82. At the other extreme, 136 of 166 school districts have minority-student populations of less than 10 percent; 98 have minority populations of less than 5 percent. ("Segregation of Public Schools Threatens Connecticut's Future" 1993)

Despite Weicker's efforts, the schools were unable to accomplish desegregation: in 1996 the state court ordered the Hartford schools to alleviate the situation. While perhaps a telling example, Connecticut is hardly alone in its struggles with segregation. For many, the vision of an integrated society now often seems like a sugarcoated dream, and even the NAACP is showing some strain, being pressured by significant portions of its membership to back off its integrationist stance to support new versions of the separate but equal scheme. The language of social change has changed along with the strategies for accomplishing it. If integration and desegregation were the call to arms of the civil rights movement, self-esteem claims equal prominence in contemporary discussions of racial problems and their solutions.

The commodification of race and the racialization of commodities have come hand-in-hand with a turning away from the emphases of civil rights-oriented movements. Ethnically correct dolls neatly transform the Clarks' program of social transformation into a commodity aimed at influencing individuals. Thus, psychologists (Hopson and Hopson 1991) who replicated the Clark studies focus their attention on ways that parents can intervene in children's play to reinforce positive self-image, by noting that their children are beautiful or nice. Few could take issue with this suggestion, but social change as an equally important avenue through which to address the problem of systemic racism receives much less emphasis. In their book *Different and Wonderful: Raising Black Children in a Race Conscious Society,* the Hopsons write, "You do not want your child to grow up thinking that only White dolls, and by extension White people, are attractive and nice" (127). In contrast, the point that the Clarks made in their studies of children's self-concept was quite the opposite: that children chose the white dolls as being beautiful because they knew that whiteness was valued by the society at large.

The idea that children benefit by having a doll that "looks like me" to love and play with is not what I am criticizing here. The move away from insisting on massive restructuring of society to intensive remolding of self may stem, in part, from the successes of the civil rights movement: with many of the legal and social barriers to participation in American society at least lowered, if not (officially, at least) removed, more energy can be aimed at individual, rather than collective, needs. And yet this emphasis on issues such as self-esteem may also stem from the failures of the civil rights project. With affirmative action under attack and extensive restructuring of federal entitlement programs, the gains of the civil rights movement seem incremental at best. Lisa Sullivan writes that this problem is in many ways generational, and that "many believe that traditional Black leaders lack the capacity, desire, and ingenuity to address the contemporary crises that destabilize Black working-class life and destroy Black neighborhoods and families" (1996, 7). Whatever the cause, there is currently a greater emphasis on an inward attention to the destruction that racism can produce. Whereas the Clarks pointed to the larger society as the most problematic element in children's self-image, the problem has come to be seen as being located in the toys themselves: that is, interpretations seem to assert that minority children's self-image suffers in part because of the toys that they play with. A strategy that emphasizes the consumption of racialized commodities reverses the direction of causality from that suggested by the original Clark studies: it is now the toys that are culpable in shaping children's self-concept, not the society that produces them.

Manufacturers of ethnically correct dolls and toys argue that by producing culturally appropriate products children can purchase the tools of self-esteem. The way in which the relationship between a child and a doll can have an effect upon the child's relationship with the world at large remains especially fuzzy in toymakers' assertions about the value of these objects, often being summed up as "they have more fun when they play," as Olmec packaging states. If, as in Hartford, kids play with ethnically correct toys but attend racially and economically segregated schools, the consumption of racialized commodities seems unlikely to change children's perceptions of themselves or the world around them in any meaningful way.

Kenneth Clark closed the text of the report upon which the Supreme Court based the *Brown* decision with these words:

> Our society can mobilize itself to wage a dramatic and successful war against racial prejudice and its effects upon human beings. In doing so it will eliminate the situation where the prejudiced individuals are the ones who have higher status, and where they compel others to conform to their prejudices. A mobilization of the total society against prejudice will be successful to the extent that it gives moral, legal, and social status to unprejudiced individuals, making them unafraid to express their belief in decency and justice and to behave in accordance with their belief. (1955, 139)

While manufactured with consistent references to the work of the Clarks, and in particular their "doll studies," ethnically correct dolls embody a fundamentally different social project. The effort to manufacture racial diversity in the form of ethnically correct dolls is not in the end an effort to transform the assumptions and beliefs that dominate racial discourse. Far from being significantly transformed by the commodity diversity that ethnically correct dolls offer, the market has gone multicultural only insofar as store shelves can now boast themselves to be as surely segregated as are residential neighborhoods and school systems throughout the nation. As a result, market segmentation and the social barriers of race (and class) become mutually legitimizing and more deeply entrenched, and appear to be increasingly real and permanent, rather than less so.

Yvonne Rubie, president of the International Black Toy Association, was quoted as saying, "If children grow up with things that are like themselves, they will tend to like themselves or at least identify themselves with that positive image" ("New Boom in Ethnic Toys" 1993, 66). The most startling thing about this quote is Rubie's assertion that it is children's relationships with things rather than people that is most critically important for their sense of self. This understanding certainly fits in well with the emergence of an industry ready to supply the things kids need in order to have a "positive self-image" but neatly sidesteps the question of fundamental social, political, and historical issues that also impinge on children's experiences and hence their perceptions of themselves as people in the world. This shift is typical of makers of ethnically correct toys, but these assumptions are belied by what can be seen and heard among children from places like Newhallville. Kids like Carlos, Tionna, and Natalia are keenly aware of the complexity of race, seeing Native American ancestry in a Shani doll and class-based omissions in the personality of Barbie.

Adults tend to assume that the physical aspects of toys—their gender, skin tone, hair—determine how children will use and relate to them. Part of the impetus behind the move to introduce ethnically correct dolls to the marketplace is to provide children with toys that look like them and to which children can relate. The way kids use and think about toys is much more flexible—and critical—than adults often assume, however. What Newhallville girls said and thought about Barbie, for instance, indicates that ethnically correct dolls may not provide a solution to the problems embodied in these toys, which address the issue of race but not class. While diversifying the ethnic mix available at Toys-R-Us, Wal-Mart, and Target, ethnically correct dolls and their producers do not redefine the market itself as a sphere accessible to children of color who are also poor. In all fairness, companies like Olmec cannot reasonably do so and expect to remain economically viable. Nevertheless, it is unlikely that any of the 500,000 Kenya dolls sold by Tyco in 1992 ended up in Newhallville kids' homes.

These girls were not asking for dolls who looked like them; they were expressing the desire for dolls who lived like them and the kids they know in their neighborhood—people who get pregnant, experience abuse, and whose clothes and style are "dope" and "slammin'." Dolls from Mattel's Shani line, though "ethnically correct," still live lives fantasized about by the middle class of most any color. Olmec's Imani, decked out each year in a new, commemorative African-style outfit, was described this way in 1992 company materials:

> Spectacular in her gold trimmed gown, Imani is truly a Royal Princess in this outfit! The unique kente cloth fabric accents the African inspired cape design worn over a belted long sleeved jumpsuit. Her beautiful jeweled crown tops her fully rooted, long crimped hair. Imani's face has been resculpted to reflect more gorgeous features that little girls will love.

Natalia and Asia's request that they be given the opportunity to play with dolls who are like them not in looks, but in life, is more radical than the demand for equal opportunity representation of skin tones on the toy store shelf.

Similarly, many girls in the neighborhood played with their white dolls in ways totally unanticipated by the idea that white dolls limit black children's fantasies. These girls did not allow their dolls to remain white. From Cabbage Patch Kids with their yarn hair strung with beads and wrapped with foil to long-haired blonde dolls sporting intricately braided 'dos, white dolls in Newhallville were, over and over again, not quite recognized as such. They were still white, of course, and kids knew that, but the whiteness of the dolls did not stop girls from integrating them into their worlds. In so doing, these children failed to commemorate the boundaries of racial difference.

Manufacturers of ethnically correct dolls add selling appeal to their wares by embedding a social message in their products—the notion that these toys can help to correct social ills. In the case of ethnically correct dolls in particular, their benefits are metaphorically connected to civil rights issues such as enforced school segregation through references to the Clark doll studies. Yet, as these manufacturers have reminded me when pressed, they are businesses, not social service agencies. Their aim is to sell their products, not to distribute them in acts of charity. Their social conscience is a market-driven one—and one that sometimes drives them to contradict their own agenda in ways that, if not exactly startling, are worth noting.

The notion that the toybox is or should be a democratic space mirrors the commonly held notion that the consumer world is similarly democratic—a place and sphere of equal opportunity for anyone with a few bucks to spend. Makers of ethnically correct dolls do little to discourage this notion of the democratic marketplace, emphasizing instead the growing power of minority consumers as part of the buying public. For poor minority children, the entry of minority toys and toymakers into the industry has made little, if any, impact on their own toy collections or, for that matter, their self-esteem.

These children have diversified the social world their playthings represent in ways that are ultimately more radical than those proposed by the makers of ethnically correct dolls. In confronting the market itself as an exclusionary sphere, describing Barbie as "nice" to the public at large and then wondering why there is no abused or pregnant Barbie, these girls reject the notion that their "self-esteem" can be boosted through consumer items that address issues of race but not class. In making their white dolls live in black worlds, they similarly reconfigure the boundaries of race, which minority toymakers portray as being immutable. In so doing, these girls demonstrate and fashion an understanding of the social construction of not only their own blackness, but of whiteness as well. The more rigid understanding of race evidenced by toymakers is, in comparison, one based on notions of the fixity of genetics, an attempt to turn racism on its head but not an attempt to reimagine race itself. Toymakers have remolded their products, but not the parameters of the debate.

Conclusion

For Asia, shopping is infused with racism; for Tarelle, going to the corner store is at once an adventure in independence and a trial where the temptations and dangers of the drug economy must be negotiated; for Natalia, Barbie dolls are representatives of a world both foreign and hostile. In recognizing that these children's consumer lives are shaped by the same forces of social inequality evident in their neighborhood, educations, and even their life chances, my aim has been to highlight consumer culture as a terrain in which questions of social justice loom large. The deprivations experienced by children like those in Newhallville are deep and lasting and perhaps all the more poignant because they take place in such close proximity to wealth and comfort. More than a depoliticized cultural space in which people may choose to purchase or try on identities, fantasies, and styles, consumer culture is a medium through which multiple oppressions are brought to bear on people's lives in enduring and intimate ways.

The ethnography of consumption, then, needs to take into account more than the interactions between individuals and particular commodities, the specific moment of purchase, the malls and stores where shopping takes place. This is in part because consumption activities cannot be seen as being limited to these relatively obvious encounters; consumption begins well outside of the store and continues well after a given purchase has been made. Any particular act of consumption is a moment—a snapshot—taken at the confluence of complex social, political, and historical streams. Understanding these moments requires thinking about what is taking place within the relatively arbitrary frame (So-and-so is buying item x) as a prelude to investigation into the breadth of factors that brought that moment into being. This is why the data generated by the children's shopping trips only *begin* with the act of shopping. Newhallville children's reasons for seeking out particular items and their capacity for "spending my money wisely" are socially rooted in attempts to please caretakers, efforts to avoid the disappointment or anger of parents, the desire to share with siblings, and anticipation of the pleasures of gift-giving. These relationships, in turn, are shaped by the straitened economic circumstances of these families, circumstances ensuring that consumption is often for these children not a realm of unbridled fantasy, but rather one where fantasies must be reined in. This is not to say that questions of fashion or style, fad and fancy have no place in children's consumption. Such status items as Cross-Colours clothes and Nike sneakers were without doubt consistent objects of intense desire and scrutiny, coveted by some or lovingly cared for by others. But, as one young man pointed out in a group discussion at a neighborhood drop-in center, the emotional energy devoted to these possessions—or objects of desire—needs to be understood in its proper context. As he explained:

> White kids, they get things given to them. Their parents buy them a car, sneakers, they have everything. A black man, he has to work hard for what he gets, gold chains, sneakers. We don't have so many things. So when somebody comes along and steps on your sneakers, it's the same as if they went up to that other guy's brand-new Porsche and bashed it.

While white kids (among others) might debate the assertion that "they have everything," the important point made by this man is that people value the things they own, whether these are sneakers or Porsches. He urges us to remember consumer lives are not simply expressions of individual desire. In New Haven, these lives cannot be understood apart from such processes as urban renewal, deindustrialization, the drug economy, informal segregation, and public transportation, since these are the processes that have been critical in shaping the consumption horizons of the black community there.

One place where these processes are manifest is in geographic spaces, which are as important to consumption as are individual desires, likes, and dislikes. A racially charged downtown, a sexually threatening neighborhood, a local area thronged with liquor stores, storefront churches, and corner stores—these provide distinct geographic contexts for consumption within which multiple facets of identity are configured and reconfigured. Aside from providing children with different commodities to purchase or covet, these distinct geographic locations open up (and close off) various spaces for play, fears, and fantasies. Triumphantly slapped down on the counter in Asia's imagined rebuke of a judgmental cashier, a fifty-dollar bill can be unlike the sweaty handfuls of change the girls place on Bob's counter. The fifty-dollar bill is charged with racial conflict and the received humiliation of being thought to be poor; there is little or no shame in scraping together a pile of coins to buy cheese crackers at Bob's, where you can expect the black storekeeper to not only sell you snacks but to fill your ear with advice offered in the uncompromising tones of a strict grandfather.

This book has centered its attention on the ways in which consumption is implicated in the exercise of oppression and in responses to such oppression. Because much of the oppression operative in the consumer sphere is symbolic, much of this book has been generated in tension with stories told about the consumption of the poor and of racial minorities. I have endeavored to show in my analysis of consumption under slavery and the production of images of black pathological consumption, for instance, that such oppression is operative at both the symbolic and material levels, both of which have real and telling effects on people's lives. Such images and portrayals are an important element in the politics of consumption, a politics that portrays the consumption of the poor as being, on the one hand, problematic because they do not want enough and, on the other, dangerous because they want too much. Tales of constrained consumption are often used as examples to show why the poor cannot get ahead, and a lack of consumer desire is often seen as preventing the poor from attaining middle-class status. At the same time, we have the apocalyptic stories about the pathological consumption of the poor. Rather than not wanting enough, these poor people want too much. In this vein, terms like *compensatory consumption* surface with regularity. The beauty of this discourse is that whether consuming too little or too much, the supposed consumer orientation of the poor explains their poverty.

It must be remembered that these stories are tales mostly told by the privileged about the poor and working class. They are not the stories that the poor and working class tell about themselves. As such, they are artifacts of the power wielded in the cultural arena, where, as the proverb says, "Hunters will only remain heroes until lions begin writing history." On the one hand, these tales suggest that the poor are materially impoverished and that their imaginations lack richness. Alternatively, the implication is that the poor cannot or will not grasp the difference between fantasy and reality and, despite the real limits on their incomes, will do anything to acquire the goods they want. Without denying the grains of truth upon which such stories are based, I would like to suggest that there is an entire beach to travel between the grain at one end of this spectrum and the grain at the other. Presenting constrained consumption as a kind of irrational, primitive, and shrunken consumer desire trivializes the real limits within which the poor must attempt to provision their households, clothe their members, educate their children, and so forth. Families have a great deal at stake in instilling in their children such values as "spending my money wisely" and sharing resources among householders. Mastering these skills is, in fact, more realistic than it is fatalistic or irrational. Despite American mythological beliefs to the contrary, most of those who are born poor are likely to die poor, despite their best efforts to improve their economic and social status. Without spending their money wisely and teaching Natalia and her brother a thing or two about thrift, Natalia's elderly grandparents had hardly a hope of raising their two grandchildren on their income of $18,000 a year, despite the fact that they owned their modest home and grew vegetables on a good-sized plot alongside the house. As children revealed in their shopping trips, these are lessons they have learned well even at the age of ten. Rather than being at base a kind of limitation, this is an important form of social knowledge and cultural action, and they are skills that among the middle class would be viewed not as horizon-tightening but as signs of maturity and responsibility. Or perhaps not. Today, middle-class savings rates are the lowest in a century, consumer debt is reaching new heights, and middle-class consumption seems to be characterized by a general lack of fiscal responsibility.

Because consumption is at its root a social process, it is enmeshed with the full range of social action from positive, altruistic expressions to destructive and violent outbursts. The realm of consumption offers ample space for people to find profound meaning in their worlds and existence, to integrate (rather than fragment) a sense of self, and to utter or to perform commentaries about what they see and feel in daily living. Children in Newhallville often turned the consumer sphere to their own expressive and prosocial purposes, using shopping as a way to create connections to their family and friends, as a sphere of creative play, or a realm in which they could construct critical assessments of the world around them. The consumer lives of these children from Newhallville show the complex ways in which forces of ideology, hegemony, and power can be bent—if only temporarily—into the contours of a particular life. These children do not necessarily view racial boundaries (at least as embodied in their toys) as innate and firm, something made especially clear in their doings with their white dolls. But while putting braids on a blonde doll can bend the boundaries of race, and Carlos's comments about black Barbies can challenge the logic of racial categories, these are not commentaries that take place outside of the pressures exerted by the very racism and social inequality about which they speak. Neither do these commentaries, generated as they are by poor, young, marginalized kids, provide much hope of substantially transforming racism, sexism, economic inequality or the place of children in American society. But the meaningfulness and power of what these kids say and do should not be measured solely by their ability to transform a world that gives them only meager breathing space. The fact that these commentaries exist at all is a measure of their strength; the fact that they often exist briefly and subtly is a sign of their fragility. These moments are like pinpricks in a large piece of paper: invisible from a distance, but if you put your eye close upon it, you can get a pretty good view of what's on the other side. Tiny vistas opening onto possibility. Taking account of such tiny vistas has long been the work of anthropologists. Enlarging them is work for all of us.

Afterword:
The Return to the Scene of the Crime

When I was an undergraduate at New York University, my best friend and I decided to take an anthropology class together, a course on human evolution. In the large lecture hall, we felt invisible, and though we found the class interesting and engaging we liked to enliven the class hour for ourselves by creating imaginary scenarios through which our professor would travel. Invariably, we would imagine him clothed in a pith helmet and khaki shorts, tromping through the African savannah or the jungle. This image was especially ridiculous because our reserved professor was usually dressed in a turtleneck shirt, tweed jacket, and Frye boots, and the thought of him dressed in an outfit that would show his knees (which we imagined as very white and very knobby) would send us tumbling to the floor in not-so-silent giggles. He must have loved us.

Even in my first brushes with anthropology I had an idea of who the anthropologist was. I had absorbed the popular image of the anthropologist as intrepid (white, male) adventurer who strikes out into unknown lands among unknown peoples alone, armed only with a pencil and a notebook and, yes, dressed in a pith helmet and khaki shorts. This stereotypic anthropologist is then immersed among the new and unfamiliar smells, tastes, sights, and experiences of this "strange" culture and must learn in tiny increments at least some part of what it means to be a person in this place. In contrast to this image, but like a growing number of ethnographers, I (female, half white and half Chinese) struck out into old and familiar territory: rather than coming home from the field, I went home to do my fieldwork. When I describe my field site, I jokingly juxtapose the popular image of the anthropologist-adventurer with the apparent mundane familiarity of the site, calling my field location "exotic New Haven, Connecticut."

The resonance of this chapter's title is multiple. Because I myself grew up in New Haven I often referred to the research as the "return to the scene of the crime," meaning, the scene where my childhood took place. For me, the crimes to which the title alludes are painfully funny in a brittle sort of "ha, ha, ha" way. Many of these experiences were, at least in their basic outlines, not particularly far removed from those of the children I knew in Newhallville: an absent father, a long stint on welfare, and a family crisis that left my mother hospitalized and my brother and me in separate, informal fostering situations for more than a year. Paradoxically, I cannot claim that these experiences give me special insight into the lives of the children I knew in Newhallville, primarily because despite the outward similarity of these factors individually or all together, my class position and racial identification (voluntary or otherwise) laid out a territory radically different in terms of past experience and future effects. In summoning my own childhood experiences as a resonator to my fieldwork as the return to "the scene of the crime," my aim is not to show that I have suffered and survived but to underscore that social context makes a world of difference. The poverty and family disintegration I experienced are only similar to that of the Newhallville kids I knew at the level of raw statistics—in other words, the same "crimes" (an absent father, for instance) only become fully intelligible in the context of the different "scenes" in which they took place.

As a child growing up in New Haven, I was relatively privileged, despite an often-disordered family life. Most of the kids I went to school with were children of Yale professors or well-to-do business people, but their economic privilege did not mean their lives did not also include alcoholic and abusive parents, absent family members, plenty of drugs. In other words, every dysfunction in the book. This chaos was buffered by many factors, allowing troubled middle- and upper-class kids to be sent to the dreaded fifth floor of the Yale Psychiatric Institute—which we all called "YPI"—rather than juvenile detention, and also allowing abusive middle- and upper-class parents to go unchallenged by state intervention. During my fieldwork I found myself on more than one occasion interviewing mothers in Newhallville who had attended the same public high school that a number of my girlhood friends had attended, but without having attended any of the same classes. My girlhood friends are today doctors, lawyers, writers, entrepreneurs—all highly educated and well paid. In contrast, their schoolmates who remain in Newhallville are high school dropouts or never made it to college; they are sporadically employed, work as home health aides or not at all; many became mothers in their early teens. The high school attended by my friends and those who became my research subjects was and remains internally segregated, with classes divided by academic level, neatly overlapping with social class and to a great extent, race. Thus, New Haven itself is a crime scene, the site of historic and continuing segregation, racism, and social inequality. It is a scene that enables other levels of social crimes, in this case the ability to utterly avoid entire worlds that are enmeshed, nevertheless, with one's own.

Implicit in anthropology's valorization of the ethnographer's role in demystifying "other" cultures is the mastery of the strange and the domestication of wildness. These issues are more complex when doing fieldwork at home, and particularly when doing fieldwork not only at "home" in the most generalized sense—that is, in one's own culture (however that may be defined)—but in the same place that you call home, the very house, the very neighborhood, the very town. The argument against working "at home" is that the familiarity will dull the ethnographer's senses of observation, perception, and critique. This argument, of course, is only partially correct, as Delmos Jones has pointed out (1970). Being an outsider does not guarantee a lack of blind spots, and being an "insider" can sensitize a researcher to important subtleties that might otherwise be missed. In addition, despite the fact that New Haven was where I grew up, I did not grow up in Newhallville. The cultural and social barriers erected by various forms of segregation and isolation make even closely related communities nearly strangers to one another and despite common reference points—language, city landmarks, television shows—the world I encountered in Newhallville was not "home" for me. When I returned to work in Newhallville, I entered a New Haven that I had only dimly known existed, and had seen only as a passing vista from the window of a moving car. I had been much like the elderly ladies in the passing blue sedan whom Tionna assaulted with her shout, and people seemed to ask me, "What are you looking at?"

A key experience came outside of my formal fieldwork. Early on in my return sojourn to New Haven, I joined a local dance company that specialized in pan-African styles. The group was headed by Kym, a black woman about my age who had grown up in the Dixwell area of New Haven. The company had an on-and-off roster of about six dancers and three drummers, all of whom were juggling jobs, families, and children with rehearsals and performances. As a child in New Haven I had intensively studied ballet, a discipline for which I was not well suited, despite my determination to be a ballerina. For my first dance performance in the ten years since I'd quit intensive dance training, I was to dance with Kym and two other members of the group at a medium-security prison in Enfield, Connecticut.

The prison was a series of two- and three-story buildings that ringed a grassy compound area, which we could glimpse from the front entrance through a heavy lattice of wire studded with barbs and razors. We performed in the building's gym on a bitterly cold winter night. We dancers were the only women in the entire compound, and our attendant guards kept protectively near. We had to change clothes in an unheated and unprivate bathroom area, the drummers and guards turning their backs. Through the window in the door that led from the "weight room" to the gym, we could see that the bleachers were filling up with men, all wearing what could have been gas station attendant uniforms: dark blue pants and shirts. Kym and I waited for the performance to begin perched on the sit-up bench, our bare feet hovering above the cold cement.

After the performance, guards stood between us and the bleachers to prevent the inmates from having any contact with us, and the men were hustled out of the building and into their sleeping quarters. As we were leaving, we walked past the prisoners' barracks. It was dark outside, but the barracks buildings, where the men had been shut in, were lit from within. They could open the casement windows with a crank. With the light behind them, we couldn't see the men's faces, and the outlines of the men were traced in black against the windows. We walked among their shadows cast into the yard. Some waved to us, high-spirited and jokey, but many were shouting to Kym and the drummers in a completely different tone. One called to Kym, asking after a friend's mother, and Kym shouted back, "She's still in the hospital. She's still in a coma."

Every now and then an arm or a hand would be thrust outside of the crack in a window, reaching out toward us. Kym and Andre and Hal were a glimpse of home and those men were reaching for it. But the guards had to hustle us away—and though I was at that point eager to go, the others came away more slowly. Kym and the others were walking away from a lively, vital piece of their community, fruit fallen too far from the tree.

The experience at Enfield Prison helped me to begin to understand that the Newhallville neighborhood that seemed to be so isolated in so many ways was, in other ways, a community deeply connected to sometimes distant people and places. The hundreds of men in this single prison were an important element of people's family lives, part of a dynamic that involved the regular movement of people in and out of Newhallville itself. Going to prison was one way in which people might physically move out of the community and, like other hard-hit areas of New Haven, the gaps felt in Newhallville by those absent in this manner were profound.

Tensions with the police, not surprisingly, were one aspect of the prison dynamic in Newhallville. This included a hefty suspicion of outsiders, and in my early months in Newhallville that suspicion was extended to me. My rule from the beginning was this: do one brave thing a day. In the beginning, a brave thing might constitute making an appointment to speak with someone or introducing myself to someone new in the neighborhood. As the fieldwork progressed and I knew more people and had become welcome in some families' homes, I found myself having to force myself into new situations less and less; the situations found me. I felt terribly awkward and shy as I started my fieldwork, and these feelings never quite went away. Some of these feelings were purely personal, but I was also acutely aware of the inequities of conducting this kind of fieldwork, and that the investment of time I was asking from kids and their families was, in essence, their donation to my professional advancement. I felt then and still feel that it takes a lot of nerve to ask relative strangers to make that kind of investment. These tensions were exacerbated by the often unhappy relationship between Newhallville residents and Yale University, as New Haven has served as a sort of living laboratory for university students for more than a century. Many Newhallville residents resent this state of affairs openly and vehemently. On more than one occasion, I was directly confronted with the question, "Are you from Yale?" When I answered no, the response was, more often than not, "Good! Then I'll talk to you." However, my not being from Yale did little to change the power dynamics of the relationships I forged in Newhallville: various foundations, including the government, had given me the money to study the people who lived there, I was free to leave the community whenever I chose, and despite my attempts to become a fixture in the neighborhood I was a movable, temporary presence there.

I stuck out like a sore thumb. Especially in the first few months, I felt as if I might as well be walking down the street in a clown suit (or an anthropological pith helmet and khaki shorts), even though my relatively modest uniform consisted of jeans and a t-shirt. The problem wasn't so much my clothes but my obvious status as an outsider. Some people thought I was an undercover police officer for a while, others pegged me as a clueless Yale student, and others didn't know what to make of me.

Newhallville is a neighborhood where few people who do not live there can be found walking on the street—its reputation as a dangerous and unpredictable area has most outsiders who must drive through the area doing that driving fast, with the windows shut tight and the doors locked. Even teachers who are in the neighborhood every day rarely stray from the enclosure of the school grounds. I walked everywhere, an act that was meant to convince myself as much as others that I belonged. As I walked to the school every day, I made sure to say hello to every person that I passed. In the mornings these people were often waiting for the bus to go to work, and in the afternoon it was parents waiting for children to come home, elderly people watching the sights from their stoops, or knots of young men selling crack and marijuana. Initially, my greetings were usually met with surprised silence, but after a few weeks, people started responding, sometimes with a wave or a comment about my pink Converse sneakers, sometimes an invitation to sit down and watch passersby, sometimes an offer of a soda or a beer. My presence in the neighborhood began to be part of the regular routine, for me and for the people I greeted on my walks. Saying "hi" was my secret weapon, and I deployed it each and every day that I was in Newhallville.

It seemed a simple enough thing to do, walk through the neighborhood and say "hi" to everyone, not even stopping to talk most of the time. In the beginning, it fit into my "one brave thing a day" rule, but as time went on, I realized that saying "hi" was in its own way a profound sort of gesture. In a scene like that presented by New Haven, where informally maintained boundaries separate communities with an amazing effectiveness, people also maintain those boundaries in important ways. One of the most important is to pretend that people outside their own familiar worlds just do not exist. We all have done it when walking down the street, particularly if we're urbanites: not looking people in the eye as they come toward us down the sidewalk, or carefully adjusting one's stare to indicate that the people around you are physically there but socially unimportant: they don't exist. Saying "hi" to people changes this dynamic and is an acknowledgment of at least a potential social relationship, a sharing of space if not community. For people who have gotten used to being routinely ignored on the street, in schools, in stores—except as potential instigators of trouble—this kind of acknowledgment can be startling, but I found that my greeting was always effective. At first, I'm sure that people indulged me the way they do the mildly insane, but this is hardly an unfamiliar position for most ethnographers who have to develop the art of asking the insanely stupid question. When the children at the Shelton Avenue School realized that I was indiscriminately greeting everyone I passed on my way to and from their school, however, they took me under their wings, to give me the benefit of their greater knowledge and experience of the place.

Early on, the children at Shelton Avenue School began to protect me from what they viewed as my recklessness, shepherding me through the neighborhood after school to the border marked by Prospect Avenue, at the top of the hill that descended down to the East Rock neighborhood, where I lived. Although I never encountered any threatening situations, and generally felt comfortable and safe, the kids steered me away from certain street corners, groups of people, and whole areas of the neighborhood, and in so doing led me into an experience of the neighborhood that was shaped by their own sense of safety, danger, pleasure, and excitement.

One of the benefits of my return to the scene of the crime was that I was able to activate networks of friends and fictive kin who were decisive in allowing my research to go ahead smoothly, and who consistently funneled me important bits of information, particularly about local politics and the school system. One such person was an administrator in charge of elementary schools, and it was she who pointed me toward the Shelton Avenue School, where I did my research. This was a decisive event, since I had actually planned to conduct my research in an entirely different part of the city. The main activity in my initial months of fieldwork was running an oral history project as part of an afterschool program, an activity that gave me an intelligible identity to the kids and their families. As far as they were concerned, I was Miss Chin, the teacher, although as I mentioned in the introduction, the children never were fooled that I was *actually* the kind of teacher they had to mind, the way they had to hop to it when Lucy Aslan called them to order or called them onto the carpet. During the summer my status mysteriously would metamorphose into that of "camp counselor."

Acquiring this sort of identity was both a blessing and a curse. Being thought of (by the adults, at least) as a teacher was helpful in that it made parents and caretakers feel they could trust me to take care of their children, and that I had the kids' best interests at heart. It was only after I was informally given the title of "teacher" that families began to open their homes to me. However, from the perspective of caretakers, my being a teacher placed me within the institutional structure of the school, which was itself an arm of the state. While all the families were firm believers in the benefits of schooling, many had dropped out in elementary, junior, or high school, and only one or two had been to college.

Schools were, for many, threatening foreign places. A consultant working with teachers at the school attempted to illustrate to them the ways in which their policies worked to alienate families who already had a tenuous relationship with the school. He asked them whether they required parents and caretakers to sign in when they came into the school. "Of course," the teachers answered. "Why?" he asked them. One teacher explained in grave tones that a few months ago a man had entered another school with a loaded gun and shot a teacher. "Let me tell you something," the consultant responded. "Nobody who comes into the school to shoot someone is going to sign in first."

With teachers mandated to report on suspected child abuse, relations between caretakers and school personnel were additionally strained. Many of those raising school-aged children had been reared in the South, in an atmosphere where punishment involved a swift switch, not a time-out. While families understood that physical punishment was not acceptable and could result in their family's dissolution, many caretakers did not know what else to do when they needed to discipline children. They felt that the rules had been changed on them, but that the new rules were somehow secret. This left families wary of confiding problems to teachers and often unwilling to open their homes to those who, once they got their foot in the door, were likely to create havoc in their lives. This sense of danger was so pervasive that a common threat to children who misbehaved was that if they didn't calm down the "state" was going to take them away.

My delicate task with caretakers was to hang on to the goodwill generated by being thought of as a teacher while distancing myself from the institutional shadow of the school system itself. I did this by selectively doing things that were very un-teacherly: playing around with the kids, and refusing to discipline them except in cases of obvious danger; visiting people in their homes and eating meals with them; continuing to walk around the neighborhood both day and night.

The Shelton Avenue School and the Oral History Project

The problems I have outlined above in terms of school-community relations are common in urban settings such as Newhallville. In fact, because the school's principal was exceptionally charismatic and compelling, parent participation in school events and even in classrooms was impressively high. Carlos's mother, who was unable to work and on disability, often spent part of her afternoons in the classroom helping Lucy Aslan with various tasks. Other parents sought jobs as classroom aides, or took part in fairs, cleanups, and school trips.

The school was unusually progressive and was making use of a number of compatible educational philosophies. It was a Comer Model school, which was run by a school-based management committee, although one that sometimes chafed under the supervision of an unusually outspoken and charismatic principal. The classrooms with which I worked during 1991–93 were part of what was called the "constructivist" wing of the school, a series of classrooms, grades one through five, that had won a special grant to run a coordinated effort, using constructivist educational methods. Among other things, these methods emphasized small group learning, cooperative classroom experiences, and the use of centers, all techniques aimed at allowing children to enter actively into educating themselves and each other. As luck would have it, then, the school shared my own commitment toward the kinds of interaction and learning it wanted to foster among children, and between children and adults. It was a wonderful atmosphere to enter into and vastly different from other schools in similar communities. Many urban public schools are simply too overwhelmed by shortages in resources and personnel to integrate a researcher into their daily routines. At the Shelton Avenue School, however, I was able to become part of kids' daily school life.

One of my primary goals was to involve children, actively, as fellow researchers. I had several reasons for this, among them that I wanted them to get something out of participating in the project. More than this, though, I wanted them to understand what it is we were doing, and I wanted them to understand what anthropology is from the inside out, as researchers, not just research subjects. I had also made my entrance into the community via the neighborhood elementary school and wanted to integrate my research, as much as possible, into children's educational experience. These multiple goals and efforts were sometimes at odds with each other, and on occasion my commitment to making the research educationally relevant for the kids took up such enormous amounts of my time and energy that I was resentful. In the end, these efforts "paid off" better than I could have imagined.

Doing fieldwork with children poses unique challenges, to put it mildly. Despite the emphasis on participant observation, anthropological methods are heavy on talk. Long, rambling oral history or informational interviews are de rigueur in the discipline and yet entirely inappropriate for ten-year-olds, especially those I knew. In Newhallville I found there was no surer way to render chatty kids suddenly monosyllabic than to directly engage them in conversation. Some of this was cultural: this was a place where rangy conversations between adults and children were quite uncommon; what worked better was to engage kids in activity and then start talking.

One of my most important activities during my research was conducting an oral history project with two groups of children. The oral history project was undertaken as part of a citywide program called the Extended Day Academy, an afterschool program consisting of a number of classes ranging from art, music, and theater to leadership groups, computer classes, academics, and substance abuse prevention. The basic goal of the oral history project was for children to design, conduct, and analyze interviews of adults in their neighborhood, centered around the topic of what the community was like when they were young. The group of ten children met two afternoons a week for an hour during the spring of 1992. During that semester's work, the group learned about basic concepts and terminology in anthropological research (the first term being "anthropologist") and went on to write, pretest, and conduct oral history interviews throughout their community. Over the summer I transcribed the taped interviews. In the spring of 1993 I met with students again as part of the afterschool program. Because the second half of the project took place in a new school year, the group was almost entirely different, and their number had reduced to six. However, since our task in the second half was to analyze the data and write a report, having new children work on the project proved workable. In the next few sections, I go into great detail about conducting this part of my work. This detail is necessary especially since little has been written about the complexities of conducting anthropological research with children, much less the possibilities for bringing children into the discipline as researchers themselves.

Ten-year-olds as Researchers

For kids to be successful with this kind of work, they need to understand what they are doing. They must have a basic vocabulary that they share and can use, they must have a "toolkit" of ideas, concepts, and methods that they likewise share. In this, adult researchers are no different, but the complexity and scope of the work, concepts used, and so on, are understandably different. Although I controlled much of the process in that I set the schedule, introduced key ideas, and organized the final questionnaire (among other things), group decisionmaking and teamwork were a daily part of the process as we conducted the research, analyzed data, and wrote the report. In my view, it is more important to use simplified concepts and methods that children fully understand than it is to use more complicated methods and ideas that children make use of or participate in only partially. As children master and gain confidence about new materials, they often are able to move themselves onto higher levels of conceptual complexity.

There is no doubt that this method of working took more time than either simply doing the research myself, or having the children administer a preprepared questionnaire. However, in either case, the kids would have learned and understood a great deal less about the project and its relationship to their lives, and thus had more difficulty imagining how to use the skills and information independently. While it was necessary that they learn some basic concepts of social science, deciding how much they needed to know and what level of sophistication their understanding of these concepts should be was difficult. In addition, presenting a complex notion like that of "hypothesis" was something that often could take the entire hour. The challenge, then, was to plan enough time to introduce relevant concepts, develop ways to make learning and understanding both accessible and engaging, and to move the work along so that it could be completed before the end of the school year, all the while making sure that the project remained primarily the product of the kids' work, not my own. Stressing that we were a research team was an important element of each day's activities and even small responsibilities like cleaning the board meant that each kid felt important to the ongoing process of our research. Children had special tasks to accomplish each day or special responsibilities. These might include setting out or cleaning up the snack, passing out photocopied sheets, taking notes, collecting finished papers, and so on. Each child also had his or her own work folder, and we quickly established a routine where we would eat our snacks together, clean up, and then move on to the folders to begin the day's work.

We began each session with a fifteen- to twenty-minute snack time (milk and cookies) where kids could eat, relax, and chat with each other or with me. Snack was important in part because kids needed some transition and free time before we got down to work. This would be the case for any kids this age, but was especially important at Shelton Avenue School because children had no recess period during their school day, either indoors or outdoors. At school since 8:30 in the morning, by 2:30 in the afternoon they were practically bursting out of their skins with pent-up energy. The snack time was also useful because even though the program was for an hour, realistically, the concentration period for a ten-year-old who has already had a full day of school is reaching its limit at forty-five minutes—especially when the work of the oral history project was often less manifestly "fun" than something like art or sports. However, snack time was hardly unproductive and this time eventually proved to be an especially important period to listen to children's ideas about themselves and the world around them. One afternoon, for instance, children's casual conversation veered toward their sense of constant endangerment in their neighborhood and their fierce protectiveness of their mothers. I wrote in my field notes that day:

> Brandy suddenly announced, early on, that she had a dream last night where a man came into her house and started choking her mother. "So then I got a gun and shot the man," Brandy said, in the most matter-of-fact way. The conversation then focused on how each child would protect his or her mother if she were in danger. Brandy said she'd do anything she had to, saying that her mother wasn't married, was a single parent, and that if something happened to her mother she wouldn't have anyone to take care of her. This also was delivered in a matter-of-fact fashion. Darla then added that she would get a knife— no—she corrected herself, she would get a big butcher knife. Charles also said he'd get a big butcher knife and sharpen it up, and kill whoever it was. "And then I'd go to kid jail," he said, with that round-cheeked, bright-toothed grin that he's got. Until now, Tionna, whose mother *had* been killed by intruders, had been coloring and playing with another girl, as if the conversation was not taking place and even if it was, as if she were paying no attention to it. "No, you wouldn't," she piped up. "You'd go to juvenile hall." "Yeah, juvenile hall," Charles said. "My cousin is in jail," he added, as if placing a cherry atop an ice-cream sundae.

These discussions clued me into some of the personal issues being faced by children, and these issues had a clear effect on their progress at school, their ability to concentrate, their approach to interpersonal relationships, and their work on the oral history project. My experience in their classrooms had already provided me with some idea about their reading, writing, and critical skills. These were bright, energetic, and fun kids, but they also presented a range of abilities typical to the social and economic conditions of their community: some had terrible trouble writing, others were desperately shy, others had math skills that were abysmally low.

Concepts had to be introduced in ways appropriate to the group's developmental level, and in a way that was engaging and fun, as well as lasting. In introducing the idea of the hypothesis, one of my first tasks was getting the kids to pronounce what they found to be a tongue-twister-y word with ease. My basic explanation of the meaning of the word *hypothesis* was that it is a kind of guess that scientists make: it's their idea about what a solution to a particular problem might be. To give kids a concrete idea, I started the group off with a science-like example: "What do you think steam is made of?" Kids provided a number of wild guesses: "Air?" asked one. I asked them what happens when you hold something over steam, and they answered that it gets wet. "So," I said, "what do you think steam is made of?" "Water!" they shouted. "That's your guess, that's your *hypothesis*, that steam is made of water." This process had taken fifteen minutes.

Moving children into connecting this notion to the research they were doing took the remaining half hour, during which the idea of hypothesis had to continually be reintroduced and reinforced—as it was during the ensuing weeks of research. First, I asked them what kind of people we were planning to interview in the project. Grown-ups, they answered. And what are we asking them about? After some discussion, we agreed that our larger purpose was to ask them about their childhoods and what the neighborhood was like then. The next step was for kids to offer ideas about what we might find out, and each of these was written on the board:

The world was better then.

That the world was worse.

That the HIV thing wasn't out.

That there weren't drugs.

That there weren't drug dealers.

No dirty bums.

There was no drinking and driving.

No killing people.

No rap songs.

Looking at the list, I asked the group what they thought these ideas had in common. Moving kids of this age from the specificity of their observations to a generalized idea can be difficult, and guidance—often in the form of leading questions—is really important. After some discussion, I asked the group, "From what we have on the board, do you think things were the same when today's grown-ups were kids?" "No!" they answered. "So what is your *hypothesis*, what is your guess? That the world was ____?" "Different!" came the answer.

As a basic hypothesis, "the world was different when grown-ups were young" may not seem all that sophisticated. However, it is a workable hypothesis and, more important, one that children could grasp clearly and completely. In all phases of the research, it was attaining a clear and complete grasp of concepts, procedures, and information that was most important. From that base, children were able to elaborate their ideas according to their tastes and abilities and many were able to move their own work on to higher levels of interpretation and analysis or even to apply their skills and knowledge in other settings.

Developing the Questionnaire

Early in the term I had the kids fill out what I called the "sneaker survey," a short questionnaire with different types of questions related to sneaker brands, advertisements, and their opinions. The purpose of the survey was twofold: it gathered some preliminary data for my larger research project, and it served as the basis for discussions in which children were introduced to basic questionnaire design and evaluation. While the children all had a hazy idea of what an interview was, and that the purpose of the project was to actually interview people, they had no real framework for thinking about what questions to ask, why, how to ask them, or how an interview ought to be structured.

The "sneaker survey" provided kids with a hands-on tool for learning about many of these ideas, even though it was a questionnaire and not an interview: it was easy to read and it was a topic upon which they had many opinions. I had included close-ended and open-ended questions on the survey, to prepare kids for discussion of kinds of interview questions. There were also different kinds of open-ended questions, aimed at showing kids that even open-ended questions can elicit a range of information; in other words, some open-ended questions are more open than others.

Ten-year-olds are tactile and mobile, and often the best way to try to understand complicated ideas was to involve their voices or bodies. In illustrating the difference between open-ended and close-ended questions, I had them demonstrate with their hands whether a question was open- or close-ended. Likewise, when we moved on to evaluating different open-ended questions, they showed with their hands whether they thought the question was likely to elicit a lot of information (hands held far apart) or only a little (hands held close together). Other tactics along these lines included playing hangman, using colored paper and pens for different tasks, and illustrating ideas with pictures.

We had early on established the general gist of the interviews, that they would be about "what the world was like when you were young," but developing the questions for the actual interviews required that kids get more specific with their questions—their open-ended questions. In the initial phase, I broke children down into groups to generate questions and provided them some general categories if they were having trouble thinking of what to ask: games, school, clothes, friends, music. I purposefully kept the parameters vague, because I did not want to unnecessarily limit kids' ideas about what a good question might be. After a few sessions of generating questions and probes (why is that?), I organized the questions into categories, and included about five questions of my own. The bulk of the interview, however, had been generated entirely by the children themselves (the entire interview is contained in appendix B). The interview also included a separate section on demographic information. I chose not to introduce the concept "demographic" to the group, but instead discussed the importance of "background information," and over the course of two sessions children developed the background information section of the interview. The introduction to the interview was also written by one of the children and reflects the emphasis that was given to presenting children's own writing, rather than cleaning up every single grammatical glitch, or substituting more common social science phrases:

> This interview is about your childhood. All the question we asked are going to be private. If there are any questions you can not answer please just don't. But we would appreciate it if you could answer all of the questions.

Conducting Interviews

The research group conducted several practice interviews with adult visitors, group interviews with the school's principal and the city's mayor, and individual interviews with friends and family at home. The practice interviews were essential for giving kids the opportunity to get familiar with the questions, to reword them if necessary, and to gain ease in managing reading questions, processing responses, and asking probes when necessary. In the first practice session, an adult visitor was interviewed by the group as a whole, with kids asking one question at a time. I would stop them occasionally, pointing out where they could probe further, asking for more information or clarification. In the second practice session, three visitors came, and each visitor was interviewed by a small group of three or four kids; I circulated, giving children guidance and suggestions when needed. Afterwards, the groups reported back to each other on what they had learned. When the school's principal and the city's mayor came for interviews, the team of child researchers conducted the work independently, while I took photos, giving children assistance only when they asked for it.

During group interviews, each child had an assigned job in addition to asking questions for the interview. These responsibilities kept the kids working as a team and engaged each child actively in the research. Jobs included working the tape recorder, labeling the tapes and making sure I got the tapes at the end of the interview, taking notes, checking off the questions as they were asked, asking the background information questions. Children took their responsibilities very seriously. Charles, for instance, took ten and a half pages of notes during one of the group interviews.

After the series of group interviews, children were well prepared for conducting interviews independently at home. I prepared interview kits that consisted of a plastic bag containing a small tape recorder, tapes, extra batteries, a copy of the interview, and a pen. Children checked out the kits and returned them to me at an assigned time. Despite teachers' and parents' fears to the contrary, they were extremely conscientious about taking care of these materials and not one tape recorder was lost or damaged. One minor problem was that a few tapes were returned with the interviews, followed by (1) child singing popular songs into the tape recorder; (2) conversations (usually silly) between kids on the tape recorder; or (3) recordings made from local radio stations. These additional "recordings" had no impact on the interviews themselves and were often highly entertaining. The children completed a total of seventeen interviews during the first phase of the research.

Analyzing the Data

Analyzing the data and writing the report were probably the most difficult parts of the project. The conceptual tasks were entirely new for the kids, and figuring out how to find a way for the children to take charge of the material was very difficult. The work honed in on children's anxieties as well, since many had trouble reading and writing or doing math—all skills required in this stage of the research. I divided the six children who worked on data analysis and writing into pairs to work together. Each pair was provided with a full set of the interviews, and I highlighted the sections relevant to their work. We focused on coding each section, making bar graphs representing the findings, and then figuring out how to interpret them. This process took several weeks, and children needed an enormous amount of guidance and attention. The critical element here was breaking their tasks down into doable chunks, since envisioning either the entire process (data to written report) or the final product was impossible for them.

Writing the Report

To assist kids in writing their section of the report, I had them break the task down into smaller jobs, writing short sentences in answer to specific questions. I developed a form that led them into the writing process by answering a series of questions and then stringing the answers together to form a paragraph. The children already had classroom experience with writing, editing, and rewriting in "writer's workshop," and I used the language and methods of that process in the handouts and forms for report writing.

Several children were extremely uncomfortable with writing and, while able to verbally articulate their ideas and observations, could not seem to write them down coherently. In these cases (about three children) I took them through the writing form in a conversational way, asking the questions face to face and having children tell me their answers, which I wrote down verbatim. Armed with their own written-down words, children could then edit and rewrite their answers into smooth prose. This was, I believe, the single most important technique I used that allowed the report to get written.

Each section of the report was based around a bar graph that presented the basic findings of the group in relation to a specific section of the report. The classroom computers did not have a program that allowed kids to make these graphs. One day, a volunteer art teacher took the children aside and had them make large versions of their graphs for display during presentations. I scheduled a special time for each pair to come to my home to make their graphs on the computer to be included in the written report. Both in making the colorful and oversized versions of their graphs and in coming to my home to make them on the computer, kids were allowed to engage in a special activity that allowed them to really see a payoff for their work to that point. They were both activities that involved fun, and something special (Shelton Avenue School had no art program). Inclusion of these kinds of fun yet productive diversions is really central to this kind of work, not only for the kids, but for adult facilitators!

We met regularly as a whole group to share progress and to read each other the developing reports. In these sessions, children could pose questions, ask for clarification, and also see the kinds of progress being made by their peers. When the reports were well on their way, we also presented the report to Lucy Aslan's entire classroom. During the question-and-answer period that followed, the student researchers were able to see where their information was not clear, or where they needed to re-work ideas. This practice session also made the work seem much more real to them, as we were going to be presenting the work to the Ph.D. program in anthropology at City University of New York, where I was a student.

Presenting the Findings

Our first presentation was, as I have mentioned, to Lucy Aslan's class, where the children were students. One thing this first presentation illustrated to the kids was that they were in many ways still unprepared and the report was unfinished. It was a hard lesson for the kids, but almost unavoidable, since the report was unlike anything they'd done before and it was hard for them to gauge the quality or completion of their work. Presenting their report to the class made it clear that there was still a way to go. Because we were presenting to the class, however, and to their teacher, there was an element of comfort that kids were not like-ly to have in our other two presentations: one to the City-Wide Parents and Teachers' Organization meeting, and another to the faculty and students in the Ph.D. program at the City University of New York Graduate Center.

Along with Cherelle's grandmother, the children and I took the Metro-North commuter train into New York City the day of the presentation. Although the children were hardly fazed by the illustrious audience they had garnered, I was pleased and terrified to see Vincent Crapanzano, Eric Wolf, Leith Mullings, Gerald Sider, Delmos Jones, and Jane Schneider (among others) sitting expectantly in their seats when the presentation was ready to get under way. I have had few experiences more satisfying than the opportunity of seeing the faculty of the Graduate Center at the mercy of a group of ten-year-old researchers. Seated at a table in the front of the room, the children looked hardly any different from any array of experts that might have also occupied those chairs in front of the same microphones. The children presenting their portion of the report went to the podium, taking with them the large charts and displays they had made to accompany their discussion of the data and information. They fielded questions like pros, calling on those with upraised hands with an ease that belied their nervousness.

Unexpected Developments

By the fall of 1992 I was working very closely with fifth-grade teacher Lucy Aslan, who was looking for a way for more children to be involved in the kind of work I was doing with the oral history group. Together with another classroom teacher and the school's custodian (who had a high level of involvement in classroom learning!) we developed a four-week workshop on advertising in which over one hundred children would participate. Each of the adults developed an hour-long workshop related to some aspect of advertising: in one, children developed their own ads and drew pictures to illustrate them; in another, they discussed the relationship between hard sell and community violence, in another they wrote questions to ask people in the advertising industry. The children were divided into four groups and attended a different workshop each week. The culminating event brought all the children together to attend a panel discussion of three people in the advertising industry. One was a local commercial artist, one was an executive from the Mingo Group—at the time the largest minority-owned advertising agency in the United States—and another was a vice-president from the Olmec company, the largest minority-owned toy company in the United States. The children had prepared questions ahead of time, which they addressed to panel members, and they pulled no punches. A question addressed to the Mingo Group executive, for instance, asked, "Do you do ads for liquor and tobacco? And if so, why?"

Before arriving at the school, a vice-president from Olmec had sent two large cartons full of toys to Lucy Aslan's classroom. The children had been eyeing the cartons with anticipation for days. Lucy felt strongly, however, that giving the toys to the kids would give them entirely the wrong message about what we had been working on over the past four weeks, and she didn't want kids to feel that they effectively were getting prizes for their participation in what had been a very stimulating and exciting workshop. I agreed, as did the other teachers and the custodian. We wondered, however, what should be done with the toys, and how to present the problem to the children. We addressed the problem candidly and openly, expressed our reservations, and asked children to propose alternatives. What could be done with the toys to benefit the most people? After several suggestions, the children decided as a group that the best idea was to donate the toys to local day care centers.

Then came the question, how would it be decided which day care centers to give the toys to, and how many at each place? I was away during the time that these questions came up and, as it turns out, my absence was fortunate. When the classroom's student teacher asked the kids how they might make these decisions, Tarelle answered with confidence, "We'll do a research study!" The children with whom I had worked on the oral history project went on to develop a questionnaire to be administered at each day care center, looking at the number of children, the number of toys, which toys were for girls, which for boys, and so on. Based on these children's work, the toys were divvied up and readied for distribution (see table A.1).

Some people have thought that it was unfortunate to insist that kids who had so little ought to give away gifts received, especially much coveted toys. Any fears that I might have had along these lines disappeared as I accompanied Tarelle, Davy, Teyvon, and Cherelle in delivering the toys to day care centers in the neighborhood. I had not yet begun the shopping trips and had little inkling as to the importance of giving gifts for these children. As I watched their pride and pleasure in being able to give something to someone else, and particularly to younger kids to whom they felt some sort of "big kid" tie and relationship, I was struck

Table A.1. Data generated by children for distribution of Olmec toys

	Macedonia	Dear Day Care	Newhall-ville	Latch Key	Head Start	Growth Center	Little Jewels
Dolls	8	1	15	1	8		
Kids	30	12	60	32	17		
Total	22	11	45	31	9		
Work in Groups -5	17	—	40	26	4		
No. of boy dolls +3	20	14	43	29	7		
Rotate no. of stations at each center or activity	14	14	20	10	5	5	
No. of children Over 10 yrs old	—	Yes	—	Yes	—	—	
3 or under	14	10	20	6	5	5	
No. of toys given to each day care	16	10	18	8	6	6	4

that this kind of opportunity was a rare one for these children. Our analyses of the effects of poverty tend to focus on the difficulties in providing for basic needs, but poverty equally makes gift-giving—and all that implies—extremely difficult as well.

Separation

Nearly a year after I had finished my formal fieldwork, in June of 1994, I visited my advisor, Delmos Jones, at his upstate New York home, taking Tionna with me for the overnight trip. I had just decided to take a job in Los Angeles and had told Tionna that I would be moving in a few months.

She spent most of the afternoon glued to Del's computer, playing a version of Mario Brothers, advancing to the highest level and making increasingly higher scores. She could hardly be induced to come to the dinner table but eventually came to sit with the rest of us. Inevitably we got onto the subject of my new job and the changes in store for me. I talked of marriage and babies, and then dropped the comment that Tionna did not want me to have any children. "Why not?" Del asked her in a gently teasing voice. Tionna, stiff and staring down at her plate, would not answer. Tears gathered on her lids and hung suspended there, trembling. I realized with a rush that I had hardly stopped to think about what my leaving might mean for Tionna and burst into tears myself. Tionna and I huddled together at the table while Del and his wife discreetly retired to the living-room couch. Dimly I heard him telling her that "sometimes we forget that fieldwork can be a lifetime commitment." I tried to tell Tionna reassuring things, promised I would call every week and said she could call me collect anytime she wanted to. When we had calmed ourselves a little, Tionna and I took a walk. Day was melting into twilight and the nearly untraveled country roads gave us unbroken privacy. "I'll teach you a song," Tionna told me after we had walked for about fifteen minutes. "My daddy taught it to me." She began to sing in a breathy, yet clear voice:

> Come to the water and stand by my side
> Drink from the fountain you won't be denied
> I sing of the teardrops that fell from your eyes
> I died for your sins but now I'm alive
>
> So many, many times I begged you to come home
> But you wouldn't listen, you kept going on
> Put your trust in Jesus and he'll see you through
> He died for my sins and he died for yours, too

Methodically, patiently, slowly, she taught me the song and, after a few repetitions, said, "Now you try it yourself." I sang alone as she listened. We walked along the cooling road, passing stands of pine trees and empty fields, and sang together as we returned to the house, Tionna on melody, me on harmony.

Love is mysterious knowledge. I knew Tionna as well as I did in part because I came to love her; this, I believe, is crucial to the practice of anthropology and there is no point in denying it. This kind of mysterious knowledge neither replaces objectivity nor renders it impossible, although they exist in tension with each other. Learning to manage love and science in relationships, as a fieldworker must, is a little like having two brains. Not always a comfortable experience.

Working as I have with children, the burden of responsibility for the relationships I set in motion is great. Certainly not all the children I knew loved or even liked me, but some have. For Tionna in particular, whose loss of her mother has given her little faith in the mutability of separation, our parting was not easy. This, as my advisor pointed out, is one of the realities of fieldwork. Anthropology consists not only of the observation and analysis of human relationships, but their creation and maintenance, and we are often obligated to maintain these relationships as long as we live, not in the interests of science but out of simple human caring. I felt that in teaching me her song, Tionna was giving me permission to leave, and giving me something of herself to take with me. Without her permission, I would still have had to leave. With it, I felt reassured both about her future and my own.

When I returned to New Haven in the summer of 1997 for a two-week stay, I slipped right back into fieldwork mode, complete with the inefficiencies produced by anxiety and unrest stemming from several sources. Shreds of rumors came rushing in at me, filling in the gaps in my knowledge and experience that resulted from a long stretch of time away that had been punctuated by short visits to people's homes simply to drop in and say hello but not enough to find out how the neighborhood was doing. It was early June and kids all over the city were graduating from kindergarten, elementary school, junior or senior high. I spent much of my time going to these ceremonies, where I rightly figured that I would run into many of the kids and families that I had been close to in 1992 but most of whom I had lost touch with in the intervening years.

The most obvious change was that most of the kids were now about

two feet taller than I remembered them. Remembering my own annoy-
ance at the surprised protestations of my own aunties and uncles, who
used to crowd in on me at family gatherings, thrusting their faces into
my view and saying, "Betsy! What a big girl you are now!" I tried to
stop myself from erupting in a similar way, but it was all I could do to
hold my tongue. The growth of children during one's absences, it seems
to me, is one of the true mysteries of the universe, because the change is
so absolute, so dramatic, and so relentless. Our memories are slow to
catch up to such changes if we have not witnessed them. In any case, the
newly gangly boys and rounded-out girls seemed not quite to know
what to do with or about me, either.

The stark drama that is often seen to characterize urban areas does
not capture the Newhallville area at all. The changes seem to be slow,
punctuated by occasional dramatic events, but nevertheless, things seem
to be not getting worse overall rather than getting better. In the dramatic
events category, the city's police chief was revealed to be the father of the
child of a crack-addicted prostitute. Given the clear conflicts this created
for staying in his job, he chose to step down, bouncing back to become
the head of a national policy center on policing and local lawmaking.
The new chief was a local New Haven man, and people in Newhallville
seemed to like him pretty well. Certainly, tensions between New Haven
police and residents seemed to have eased somewhat, with kids enthusiastically telling me about not only the mounted police but the bicycle
police as well. The new at-ease element of this relationship may have
stemmed also from an increasing tension with the police of neighboring
towns, exacerbated by an incident where East Haven police pursued a
young New Haven man out of their jurisdiction and into New Haven.
Once the man, Malik Jones, had stopped his car, the East Haven officer
broke his car window, reached in, and shot Mr. Jones dead, even though
he was unarmed.

Kids' minds were less occupied by police violence, it seemed to me,
than they were with an impending plan to move the downtown bus stops.
The city aldermen, in concert with Yale University, had entered into negotiations with a development company (owned by Donald Trump) to re-
vamp a defunct downtown hotel into a four-star establishment. Apparently without reading the fine print, however, the board of aldermen had
approved a plan that required moving the town's downtown bus
stops—the major transfer point for most routes—three blocks away.
The move was clearly racist and classist in the eyes of many residents,

and beleaguered alderpersons were furiously attempting to backpedal on the bus stop issue while retaining the hotel development project.

I did not get to see Tionna, who was almost never home any longer. Since the year before she had been very involved with her boyfriend, and they spent all their time together. Her grandmother, Celia, was still out of work. Ella's knees seemed little better, and she kept tabs on the neighborhood from her porch and via her telephone. Her aging Cadillac ran less and less reliably, and the family depended on the bus most of the time.

Cherie's house was vacant and empty, and nobody seemed to know where she was.

I went to see Stephen graduate from eighth grade at a nearby private school where he had been a scholarship student, and where I had been a student myself in second through fourth grades. He was known as "Mister Personality" around school and was presented with the prize for special achievement in athletics for his performance on the basketball, lacrosse, and soccer teams. His parents had bought land in a nearby suburb and were just finishing their house, finally moving out of Newhallville as they had hoped to do for so long.

Natalia became pregnant at twelve and had the baby when she was just thirteen. Her family did not know about the pregnancy until she was seven and a half months along—and all of this made her lighthearted banter before I left New Haven seem more like an ominous premonition. She and the baby were living with her mother, and Natalia was still in school. Her daughter's name was one Natalia had heard on a television program. Natalia's grandfather had suffered a series of strokes and could now barely tend the large garden to which he had devoted most of his energies in retirement. His wife, Lily, was her husband's primary caretaker during the day, and nights she continued to work at a minimum-wage job, as did Natalia's mother, who had kicked her boyfriend out of her home.

Cherelle and her grandmother had moved "down South," preceded by Cherelle's father, to a home long owned by the family. Their three-family house in Newhallville had not sold after two years on the market. Cherelle was always a good student but not all that fixated on school, and her tendency toward being "boy crazy" was rumored to be still in action, but under the strict eye of her grandmother there was little room for overstepping her boundaries.

Carlos was still living with his mother and sister in the same apartment, and he worked after school as an assistant to one of the teachers from his elementary school. Another of the children from the study was now living in an informal fostering situation with one of his elementary schoolteachers.

During that visit, I spent the most time with Teyvon, who accompanied me around Newhallville while I mapped occupied and empty housing, vacant lots and businesses. He took charge of one of my cameras, and after an afternoon of shooting mostly abandoned buildings, he stopped himself short, saying, "I'd better not just look at the stereotype." Since I had been in New Haven Teyvon's family had moved twice. The first move had been to a home that his mother, Vanessa, bought from an aged couple living in nearby Fair Haven. The house proved to be more trouble than she had bargained for, and she "let it go," moving back into Newhallville into a rented apartment. Teyvon had been working a regular summer job for several years, saving his money, and buying most of his own clothes. At the end of his sophomore year in high school, Teyvon called me at five in the morning to tell me that he'd been on the honor roll for all four marking periods, and then listed for me a long string of honors and awards he'd received that year. As if to complete the circle, he continued to work summers at the same school I attended when I was a girl younger than he is now. At this writing, in 2000, he has begun his first semester as a student at the college where I teach.

Appendixes

Selected Household Characteristics of Main Study Group

Household Population

Child	Size	Number of Children	Primary Caretaker(s)	Other Resident Adults	Rent/Own Home	Occupation/Employment	Own Car?
Asia	5	2	Mother	Mother's sister and brother	Rent	State aid	Yes
Carlos	3	2	Mother	None	Sec. 8/rent/FOH[a]	State aid	No
Cherelle	3	1	Paternal grandmother	Father's brother	Own	Caterer and seamstress	Yes
Cherie	2	1	Mother	None	Sec. 8/rent/FOH	State aid	No
Davy	5	4	Mother	None	—[b]	State aid	No
Gerald	5	3	Mother, father	None	Own	Secretary, building maintenance	Yes
Kiana	3	2	Mother	None	Rent/FOH	Group home supervisor	Yes
LaQuisha	5	3	Mother	Mother's partner (part-time)	Sec. 8/rent	State aid	—
Marelle	3	2	Mother	None	Sec. 8/rent	State aid	No
Michelle	5	3	Mother, father	None	Own	Secretary	Yes (2)
Natalia	4	2	Maternal grandparents	None	Own	Domestic worker, retired utilities clerk	Yes

Name							
Nerissa	3	2	Mother	None	Rent	—	Yes
Nyzerraye	4	1	Maternal grandparents	Mother's sister	Own	Retired schoolteacher, retired firefighter	Yes
Ricky	6	4	Mother	Mother's partner	Sec. 8/rent	State aid	No
Sam	5	—	Mother's sister	—	—	State aid	—
Shaquita	5	3	Maternal grandparents	None	Own	Domestic worker, retired construction contractor	Yes
Stephen	5	3	Mother, father	None	Own	Accountant, police officer	Yes (2)
Tanika	4	2	Mother, father	None	Own	Secretary, mechanic	Yes
Tarelle	6	4	Mother	Mother's sister	FOH/rent	Nurse	Yes
Terry	2	—	Mother's sister	None	—	State aid	—
Teyvon	4	3	Mother	None	Sec. 8/rent	Student, state aid	No
Tionma	3	1	Maternal grandmother and great-grandmother	None	Own	State aid, retired cafeteria worker	Yes

[a]Sec. 8 = Section 8 voucher; rent/FOH = Living in a multi-unit home owned by a family member and paying market rent.
[b]Missing information.

This Is Our Community and This Is What We Think: Kids as Collaborators in Anthropological Research

Natalia Brooks, Cherelle Brown, Gerald Downs, Tarelle Evans, Carlos Rodriquez, and Tionna Warner, with Elizabeth Chin

This project has been a collaborative research effort between a group of children and an anthropologist. We have called the work the "Children's Oral History Project." In the spring of 1992, a group of twelve third- and fourth-grade children learned how to do social science interviews, then wrote an interview, the subject of which was "what it was like when you were growing up." The children interviewed all sorts of people who were members of generations older than themselves, conducting it with seventeen respondents altogether. Some of these interviews were done in groups at the school, some were done by individual children at home. All the interviews were audiotaped.

In the spring of 1993, after the interviews had been transcribed, a group of six fifth-graders, three of whom had worked on the project the year before, began the long and difficult task of coding and analyzing the interview material. We worked an hour a day, three days a week, for three months. Students worked in pairs on different sections of the interview: Carlos and Gerald on background information, Cherelle and Tarelle on whether things are better or worse now for kids, and Natalia and Tionna on toys people had, clothes they wore, and whether they got allowance.

In the preliminary report that follows, all of the work was done by the student researchers. They wrote, rewrote, and edited this report themselves. Sometimes, when kids clearly had ideas but were having trouble writing them, they dictated what they had to say and I typed it into the computer. Most of them typed their own part of the report. All of them constructed their own tables and figures, first by hand on graph paper, and then by inputting information into my computer to make the graphs included in this report. (Cherelle and Tarelle did not prepare a computer-generated summary of their information; instead, they made a large cardboard and colored-paper display that included a graph. This has not been reproduced here.)

I would like to emphasize one thing: the children did a better job conducting this research than I ever could have. Their point of view and insight both as children and as members of the community we were researching gave them countless advantages over me—as an outsider—as they first conducted the interviews and later analyzed them.

Carlos

Hi. My name is Carlos and my partner is Gerald. He will be telling you what he will be doing later. We are going to talking about the background information. O.K., let's get started.

We interviewed seventeen people. Seven were males and ten were females.

Next I'm going to tell you about the graphs I made. I made graphs about jobs, children, and education. The education graph (fig. 1) tells who went to high school, college, and who got a Ph.D. First one person had some high school. Seven people finished high school. Two had some college, and two had A.A. degrees. Three people finished college. One person got a Ph.D.

The children graph (fig. 2) tells you how many people had babies. Four people didn't have babies, twelve people did.

The last graph I am going to tell you about is the job graph (fig. 3). Eleven people had a job, four people didn't have jobs.

Highest Grade

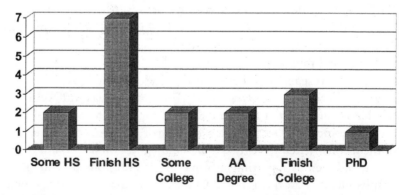

Figure 1. Education

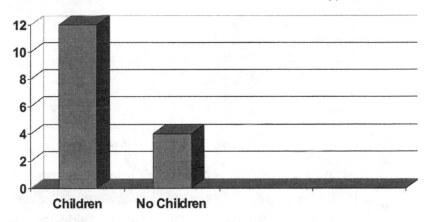

Figure 2. Children

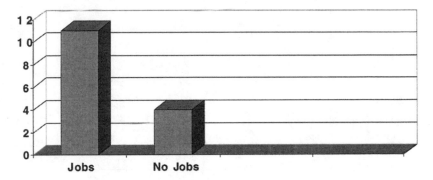

Figure 3. Jobs

Gerald

I worked on background information. I made a graph about marital status (fig. 4), and I made a chart about the sex, the ages, and I found the average age (fig. 5). I found out how the people we interviewed were related to the interviewers. It was important to ask these questions because we want to know about these people. We want to know what they do. Do they live alone, what's their highest grade, do they have a job?

In my graph about marital status I found out how many people were married, single, divorced, or widowed. There were four people married, eight people were single, three people were divorced, one person was widowed. The three people who were divorced were all male.

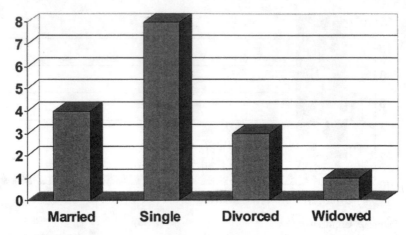

Figure 4. Marital Status

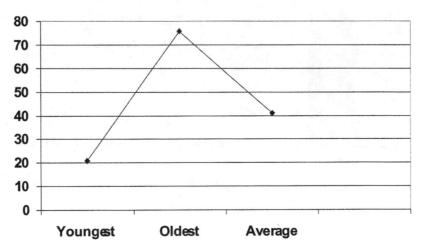

Figure 5. Age Information

I found out about the oldest age, the youngest age, and the average age of everybody interviewed. The oldest age of people was 76. The youngest age was 21 out of three people. Out of all the ages of those people I found out the average age, and it was 41.

Of all the people we interviewed, there are seven parents, four friends, one grandfather, one principal, and one uncle. It's funny. Everybody we interviewed had something in common: they're all black.

Cherelle

I'm Cherelle, this is my partner, Tarelle. My partner and I worked very hard on the better and worse graph. The better and worse graph means like what's better in the world. For an example, I asked, did life change since you were a kid?; are things better now or worse? It's important to ask these questions because you have to know how other people think and how people might say things.

One person said something about teenage pregnancy. This one person said it is sad these days kids as teens are getting pregnant and having AIDS. Almost everyone said drugs are very big now. People are killing people for drugs. A lot of kids are disrespectful and don't care what anyone says. Even now kids carry weapons to school and that's a bad thing too. That's about it for the worse graph too. I'm going to begin on what one other person said, kids have lunch in school these days, everyone can have a decent job. That's about it for our graph.

I would like to talk about some of the things I learned last year in the oral history class doing interviews. I learned what the news people go through when they interview people and ask questions. That gave me an idea and made me think about what I should ask people. It's better to have long than short answers. We need more details. If I asked, "how did you grow up?" and they said "we grew up nice," I'd ask, "in what ways?" to make it longer.

Tarelle

Hi, my name is Tarelle, and this is my partner, Cherelle. We worked on the better and worse part of the interviews. Better and worse is something about the olden day. For example, I was asking people do they think it is better or worse for kids these days? I was trying to find out what the people community had to say and their opinions. Is it really better or worse nowadays? I thought it was important to ask these questions and could know how people feel about the Newhallville area. I was shocked at some people's answers. Because some people said some pretty dumb things. I was expecting people to say things like drugs, kidnapping, black killing black, AIDS, and last but not least, teenage pregnancy. Those are the main things going on in the area. I keep asking myself, is it really better or worse these days and times. A majority of people said it was worse and I think it is true. This is something to think about. I expected more from the people that live in Newhallville. I expected them to say the true thing that goes. Because some people I interviewed didn't tell the truth. But some said some pretty dumb things. Example: Donny said it's better now because kids eat lunch in school. And that's certainly not the kind of answer I'm looking for. That's something like kind of dumb to say. It's just that ain't something that a grown person should be saying, not an adult. They could say it's better because people have jobs, or it's better because kids get to do more stuff than we did and have after school programs and stuff like that.

There are questions I'm still trying to figure out. Is it really better? Or worse? Can the neighborhood get better? or worse? I think the neighborhood could get better. And in a way I think it could get worse. Because it could get worse in a way that people could start killing more and setting up things, setting up stuff like you stay at this corner, you stay at that corner. Like little kids selling drugs and stuff like that. Then kids could start getting killed and all that. And I think it could get better when they start building police substations.

I think the people in the interviews felt the neighborhood is going down. I hope that when they build these police substations, the neighborhood will come back up. I have no problem with the neighborhood. To me the neighborhood is straight. The only thing the matter with the neighborhood is the drugs, the chaos and the violence. Because some people realize what they are doing wrong because most of the people out there, parents, go to church, and I know they brought them up right. I think the people in the interviews felt the same way.

I think the people in the interviews thought the neighborhood was sort of good and bad. I think they thought that it's like a good and bad place to grow up. I think the people we interviewed think that kids under age shouldn't be hanging out so much. Because they pick up bad habits. They hear the foul language and everything.

By interviewing people now I know their opinions, and what they think of the neighborhood. I think this was a great idea. Thank you.

Natalia

Hello, my name is Natalia. I worked on toys, favorite toys, and toys people wanted but never got. We wanted to know about the people when they were young because we were trying to find out what kind of toys people had back in the old days. I thought that some people would say they didn't have no toys. And I thought that they would say they had toys like we have now, but they didn't.

The first thing I worked on was toys. We asked questions like "What kind of toys did you have?" (fig. 6). Another question we asked was "what was your favorite toy?" (fig. 7). It tells me that many people back in the old days didn't have as many toys like kids do nowadays. There was only one person who picked Lincoln logs. Nine people said they had dolls and that was the highest amount. Most kids nowadays play with dolls and bikes, but some boys play with G.I. Joes.

Well the next thing I worked on was favorite toys. Many people didn't name very many toys. Lincoln logs got one again. The highest amount was two, and that was dolls. I didn't think there would be only two people picking dolls as their favorite toys. I thought since nine people picked

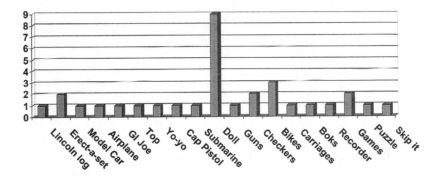

Figure 6. Toys

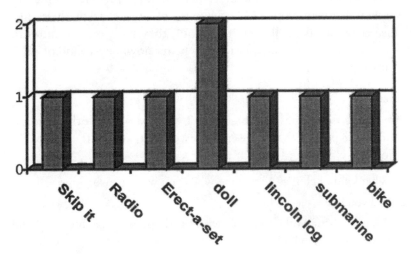

Figure 7. Favorite Toys

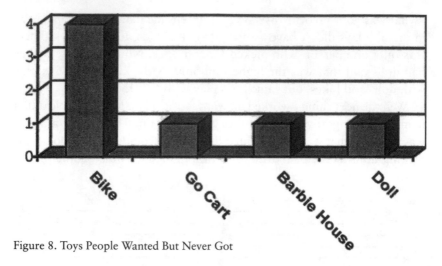

Figure 8. Toys People Wanted But Never Got

dolls in toys, there would be at least the same amount of people picking dolls in favorite toys. The favorite toys were skip-it, radio, erect-a-set, doll, Lincoln logs, submarine, and bike.

Well I'm going to go to my last report and that is toys people wanted but never got (fig. 8). The least amount of toys people wanted but never got was one, and that was go-cart, Barbie house, and a doll. The highest amount of toys people wanted and never got was four, and that was a bike. I remember I wanted this bike but never got it.

I think kids nowadays have more toys than people back in the old days. I wouldn't want to be a kid back in the old days, back in their time. Because they had to walk long to school, they had to walk miles to school, that's a matter of fact. I think it's better nowadays. Kind of. Well that's my report for now.

Tionna

Hi, my name is Tionna. The part that I worked on is clothes and allowance. The people that were interviewed were asked the following questions for clothes and allowance:

1. What kind of clothes were there when you were growing up?
2. Did you like your clothes?
3. What kinds of clothes did you wear? Did you wear bellbottoms? Did you wear fancy clothes?
4. Did your mother ever make you wear clothes you didn't want to?

5. Did the children talk about your clothes?

6. Did you spend money on your clothes? What was the highest amount you spent on your clothes?

7. How much did you get for your allowance?

8. What stores did you like to go to?

9. What did you buy at those stores?

I think it was most important to ask these questions because we wanted to know if their clothes were different from nowadays, and we wanted to know if they got allowance because most people do these days. We wanted to know if it was the same back then.

Now I'm going to tell you about what people said about clothes (fig. 9). These are the clothes people mentioned: khaki pants, tan pants, knit shirts, bellbottoms, fish tail skirts, crinolines, popcorn skirts, skirts, ties, jeans, shorts, platform shoes, wide lapeled jackets, wide lapeled shirts, hand-me-downs, dresses, ankle socks, suspenders, leather coats, cotton skirts, suits, job master shoes, boat shoes, sandals, t-shirts, sweat shirts, suede leather coats, shark skin pants, blind knight sweater, cotton flannel skirts, black bloomers, and blouse.

Now here are some materials people mentioned: shark skin, silk, polyester, and double knits.

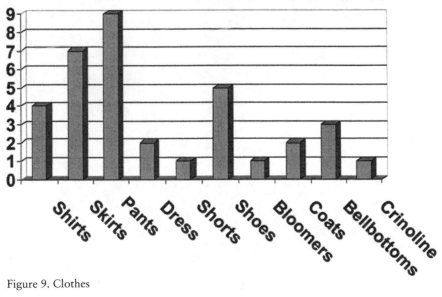

Figure 9. Clothes

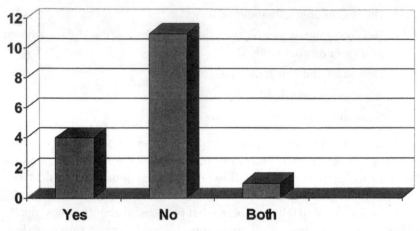

Figure 10. Allowance

Now I'm going to tell you about allowance (fig. 10). If people got allowance or did not get allowance. On my allowance graph, eleven people said they didn't get allowance. Four people said they did get allowance. One person said both.

Kids nowadays have more money to spend. The people who got allowance said they earned it. One person said they shined shoes for allowance. Another person established a paper route. Two other people said they earned allowance but they didn't say how. Thank you.

Project Interview for Children's Oral History Project

Children's Oral History Project
Project Interview
Draft 4/9/92

Name of person interviewed _____

Date interviewed _____

Interviewed by _____

Is the person male or female? (Check one) Male___ Female___

Introduction

(Make sure you have had the person you are interviewing sign the consent form!)

This is an interview about your childhood. The questions we ask are going to be private. Your name will never be used if we write about or talk about what you say in this interview. If there are any questions you prefer not to answer you don't have to. But we would appreciate if you could answer all of the questions.

General Questions

1. When you were growing up, did you think it would be hard? Why did you think that?
2. Do you think life has changed for children since you were little? In what ways?
3. Do you think things are better now for children or worse? Why is that? What things do you think are (better) (worse)?

Questions about Growing Up

4. When you were growing up, where did you live? What was it like there?

5. Did you have a lot of friends when you were a kid?

6. What kind of games did you and your friends play? Can you give me examples? Can you think of any others?

7. When did you meet your first true friend? What was that person's name? How did you meet? What kinds of things did you do together?

8. Did you ever have a fight with your best friend? What happened?

Questions about School

9. What school (or schools) did you go to when you were little?

10. Did you like school?

11. How was your behavior in school?

12. Did you ever get suspended?

13. Have you ever been to the principal's office?

14. What were the names of your favorite teachers? What did you like about those teachers?

15. When you were growing up, did you want to be a teacher?

Questions about Clothes

16. What kinds of clothes were there when you were growing up?

17. Did you like your clothes?

18. What kinds of clothes did you wear? Did you wear bell-bottoms? Did you wear fancy clothes?

19. Did your mother ever make you wear clothes that you didn't want to?

20. Did the children talk about your clothes?

21. Did you spend money on your clothes? What was the highest amount of money you spent on your clothes?

Questions about Money

22. How much did you get for your allowance?

23. What stores did you like to go to?

24. What did you buy at the store?

Questions about Toys

25. What toys did you have? (Try to have the person list as many as you can think of. Ask them about each toy: Where did you get it? Why did you like it?)
26. Why did you like it so much?
27. When you were little, was there a toy you really wanted but never got?

Questions about TV

28. What did you watch on TV?
29. What were your favorite programs?
30. Did you ever hear Martin Luther King on television?

Questions about Music

31. What kind of music did you listen to when you were little?

Background Information

32. What year were you born?
33. We would like to know if you are:
    Married ___   Single___
    Divorced ___   Widowed___
    No Answer___
34. We would like to know if you have any children.
    Yes ___ No___ No answer___
35. Do you have a job?
    Yes ___ No___ No answer___
    [If YES, ask 35a]
35a. What job do you work for?
36. What is the highest grade or degree that you finished in school?
37. Do you live by yourself?
    Yes ___ No___ No answer___
    [If No, ask 37a]
37a. Who do you live with?
[Ask 38 if you don't know what race the person is]
38. What race are you?

That was my last question. Thank you for doing this interview with me. I enjoyed talking with you very much.

Notes

Preface

1. Some of the best current theoretical work that critically examines the importance of children in social life (and also in social theory) includes the work of James and Prout (1990) and James, Jenks, and Prout (1998). A collection of essays entitled *Children and the Politics of Culture* is also important and lays out issues and questions particularly well in the introductory essay by Sharon Stephens (1995). In anthropology, a collection edited by Helen Schwartzman (in press) includes ethnographic and theoretical essays that make clear the importance of both children and childhood to the discipline.

1. Consumption in Context

1. A number of authors have written about the black-consumer-as-shoplifter issue, most notably Regina Austin (1994a, b) and John Fiske (1994).

2. Anthropologists have done an admirable job of documenting the great variety of ways people from diverse cultures deal with commodities and consumption, primarily by showing the ways in which indigenous conceptual and cultural frameworks differ from those of the West, or, conversely, the ways that "others" have appropriated and transformed western commodities (cf. Creighton 1992; Heath 1992; Taussig 1980). In analyzing cargo cults, for instance, anthropologists have put the study of consumption in the context of political economy and understood consumption as a process tied to the inequality between a hegemonic western culture and a less powerful "other" culture (Worsley 1957). Inequality in the sphere of consumption thus is most commonly portrayed as existing between cultures, but not within them. This point of view leads to a tendency to see the politics of consumption as the hegemonic incursions of European and North American goods, values and media, with people attempting to maintain their cultural integrity in the face of those products even as they incorporate them into their lives (cf. Heath 1992; Hugh-Jones 1992; Turner 1992). More often

than not, these confrontations have taken place under circumstances of colonialism, genocide, slavery, economic or martial battle. When viewed from a global
and long-term historical perspective, the similarities between dilemmas faced by
the migratory North American Naskapi Indians entering the fur trade and East
Indian states under British colonial rule are striking (Wolf 1982). Moreover,
changes in western consumption—the drinking of sugared tea among the British
working class, for example—have been seen to be fundamental to changes in
production in industrialized centers, as well as a powerful means of drawing
such areas as India and the Caribbean into the capitalist system (Mintz 1985).
That is, consumption has been critical in the emergence of modernity.

3. Studies of "Third World Consumer culture" (Belk 1988) have pointed
out that even in cultures making use of western commodities, their uses and
meanings "are bound up with pre-existing systems of exchange, display, and
consumption" (Arnould and Wilk 1984, 748–49). In anthropology, the incor-
poration of a modern/primitive dichotomy in the analysis of consumption has
proven extraordinarily difficult to dislodge (Weismantel 1997). Western consumption is portrayed as being relatively undifferentiated and, in some cases,
appears as an almost reified, static entity. Commodity consumption in a cross-
cultural context has thus been understood as a strange mix of authenticity, imitation, and contagion. It is at once the western intrusion into and distortion of
"pure" cultural forms and the local imitation of authentic western templates
(however objectionable these templates may be). Ethnographic explorations of
economic systems featuring wealth and trade based upon unalienated commodities provide contrast to—and shed light upon—the unique nature of commodity
consumption under capitalism. For example, Melanesia has long been the site
of a wide range of studies examining aspects of such economies including gender, the role of gifts, commodities, barter, and trade (Cheal 1988; Gell 1992;
Malinowski 1922; Valerio 1994; Weiner 1985). So, while the often-romantic
distinction made between economies and forms of consumption that are "primitive" on the one hand and capitalist (as opposed to socialist or communist) on
the other is perhaps a little too neat (Philibert 1990), this does not mean that all
commodity consumption can be reduced to its origin in western culture.

4. Miller (1995a) notes some of the central problems with this dichotomous
anthropological understanding of consumption: "Central Africans in suits, In-
donesian soap operas, and South Asian brands are no longer inauthentic copies
by people who have lost their culture after being swamped by things that only
North Americans and Europeans 'should' possess. Rather there is the equality
of genuine relativism that makes none of us a model of real consumption and
all of us creative variants of social processes based around the possession and
use of commodities" (144).

Miller's observation that "none of us [is] a model of real consumption"
bears repeating. And yet, Miller's "central Africans in suits," for instance, do
not and cannot exist apart from a cultural politics and political economy that

at some level does indeed measure them against notions of what people like them "should" possess. His notion of "the equality of genuine relativism" appears to gloss over prickly historical details. The European history of those suits and the problems that history poses for their wearers cannot be settled merely by recognizing that central Africans can and do legitimately dress in suits rather than bou-bous or loincloths; likewise, notions of "style" do not adequately account for the cultural politics inherent in the mass merchandising of African-inspired fashions to the American buying public.

5. These critiques can appear, at times, quite elitist, especially today when appreciations of popular culture have alerted us to the ways in which reception and resistance can go to work transforming the millions of indistinguishable industrially produced items into (almost) endless variations. And yet, it is too simple to dismiss the Frankfurt school analyses of what is wrong with consumer culture as simply nostalgia for some golden age that probably never existed in the first place. Adorno's condemnation of popular jazz can seem not only elitist but downright racist at moments, and his continual citing of particular passages of Brahms or Haydn seems only to confirm his status as a musical snob (Adorno 1993). Although one might wish that he showed some signs of thinking that other forms of music aside from western classical orchestral works qualify as worthy, his larger point is that in the kind of music he praises, music played live by musicians who are faced with an emotionally engaged, intellectually stimulated audience, a kind of total—and spiritual—experience can take place. His problem with jazz was not so much, I would like to think, about all jazz, but rather bad jazz, since he is most disturbed by schlocky pop songs that all basically sound the same and which, when played over the radio, are not so much meant to be listened to with an open heart and rapt attention as they are to serve as background music to some conversation, a boring task, or late-night party.

6. Following in this vein, contemporary scholars like Stuart and Elizabeth Ewen make incisive critiques of the advertising industry, but are less interested in documenting the process of reception by audiences and consumers (Ewen 1976, 1988; Ewen and Ewen 1982).

7. In anthropology the debate over how to define basic needs or whether this was, in fact, possible can be seen in Malinowski's efforts to develop a theory of culture based on the premise that culture fulfills basic needs (1944). It quickly became clear, however, that everywhere so-called basic needs are culturally mediated and defined. While all humans need food, it is not enough for a given item to be edible: the tasty beetle eaten in Indonesia is classified as "filth" by the U.S. Food and Drug Administration; the brie eaten in France is viewed by many Chinese as a disgusting sludge made of food meant for baby cows and left in a cool, dark place much too long.

8. In New Haven there are 18.5 infant deaths per 1,000 live births. Some argue the infant mortality rate in the city is inflated because Yale–New Haven Hospital has one of the nation's premiere neonatal units and thus attracts a

higher concentration than normal of women with high-risk pregnancies and seriously ill infants. However, one New Haven neighborhood had an infant mortality rate almost three times higher than that of the city as a whole, with 66.7 deaths per 1,000 live births (Reguero and Crane 1994).

9. Some city attempts to rectify this situation met with violent response from other city residents. When the city notified one neighborhood that they intended to use some properties to house low-income families, the houses were burned to the ground.

10. Two of these participated in the afterschool program and oral history project.

11. Section 8 vouchers are part of a federally funded program providing rent subsidies for elderly, infirm, or low-income tenants. Under the program, residents do not pay more than 30 percent of their income for rent; the vouchers pay the difference.

12. The politics of hair in the black community deserve an entire volume. Several important treatments of black hair (so to speak) address the complex politics surrounding issues of "good" versus "bad" hair, as well as the racial and consumer implications of hair and hair styling (Mercer 1990; Rooks 1996; Willis 1990).

2. The Shadow of Whiteness

1. Many Newhallville residents felt similarly; for this and other reasons, I do not use the term *inner city* in this work. Similarly, I use both the terms *black* and *African American* to describe individuals and communities. In Newhallville, nearly all those I knew used the term *black* to describe themselves racially and ethnically.

2. White identity has also been performed and accomplished in many cases through the *emulation* of black culture, particularly through music and fashion. It is no secret that today's "Hip-Hop nation" emerged out of the poverty-stricken black and brown territory of the South Bronx. Alex Kotlowitz, for example, has commented on this dynamic (1999).

3. Another project that remains to be undertaken is that of understanding how segregation and racial oppression have shaped the consumer orientations of other races and ethnic groups, particularly Asians and Native Americans, whose ability to be consumers of education, property, and even citizenship historically have been hampered by both legal and informal means in the United States.

4. In the Caribbean, slaves were often expected to provide much of their own sustenance from garden plots and were permitted time and opportunity to travel to these plots and work them (Sheridan 1995). This strategy was less common in the United States, where slaveholders were resistant to allowing slaves the mobility they needed to travel to and from garden plots—since *hatching* plots might also be the result of such unsupervised activity. As slaveholders realized

that slave production of their own subsistence relieved them of the economic burden of buying provisions, many began to institute it as a requirement (Mullin 1995). This was more common in areas such as low country Georgia, where plantation labor was organized in terms of finishing assigned tasks rather than working for a specified amount of time. Under the task system slaves who could complete their assignments early had relatively more opportunity to grow produce that they could then consume themselves or—perhaps even more important—take to market (Wood 1995).

5. Belk (personal communication) notes that in Australia the state for a time took a similar paternalistic view toward how the undeserving poor ought to spend their aid, but have since removed restrictions on such spending. Zelizer (1994) describes food stamps as a type of "instructional currency" developed by social welfare agencies and charities for use by the poor. These currencies were alternatives to cash, which the poor were viewed as being unable to handle in a responsible manner ("responsibly" being defined, of course, by welfare agencies and charities), but providing the educational benefit of allowing the poor to develop skills in shopping and consumership.

6. There is a large literature on the related issue of the emulation of whiteness through hair styles. This is addressed to some degree in chapter six, when I examine the issue of Barbie-doll hair. In addition, the huge industry producing hair straighteners, skin-lightening creams, and so on should not be forgotten. Because I have opted to focus specifically on the slavery period, however, I cannot address those issues here.

7. I should admit that I am not unbiased toward Leona Helmsley. As a college undergraduate I coauthored a kind of hate letter, in which we accused her of something like "representing the gross underbelly of corporate capitalist greed." Needless to say, Mrs. Helmsley declined to respond.

3. "What Are You Looking At, You White People?"

1. Alternatively, it is worth thinking about what Tionna thought she was looking at, since the women in the car may not even have noticed her or judged her in any way.

2. A similar lack of children's birthday parties has been noted in a Massachusetts community much like Newhallville (Jeffers 1967).

3. In contrast, middle-class parents I interviewed were in several cases able to exactly state how much television per day or week their children watched. This specificity was the result of highly structured and enforced television-watching rules.

4. None of the families I knew celebrated any of the other winter holidays such as Kwanzaa or Hanukkah.

5. Over $10 billion is spent on toys alone during the Christmas season, an average of just over $350 per child aged 6 to 13 in the United States (Pope 1993).

Few Newhallville families even approached this average expenditure for their children at Christmas.

4. Hemmed In and Shut Out

1. One such plan, it was rumored, featured a design in which it was impossible to gain access to the mall except by car. Such a plan was clearly aimed at preventing the "wrong" kind of customer from gaining easy access to the mall.

2. Plate 51 in *And Their Children after Them* (Maharidge and Williamson 1989) shows a similar array of single-brand items in a store in Parsons Cove, a poor, rural town in Alabama.

3. Belk (1994) describes similar tactics by malls elsewhere at Halloween. He points out that these efforts by malls are at some level an attempt to undermine trust between neighbors and to transfer that trust to mall merchants, who hope to some degree that "free" provision of Halloween candy will garner them loyal customers.

5. Anthropologist Takes Inner-City Children on Shopping Sprees

1. It has been argued that so-called windfall monies like those I provided children for the shopping trips are spent differently than everyday money (Bodkin 1959). However, Bodkin's argument is focused on the spending of adults, not children, who do not generally receive regular wages but often receive various forms of nonwage income in the form of gifts, allowance, or windfall. Zelizer (1989) argues that each of these kinds of "special monies" carries with it particular symbolic and social meanings and implications. The patterns evident in my analysis of these children's shopping trips are not in conflict with the $20 being windfall income or a form of "special money."

2. Some people have suggested to me that perhaps children bought gifts and "spent their money wisely," as they often said in Newhallville, to impress me. Perhaps. Yet if this was the case, an explanation is still needed as to why children thought that gift giving and careful shopping would be "good" for them, and it is an explanation that leads right back into children's social and kinship networks. In other words, the notion of "observer influence" neither accounts for nor explains the patterns that emerge in looking at children's purchases on these trips.

3. In *A Theory of Shopping*, Daniel Miller (1998) similarly notes that residents of one North London street used shopping as a way to show their love for kin, "express care and concern" (35), attempt to transform or educate household members, among other things. Fischer and Arnold (1990) also document the ways in which women engage in Christmas gift shopping as "more than a labor of love."

4. While Teyvon did not buy the silly sipper he received with his purchase of shorts, he did say he planned to give it away to his cousin, and it can be considered another gift.

6. Ethnically Correct Dolls

1. The studies have provoked a large and still growing literature that has challenged the original research (Burnett 1995), argued for recognizing the importance of social history and gender (Fine and Bowers 1984), and examined cross-cultural validity problems (Gopaul-McNichol 1995). The Clarks' original ideas about self-hatred and self-rejection came under special criticism in the 1970s and 1980s (Banks 1976; McAdoo 1985; Porter and Washington 1979). It was the Clarks' own assessment that other methods they had used were more effective in exploring the complexities of children's racial identification (Clark and Clark 1940; Clark and Clark 1950), and yet the doll studies remain for the public the most compelling demonstration of the negative effects of racism on black children's self-concept or what is more often now referred to as their self-esteem.

2. Makers of ethnically correct dolls do not focus exclusively on African Americans, and also include Latino and Asian toys. These account for a much smaller segment of the market and hence production and products.

3. It is true that minority toymakers, more than their mainstream counterparts, put an emphasis on trying to make their products available to their target customers, even if a nearby store may not stock their goods. Olmec and other minority-owned toy companies have long emphasized mail-order business as a way to make their toys available to communities that may not have easy access to major retailers. In Newhallville at least, mail order was not an option many either knew about or employed. Though mail order increases convenience for shoppers, it still requires resources more readily available to middle-class buyers than to poor or working-class customers. For the middle class who can place a call and use a credit card, or write a check and put the order in the mail, mail order may be an easy option. For many Newhallville families the equipment and resources required to make use of the conveniences—phones, checkbooks, and credit cards—are often unavailable to a given household. It is this sort of economic and business-oriented limitation that has most profoundly shaped ethnically correct dolls—more even, I will argue, than their refashioned appearances with their lips, noses, and face shapes that are distinctly black, Hispanic, or Asian.

4. See, for example, Benson 1986; Leach 1984; Williamson 1980. Also, some essays in *Lifestyle Shopping* (Shields 1992) address the question of masculinity and shopping.

5. None of these engineering changes, DuCille notes, prevent the Shani dolls from being able to wear the clothes that any other Barbie would. The limits of racial representation are imposed by the needs of commerce not only within Mattel, between the Barbie and Shani lines, but between companies as well. With Barbie setting the standard for the 11½-inch fashion doll, Olmec's Imani doll also can wear Barbie's clothes, and this is mentioned on the front of Imani's package.

6. I should note that Urla and Swedlund (1995) have actually measured Shani with calipers in an anthropometric comparison with Barbie. They did find measurement differences, and actually found Shani's butt to be smaller than Barbie's by a few hundredths of an inch.

7. In addition, Kobena Mercer's observation (1990) that no black hairstyle is inherently "natural" applies just as well to white hair. White-girl hair, especially in the long and flowing form represented by Barbie, takes nearly as much work to maintain as any "typically" black hairstyle. Prone to snarling itself into impossibly tangled rat's nests, long hair has provided many (white) girls with the painful memory of their frustrated mothers summarily chopping their hair off rather than continuing to struggle with keeping it combed and orderly. In the long and flowing version, this kind of hair is no more a natural or easy assertion of whiteness than the Afro or dreadlocks are an easy or natural assertion of blackness (in any case the tradition of long flowing hair is much more prevalent among Chicanos and Asians than it is among whites).

8. In discussing the Clarks' work, I use the racial terminology in the original research rather than contemporary terms that do not capture the historical context in which the Clark studies were conducted.

Bibliography

Abu-Lughod, Lila. 1990. "The Romance of Resistance: Tracing Transformations of Power through Bedouin Women." *American Ethnologist* 17, no. 1:41–55.

Adorno, Theodor W. 1993. "On the Fetish Character in Music and the Regression of Listening." Pp. 270–99 in *The Essential Frankfurt School Reader*, ed. Andrew Arato and Eike Gebhardt. New York: Continuum.

Alwitt, Linda F. 1995. "Marketing and the Poor." *American Behavioral Scientist* 38, no. 4:564–77.

Andreasen, Alan R. 1975. *The Disadvantaged Consumer.* New York: Free Press.

———. 1976. "The Differing Nature of Consumerism in the Ghetto." *Journal of Consumer Affairs* 10:179–89.

———. 1986. "Disadvantaged Consumers in the 1980s." Pp. 113–28 in *The Future of Consumerism,* ed. Paul N. Bloom and Ruth Belk Smith. Lexington, Mass.: Lexington Books.

Arnould, Eric, and Richard B. Wilk. 1984. "Why Do the Natives Wear Adidas?" *Advances in Consumer Research* 11:748–52.

Auletta, Ken. 1982. *The Underclass.* New York: Random House.

Austin, Regina. 1994a. "'A Nation of Thieves': Consumption, Commerce, and the Black Public Sphere." *Public Culture* 7, no. 1:225–48.

———. 1994b. "'A Nation of Thieves': Securing Black People's Right to Shop and Sell in White America." *Utah Law Review* 1:147–77.

Baker, Russell. 1992. "The Beethoven Defense." *New York Times* (July 23), L19.

Banks, W. C. 1976. "White Preference in Blacks: A Paradigm in Search of a Phenomenon." *Psychological Bulletin* 83(b):1179–86.

Baudrillard, Jean. 1981. *Simulacres et Simulation.* Paris: Galilee.

———. 1986. *Amerique.* Paris: Grasset.

———. 1988. *The Ecstasy of Communication.* New York: Semiotex(tc).

Bauman, Zygmunt. 1993. "From Pilgrim to Tourist—or a Short History of Identity." Pp. 18–36 in *Questions of Cultural Identity,* ed. Stuart Hall and P. DuGay. London: Sage.

Belk, Russell. 1988. "Third World Consumer Culture." *Marketing and Development* 1:103–27.

———. 1994. "Carnival, Control, and Corporate Culture in Contemporary Halloween Celebrations." Pp. 105–32 in *Halloween and Other Festivals of Life and Death*, ed. Jack Santino. Knoxville: University of Tennessee Press.

———. 1995. "Studies in the New Consumer Behaviour." Pp. 58–95 in *Acknowledging Consumption*, ed. Daniel Miller. New York: Routledge.

Belk, Russell W., and Wendy Bryce. 1993. "Christmas Shopping Scenes: From Modern Miracle to Postmodern Mall." *International Journal of Research in Marketing* 10:277–96.

Benson, S. P. 1986. *Counter Cultures: Saleswomen, Managers, and Customers in American Department Stores, 1890–1940*. Urbana: University of Illinois Press.

Bodkin, R. G. 1959. "Windfall Income and Consumption." *American Economic Review* 49:602–14.

Bourdieu, Pierre. 1977. *Outline of a Theory of Practice*. Cambridge: Cambridge University Press.

———. 1984. *Distinction: A Social Critique of the Judgement of Taste*. London: Routledge and Kegan Paul.

Bourgois, Philippe. 1995. *In Search of Respect*. New York: Cambridge University Press.

Burke, Timothy. 1996. *Lifebuoy Men, Lux Women: Commodification, Consumption, and Cleanliness in Modern Zimbabwe*. Durham, N.C.: Duke University Press.

Burnett, Myra N. 1995. "Doll Studies Revisited: A Question of Validity." *Journal of Black Psychology* 21, no. 1:19–29.

Caplovitz, David. 1967. *The Poor Pay More*. New York: Free Press.

Carpenter, John, and Curtis Lawrence. 1998. "Boys Linked to Murder; Girl, 11, May Have Been Killed for Bike." *Chicago Sun-Times* (August 10), 1.

Carrier, James G., and Josiah McC. Heyman. 1997. "Consumption and Political Economy." *Journal of the Royal Anthropological Institute* 3, no. 2:355–73.

Charles, Eleanor. 1994. "Yale Works to Break Down the Town-Gown Barrier: Improvement of New Haven's Broadway Is Among the New Plans." *New York Times*, September 25, R9.

Cheal, D. 1988. *The Gift Economy*. London: Routledge.

City of New Haven. 1982. *Inside New Haven's Neighborhoods: A Guide to the City of New Haven*. New Haven: New Haven Colony Historical Society.

City of New Haven Blue Ribbon Commission. 1990. "Final Report of the Blue Ribbon Commission Appointed by Mayor John C. Daniels." City of New Haven.

Clark, Kenneth B. [1955] 1963. *Prejudice and Your Child*. Boston: Beacon Press.

Clark, Kenneth B., and Mamie Phipps Clark. 1939. "The Development of Con-

sciousness of Self and the Emergence of Racial Identification in Negro Preschool Children." *Journal of Social Psychology, SPSSI Bulletin* 10:591–99.

———. 1940. "Skin Color as a Factor in Racial Identification of Negro Preschool Children." *Journal of Social Psychology, SPSSI Bulletin* 11:159–69.

———. 1947. "Racial Identification and Preference in Negro Children." Pp.
169–78 in *Readings in Social Psychology,* ed. T. M. Newcomb and E. L.
Hartley. New York: Henry Holt.

———. 1950. "Emotional Factors in Racial Identification and Preference in
Negro Children." *Journal of Negro Education* 19, no. 3:341–50.

Clifton, James M. 1978. *Life and Labor on Argyle Island: Letters and Documents of a Savannah River Rice Plantation, 1833–1867.* Savannah, Ga.:
Beehive Press.

Conklin, Beth A. 1997. "Body Paint, Feathers, and VCRs: Aesthetics and Authenticity in Amazonian Activism." *American Ethnologist* 24, no. 4:711–37.

Creighton, M. 1992. "The Depato: Merchandising the West While Selling Japan-
eseness." Pp. 42–57 in *Re-made in Japan,* ed. J. Tobin. New Haven: Yale
University Press.

Dahl, Robert A. 1961. *Who Governs? Democracy and Power in an American
City.* New Haven: Yale University Press.

Dávila, Arlene. Forthcoming. *Latinos, Inc.: The Marketing and the Making of
a People.* Berkeley: University of California Press.

di Leonardo, Michaela. 1987. "The Female World of Cards and Holidays:
Women, Families, and the Work of Kinship." *Signs* 12, no. 3:440–53.

Dowdy, Zachary R. 1998. "Racial Bias in Coverage by Media of Kids Who
Kill." *Sacramento Bee* (July 5), F1.

DuCille, Ann. 1996. *Skin Trade.* Cambridge: Harvard University Press.

Dugger, Celia W. 1994. "A Boy in Search of Respect Discovers How to Kill."
New York Times (May 15), A1, 36.

Edin, Kathryn. 1991. "Surviving the Welfare System: How AFDC Recipients
Make Ends Meet in Chicago." *Social Problems* 38:462–74.

Everett, Peter S. 1994. "Violence Comes to the Mall." *Trial* 30:62–65.

Ewen, Stuart. 1976. *Captains of Consciousness: Advertising and the Social
Roots of the Consumer Culture.* New York: McGraw-Hill.

———. 1988. *All Consuming Images: The Politics of Style in Contemporary
Culture.* New York: Basic Books.

Ewen, Stuart, and Elizabeth Ewen. 1982. *Channels of Desire: Mass Images
and the Shaping of American Consciousness.* New York: McGraw-Hill.

Fainstein, Norman I., and Susan S. Fainstein. 1974. *Urban Political Movements: The Search for Power by Minority Groups in American Cities.*
Englewood Cliffs, N.J.: Prentice-Hall.

Fine, Ben. 1995. "From Political Economy to Consumption." Pp. 127–63 in
Acknowledging Consumption, ed. Daniel Miller. New York: Routledge.

Fine, Michelle, and Cheryl Bowers. 1984. "Racial Self-Identification: The Effects of Social History and Gender." *Journal of Applied Social Psychology* 14, no. 2:136–46.

Fischer, Eileen, and Stephen J. Arnold. 1990. "More than a Labor of Love: Gender Roles and Christmas Gift Shopping." *Journal of Consumer Research* 17:333–45.

Fiske, John. 1989. *Reading the Popular.* Winchester, Mass.: Unwin Hyman.

———. 1993. *Power Plays, Power Works.* London: Verso.

———. 1994. "Radical Shopping in Los Angeles: Race, Media and the Sphere of Consumption." *Media, Culture, and Society* 16:469–86.

Fogelson, Robert M., ed. 1969. *The Los Angeles Riots.* New York: Arno Press.

Fox-Genovese, Elizabeth. 1988. *Within the Plantation Household: Black and White Women of the Old South.* Chapel Hill: University of North Carolina Press.

Gell, A. 1992. "Inter-Tribal Commodity Barter and Reproductive Gift-Exchange in Old Melanesia." Pp. 142–68 in *Barter, Exchange, and Value,* ed. C. Humphrey and Stephen Hugh-Jones. Cambridge: Cambridge University Press.

Genovese, Eugene. 1965. *The Political Economy of Slavery: Studies in the Economy and Society of the Slave South.* New York: Vintage.

———. 1974. *Roll, Jordan, Roll: The World the Slaves Made.* New York: Pantheon Books.

Gilens, Martin. 1996. "Race and Poverty in America: Public Misperceptions and the American News Media." *Public Opinion Quarterly* 60 (Winter): 515–41.

Gilroy, Paul. 1993. *The Black Atlantic: Modernity and Double Consciousness.* Cambridge: Harvard University Press.

"Gingrich Links Slaying of Family to 'Welfare State.'" 1995. *Los Angeles Times* (November 22), A10.

Gopaul-McNichol, Sharon-Ann. 1995. "A Cross-Cultural Examination of Racial Identity and Racial Preference of Preschool Children in the West Indies." *Journal of Cross-Cultural Psychology* 26, no. 2:141–52.

Goss, John. 1993. "The 'Magic of the Mall': An Analysis of Form, Function, and Meaning in the Contemporary Retail Built Environment." *Annals of the Association of American Geographers* 83, no. 1:18–47.

Gregory, Stephen. 1998. *Black Corona: Race and the Politics of Place in an Urban Community.* Princeton, N.J.: Princeton University Press.

Halton, Eugene. 1992. "A Long Way from Home: Automatic Culture in Domestic and Civic Life." Pp. 1–9 in *Meaning, Measure and Morality of Materialism,* ed. Floyd Rudmin and Marsha Richins. Provo, Utah: Association for Consumer Research.

Hannerz, Ulf. 1969. *Soulside: Inquiries into Ghetto Culture and Community.* New York: Columbia University Press.

Hartigan, John, Jr. 1997. "Green Ghettoes and the White Underclass." *Social Research* 64, no. 2:339–65.

Harvey, David. 1989. *The Condition of Postmodernity.* Oxford: Basil Blackwell.

Haug, Wolfgang Fritz. 1986. *Critique of Commodity Aesthetics: Appearance, Sexuality and Advertising in Capitalist Society.* Minneapolis: University of Minnesota Press.

Heath, D. 1992. "Fashion, Anti-Fashion and Heteroglossia in Urban Senegal." *American Ethnologist* 19:19–33.

Hebdige, Dick. 1979. *Subculture: The Meaning of Style.* London: Methuen.

Hill, Ronald Paul, and Debra Lynn Stephens. 1997. "Impoverished Consumers and Consumer Behavior: The Case of AFDC Mothers." *Journal of Macromarketing* 17, no. 2:32–48.

Holcomb, B. 1986. "Geography and Urban Women." *Urban Geography* 7:448–56.

Honeycutt, Andrew. 1975. "An Ethnographic Study of Low Income Consumer Behavior." DBS dissertation, Harvard University, Cambridge.

Hopson, Derek, and Darlene Powell Hopson. 1991. *Different and Wonderful: Raising Black Children in a Race Conscious Society.* New York: Prentice-Hall.

Hugh-Jones, Stephen. 1992. "Yesterday's Luxuries, Tomorrow's Necessities: Business and Barter in Northwest Amazonia." Pp. 42–74 in *Barter, Exchange, and Value,* ed. C. Humphrey and Stephen Hugh-Jones. Cambridge: Cambridge University Press.

Jackson, Peter, and Nigel Thrift. 1995. "Geographies of Consumption." Pp. 204–37 in *Acknowledging Consumption,* ed. Daniel Miller. New York: Routledge.

Jacobs, Harriet. 1988. *Incidents in the Life of a Slave Girl.* New York: Oxford University Press.

James, Allison, Chris Jenks, and Alan Prout. 1998. *Theorizing Childhood.* New York: Teachers College Press.

James, Allison, and Alan Prout, eds. 1990. *Constructing and Reconstructing Childhood: Contemporary Issues in the Sociological Study of Childhood.* London: Falmer Press.

Jeffers, Camille. 1967. *Living Poor: A Participant Observer Study of Choices and Priorities.* Ann Arbor: Ann Arbor Publishers.

Jones, Delmos. 1970. "Towards a Native Anthropology." *Human Organization* 29, no. 4:251–59.

Jones, LeAlan, and Lloyd Newman. 1997. *Our America: Life and Death on the South Side of Chicago.* New York: Washington Square Press.

Jones, Lisa. 1990. *Bulletproof Diva.* New York: Doubleday.

Katz, Michael, ed. 1993. *The "Underclass Debate."* Princeton, N.J.: Princeton University Press.

Kelly, Dierdre M. 1996. "Stigma Stories: Four Discourses about Teen Mothers, Welfare, and Poverty." *Youth and Society* 27, no. 4:421–49.

Kincaid, Jamaica. 1988. *A Small Place.* New York: Penguin.

Kopytoff, Igor. 1986. "The Cultural Biography of Things: Commoditization as Process." Pp. 64–91 in *The Social Life of Things: Commodities in Cultural Perspective,* ed. Arjun Appadurai. New York: Cambridge University Press.

Kotlowitz, Alex. 1991. *There Are No Children Here.* New York: Doubleday.

———. 1999. "False Connections." Pp. 65–72 in *Consuming Desires: Consumption, Culture, and the Pursuit of Happiness,* ed. Roger Rosenblatt. Washington, D.C.: Island Press.

Kozol, Jonathan. 1967. *Death at an Early Age.* New York: Bantam.

———. 1991. *Savage Inequalities.* New York: Crown.

Leach, William R. 1984. "Transformations in a Culture of Consumption: Women and Department Stores, 1890–1925." *Journal of American History* 71, no. 2:319–42.

Leacock, Eleanor Burke, ed. 1971. *The Culture of Poverty: A Critique.* New York: Simon and Schuster.

Lee, Felicia R. 1991. "For Gold Earrings and Protection More Girls Take to Violence." *New York Times* (November 25), A1, B7.

Leiman, Melvin M. 1993. *The Political Economy of Racism.* Boulder, Colo.: Pluto Press.

Lewis, George H. 1989. "Rats and Bunnies: Core Kids in an American Mall." *Adolescence* 24, no. 96:881–89.

Lewis, Oscar. 1966. *La Vida: A Puerto Rican Family in the Culture of Poverty— San Juan and New York.* New York: Random House.

Liebow, Elliott. 1967. *Tally's Corner: A Study of Negro Streetcorner Men.* Boston: Little, Brown.

Lord, M. G. 1994. *Forever Barbie: The Unauthorized Biography of a Real Doll.* New York: William Morrow.

Los Angeles Board of Police Commissioners. 1992. "The City in Crisis: A Report." Los Angeles: The Police Foundation, Inc., 1992.

MacLeod, Jay. 1987. *Ain't No Makin' It.* Boulder, Colo.: Westview Press.

Maharidge, Dale, and Michael Williamson. 1989. *And Their Children After Them.* New York: Pantheon Books.

Malinowski, Bronislaw. 1922. *Argonauts of the Western Pacific.* London: Routledge and Kegan Paul.

———. 1944. *A Scientific Theory of Culture.* Chapel Hill: University of North Carolina Press.

"Mall Wins Ruling on Limiting Bus Service." 1995. *New York Times* (August 27), A36.

Marcuse, Herbert. 1964. *One Dimensional Man.* Boston: Beacon Press.

Marx, Karl. [1852] 1963. *The Eighteenth Brumaire of Louis Bonaparte.* New York: International.

———. 1969. *Theories of Surplus Value, Part II.* London: Lawrence and Wishart.

McAdoo, Harriette Pipes. 1985. "Racial Attitude and Self-Concept of Black Children Over Time." Pp. 213–42 in *Black Children: Social, Educational, and Parental Environments,* ed. Harriette Pipes McAdoo and John Lewis McAdoo. London: Sage.

McCracken, Grant. 1988. *Culture and Consumption.* Bloomington: Indiana University Press.

McLaren, Peter, and Janet Morris. 1997. "Mighty Morphin' Power Rangers: The Aesthetics of Phallo-Militaristic Justice." Pp. 115–28 in *Kinderculture: The Corporate Construction of Childhood,* ed. Shirley R. Steinberg and Joe L. Kincheloe. Boulder, Colo.: Westview Press.

Mercer, Kobena. 1990. "Black Hair/Style Politics." Pp. 247–64 in *Out There: Marginalization in Contemporary Cultures,* ed. Russell Ferguson, Martha Gever, Trinh T. Minh-ha and Cornel West. New York and Cambridge, Mass.: The New Museum of Contemporary Art and MIT Press.

Miller, Daniel. 1995a. "Consumption as the Vanguard of History: A Polemic by Way of an Introduction." Pp. 1–57 in *Acknowledging Consumption: A Review of New Studies,* ed. Daniel Miller. New York: Routledge.

———. 1995b. "Consumption and Commodities." *Annual Reviews in Anthropology* 24:141–62.

———. 1997. "Could Shopping Ever Really Matter?" Pp. 31–55 in *The Shopping Experience,* ed. Pasi Falk and Colin Campbell. Thousand Oaks, Calif.: Sage.

———. 1998. *A Theory of Shopping.* Ithaca, N.Y.: Cornell University Press.

Miller, Daniel, Peter Jackson, Nigel Thrift, Beverley Holbrook, and Michael Rowlands. 1998. *Shopping, Place and Identity.* New York: Routledge.

Minerbrook, Scott. 1992. "Why a City Alone Cannot Save Itself: The Story of New Haven Shows How Big Social and Economic Forces Overwhelm Local Leaders." *U.S. News and World Report,* November 9, 36–40.

Mintz, Sidney. 1985. *Sweetness and Power.* New York: Viking Penguin.

Mitchell, Mary A. 1998. "Innocence Dies on a Summer Day." *Chicago Sun-Times* (August 13), 25.

Moore, Henrietta L. 1988. *Feminism and Anthropology.* Minneapolis: University of Minnesota Press.

Moynihan, Daniel Patrick. 1965. *The Negro Family: The Case for National Action.* Washington, D.C.: Office of Policy Planning and Research, U.S. Department of Labor.

Mullin, Michael. 1995. "Slave Economic Strategies: Food, Markets and Property." Pp. 68–78 in *From Chattel Slaves to Wage Slaves: The Dynamics of Labour Bargaining in the Americas,* ed. Mary Turner. Bloomington: Indiana University Press.

Mullings, Leith, ed. 1987. *Cities of the United States: Studies in Urban Anthropology.* New York: Columbia University Press.

"New Boom in Ethnic Toys: Experts Say the Trend Is More than Skin Deep." 1993. *Ebony,* November 1993, 64–66.

New Haven Downtown Council. 1992. *Major Employers in New Haven County.* New Haven.

Nightingale, Carl. 1993. *On the Edge: A History of Poor Black Children and Their American Dreams.* New York: Basic Books.

Northrup, Solomon. 1968. *Twelve Years a Slave.* Baton Rouge: Louisiana State University Press.

Okongwu, Anne. 1996. "Keeping the Show on the Road: Female-Headed Families Surviving on $22,000 a Year or Less in New York City." *Urban Anthropology* 25, no. 2:115–63.

Pan, Zhongdang, and Gerald M. Kosicki. 1996. "Assessing News Media Influences on the Formation of Whites' Racial Policy Preferences." *Communication Research* 23 (April): 147–78.

Park, Robert, Ernest Watson Burgess, Roderick Duncan, and Louis Wirth, eds. 1925. *The City.* Chicago: University of Chicago Press.

Philibert, Jean-Marc. 1990. "Consuming Culture: A Study of Simple Commodity Consumption." Pp. 449–78 in *Customs in Conflict: The Anthropology of a Changing World,* ed. Frank Manning and Jean-Marc Philibert. Peterborough, Ont.: Broadview Press.

Pope, Kyle. 1993. "Better to Receive: How Children Decide on Gifts They Want, and Plot to Get Them." *Wall Street Journal* (December 23), A1, A5.

Porter, J., and R. Washington. 1979. "Black Identity and Self Esteem: A Review of Studies of Black Self-Concept." *Annual Review of Sociology* 5:53–54.

Rand, Erica. 1995. *Barbie's Queer Accessories.* Durham, N.C.: Duke University Press.

Reece, Bonnie B. 1986. "Children and Shopping: Some Public Policy Questions." *Journal of Public Policy and Management* 5:185–94.

Reguero, Wilfred, and Marilyn Crane. 1994. "Project MotherCare: One Hospital's Response to the High Perinatal Death Rate in New Haven, CT." *Public Health Reports* 109, no. 5:647–52.

Rooks, Noliwe M. 1996. *Hair Raising: Beauty, Culture, and African American Women.* New Brunswick, N.J.: Rutgers University Press.

Rose, Damaris. 1984. "Rethinking Gentrification: Beyond the Uneven Development of Marxist Urban Theory." *Society and Space* 2:47–74.

Rutz, Henry, and Benjamin Orlove. 1988. "Thinking about Consumption: A Social Economy Approach." Pp. 121–38 in *The Social Economy of Consumption,* ed. Henry Rutz and Benjamin Orlove. New York: Routledge.

Schwartzman, Helen. In press. *Children and Anthropology: Perspectives for the 21st Century.* Westport, Conn.: Bergin and Garvey.

"Segregation of Public Schools Threatens Connecticut's Future." 1993. *New Haven Register* (January 10), B3.

Shapiro, Carolyn. 1993. "Cultural Marketing: In Designing Toys for African-American Consumers, Authenticity Is More than Skin Deep." *Toy and Hobby World* (June): 26–28, 73–74.

Sharff, Jagna. 1998. *King Kong on 4th Street: Families and the Violence of Poverty on the Lower East Side.* Boulder, Colo.: Westview Press.

Sheridan, Richard B. 1995. "Strategies of Slave Subsistence: The Jamaican Case Reconsidered." Pp. 48–67 in *From Chattel Slaves into Wage Slaves: The Dynamics of Labour Bargaining in the Americas,* ed. Mary Turner. Bloomington: Indiana University Press.

Sherry, John F., Jr., ed. 1995. *Contemporary Marketing and Consumer Behavior: An Anthropological Sourcebook.* Thousand Oaks, Calif.: Sage.

Shields, Rob. 1992. *Lifestyle Shopping.* New York: Routledge.

Sholle, David. 1990. "Resistance: Pinning Down a Wandering Concept in Cultural Studies Discourse." *Journal of Urban and Cultural Studies* 1, no. 1:87–105.

Singleton, T. A. 1995. "The Archaeology of Slavery in North America." *Annual Review of Anthropology* 24:119–40.

Slater, Eric. 1998. "Boys, 7 and 8, Accused of Killing Girl, 11; Crime: They Are the Youngest Murder Suspects in the History of Chicago." *Los Angeles Times* (August 11), A1.

Smith, Neil. 1992. "New City, New Frontier: The Lower East Side as Wild, Wild West." Pp. 61–93 in *Variations on a Theme Park: The New American City and the End of Public Space,* ed. Michael Sorkin. New York: Hill and Wang.

Smith, Venture, James Mars, William Grimes, the Rev. G. W. Offley, and James L. Smith. 1971. *Five Black Lives: The Autobiographies of Venture Smith, James Mars, William Grimes, The Rev. G. W. Offley, James L. Smith.* Documents of Black Connecticut. Middletown, Conn.: Wesleyan University Press.

Sorkin, Michael, ed. 1992. *Variations on a Theme Park: The New American City and the End of Public Space.* New York: Farrar, Straus and Giroux.

Stack, Carol. 1974. *All Our Kin.* New York: Harper and Row.

Staples, Brent. 1994. "Into the Ivory Tower." *New York Times* (February 6), sec. 6, p. 24.

———. 1996. "The Littlest Killers." *New York Times,* (February 6), A22.

Stephens, Sharon, ed. 1995. *Children and the Politics of Culture.* Princeton, N.J.: Princeton University Press.

Stern, Susan. 1998. *Barbie Nation.* New York: New Day Films.

Sturdivant, Frederick D. 1969. *The Ghetto Marketplace.* Toronto: Collier-Macmillan Canada.

Sullivan, Lisa Y. 1996. "The Demise of Black Civil Society: Once Upon a Time When We Were Colored Meets the Hip-Hop Generation." *Social Policy* 27, no. 2:6–10.

Susser, Ida. 1982. *Norman Street: Poverty and Politics in an Urban Neighborhood.* New York: Oxford University Press.

———. 1996. "The Construction of Poverty and Homelessness in U.S. Cities." *Annual Review of Anthropology* 25:411–35.

Taussig, Michael T. 1980. *The Devil and Commodity Fetishism in South America.* Chapel Hill: University of North Carolina Press.

"A Teen-Age Pall at the Mall: After-School Gatherings Please Youths But Are Worrying Many Others." 1993. *New York Times* (November 23), B1, 5.

Terry, Don. 1996. "Prison for Young Killers Renews Debate on Saving Society's Lost." *New York Times* (January 31), A1.

Turner, Terrence. 1992. "Defiant Images: The Kayapo Appropriation of Video." *Anthropology Today* 8, no. 6:5–16.

U.S. Bureau of the Census. 1980. *1980 Census of Population and Housing.* Washington, D.C.: U.S. Government Printing Office.

U.S. Department of Commerce. 1993. *Detailed Housing Characteristics: Connecticut.* Washington, D.C.: U.S. Government Printing Office.

Urla, Jacqueline, and Alan C. Swedlund. 1995. "The Anthropometry of Barbie: Unsettling Ideals of the Feminine Body in Popular Culture." In *Deviant Bodies: Critical Perspectives on Difference in Science and Popular Culture,* ed. Jennifer Terry and Jacqueline Urla, 277–313. Bloomington: Indiana University Press.

Valerio, V. 1994. "Buying Women but Not Selling Them: Gift and Commodity Exchange in Huaulu Alliance." *Man* 29:1–24.

Van Sertima, Ivan. 1976. *They Came Before Columbus.* New York: Random House.

Veblen, Thorstein. 1912. *The Theory of the Leisure Class: An Economic Study of Institutions.* New York: Macmillan.

Vincent, Joan. 1993. "Framing the Underclass." *Critique of Anthropology* 13, no. 3:215–30.

Visweswaran, Kamala. 1994. *Fictions of Feminist Ethnography.* Minneapolis: University of Minnesota Press.

Wacquant, Loic, and William Julius Wilson. 1989. "The Cost of Racial and Class Exclusion in the Inner City." *Annals of the American Academy of Political and Social Science* 501 (January): 8–25.

"Wary Mall Bans Backward Caps." 1995b. *New York Times* (January 9), 19.

Weiner, Annette. 1985. "Inalienable Wealth." *American Ethnologist* 12:210–27.

Weismantel, Mary. 1997. Review of Jonathan Friedman, ed., *Consumption and Identity. Man* 3, no. 2:380–81.

White, Shane, and Graham White. 1995. "Slave Hair and African American Culture in the Eighteenth and Nineteenth Centuries." *Journal of Southern History* 61, no. 1:45–76.

"White Person Slips, Falls: Shoppers Shudder; Is Downtown Safe?" 1992. *New Haven Advocate,* April 1, 1.

Williams, Brackette. 1996. "Skinfolk, not Kinfolk: Comparative Reflections on the Identity of Participant-Observation in Two Field Situations." Pp. 72–95 in *Feminist Dilemmas in Fieldwork,* ed. Diane L. Wolf. New York: Westview.

Williams, Brett. 1988. *Upscaling Downtown: Stalled Gentrification in Washington, D.C.* Ithaca, N.Y.: Cornell University Press.

Williams, Rosalind H. 1982. *Dream Worlds: Mass Consumption in Late Nineteenth-Century France.* Los Angeles: University of California Press.

Williamson, Judith. 1980. *Consuming Passions: The Dynamics of Popular Culture.* London: Marion Boyars.

Willis, Paul. 1977. *Learning to Labour.* New York: Columbia University Press.

Willis, Susan. 1990. "'I Want the Black One': Is There a Place for Afro-American Culture in Commodity Culture?" *New Formations* 10 (Spring): 147–77.

———. 1991. *A Primer for Daily Life.* New York: Routledge.

Wilson, William Julius. 1987. *The Truly Disadvantaged: The Inner City, the Underclass, and Public Policy.* Chicago: University of Chicago Press.

———. 1988. "The American Underclass: Inner-City Ghettos and the Norms of Citizenship." Godkin Lecture, John F. Kennedy School of Government, Harvard University, 1988.

Wiseman, Frederick. 1997. *Public Housing.* Cambridge, Mass.: Zipporah Films, dist.

Wolf, Eric. 1982. *Europe and the People without History.* Berkeley: University of California Press.

Wood, Betty. 1995. "'Never on a Sunday?': Slavery and the Sabbath in Low-country Georgia 1750–1830." Pp. 79–96 in *From Chattel Slaves to Wage Slaves,* ed. Mary Turner. Bloomington: Indiana University Press.

Worsley, Peter. 1957. *The Trumpet Shall Sound.* London: MacGibbon and Kee.

Yarrow, Andrew L. 1992. "Soaring Taxes Steal Cafés' Sizzle." *New York Times* (June 18), B6.

Zelizer, Viviana. 1989. "The Social Meaning of Money: 'Special Monies.'" *American Journal of Sociology* 95:342–77.

———. 1994. *The Social Meaning of Money.* New York: Basic Books.

Index

abandoned buildings, increase in, 16
Adorno, Theodor, 229n.5
advertising: to children, 67–68;
    workshop on, 199–201
affirmative action, 169
African Americans, influence of
    historical experiences on, 3. *See
    also* segregation; slavery and
    consumption
Ain't No Makin' It (MacLeod), 46
Air Jordans, 48, 137; assumptions
    made about, 60–61
All Our Kin (Stack), 45–46
American myth about the poor,
    56–57
Andreasen, Alan, 11, 59
anthropologist, complexity of en-
    gagement between subject and,
    63. *See also* fieldwork at home
anticonsumer, 43
apprehensions of selves and society,
    experience in different consump-
    tion sites and, 92
Aslan, Lucy, 18, 187, 198, 199
Auletta, Ken, 44
Austin, Regina, 12, 28–29
author, background of, 21–23,
    181–83. *See also* fieldwork at
    home

awareness, children's: of blackness in
    mall vs. Newhallville, 111, 115;
    of costs of their care and mainte-
    nance, 5, 70, 86; of responsibilities
    as members of families and kin
    networks, 70, 139

baby in the garbage can scenario,
    87–88
Baker, Russell, 106
Barbie doll: assumption of white-
    ness embodied in, 143–44, 149;
    Christmas gifts related to, 83; dif-
    ference between Shani lines and,
    155, 157–61; fantasy life offered
    by, 80; impressions of black girls,
    1–2, 12; range of consumer en-
    gagements with, 10
Barbie-doll hair, 25, 159–61
Barbie's Queer Accessories (Rand),
    161
bargains, adept eye for, 137
basic needs, cultural mediation of,
    229n.7
Baudrillard, Jean, 8–9, 46
beauty, white-dominated norm of,
    159
Belk, Russell, 81
birthdays, celebrating, 70–72

ELIZABETH CHIN is associate professor of anthropology at Occidental College in Los Angeles.